WHO ARE YOU WHO ARE SO WISE IN THE SCIENCE OF TEACHING?

or

The Expert in Classroom Instruction by Knowledge, Skill, Experience, Training, or Education:
Laying the Foundation for Effective Certificated Employee (Teacher) Evaluation under the Law

Rex R. Schultze, J.D.

With James B. Gessford, JD, and Kevin M. Riley, EdD, and Other Distinguished Educators

Fulton Books, Inc.
Meadville, PA

Published by Fulton Books 2020

ISBN 978-1-64952-166-8 (paperback)
ISBN 978-1-64952-167-5 (digital)

Praise for *Who Are You Who Are So Wise in the Science of Teaching? or The Expert in Classroom Instruction by Knowledge, Skill, Experience, Training, or Education*

I think this [book] is AMAZING and is a huge contribution
to Nebraska education. Congratulations!
—Dr. Melissa Wheelock; administrator; Educational
Service Unit No. 10; Kearney, Nebraska

This is a "must read" for all school building administrators and central
office HR personnel. Rex's focus on the improvement of instruction
is the best and most effective approach to teacher evaluation.
—Mikaela Vobejda, principal, Golden Hills Elementary,
Papillion-LaVista Public Schools

Exceptional work.
—Dr. Kevin Riley; professor of educational administration;
University of Nebraska–Omaha; Omaha, Nebraska

Your book is amazing!!! It is exactly what every school administrator
needs to support them with the teacher evaluation process.
—Dr. Randy Gilson; superintendent of schools;
Blair Public Schools; Blair, Nebraska

In Rex's book "The Expert [by knowledge, skill, experience, training, or education!]", he
challenges districts and administrators to define what effective teaching looks like and
sounds like in order to provide timely and targeted feedback to teachers as they improve
their instructional practice. As someone who has had the honor and privilege to work
alongside Rex, I appreciate his approach to teacher evaluation and his ability to use
storytelling to share his expertise. I hope this book is utilized in graduate leadership courses
and it raises awareness to put an emphasis on the importance of teacher evaluation.
—Dr. Derrick Joel; superintendent of schools; Raymond
Central Public Schools; Raymond, Nebraska

Thank you for sharing the draft of the book with me. I found it to be
VERY rewarding and caught myself getting drug into the details when
I should be reading for general concepts… It is a good read.
—Dr. Michael Teahon, EdD; department chair,
associate professor, educational administration; College
of Education–University of Nebraska at Kearney

To my parents, Dr. Robert R. Schultze, E. Ed., and Barbara B. Marsh Schultze, MS—life-long educators.

Dr. John McQuinn, principal, Bryan Senior High School in Omaha, Nebraska—challenger, mentor, and advisor.

Barbara Dayton Lebedz, teacher, Bryan Senor High School in Omaha, Nebraska—the best and most dedicated master teacher ever.

And Edwin C. Perry, JD, and James B. Gessford, JD—mentors and exemplars in the practice of the school of law.

Federal Rules of Evidence—Rule 702. Testimony by Expert Witnesses

A witness who is qualified as an expert by knowledge, skill, experience, training, or education may testify in the form of an opinion or otherwise if:

(a) the expert's scientific, technical, or other specialized knowledge will help the trier of fact to understand the evidence or to determine a fact in issue;

(b) the testimony is based on sufficient facts or data;

(c) the testimony is the product of reliable principles and methods; and,

(d) the expert has reliably applied the principles and methods to the facts of the case.

CONTENTS

Part 5: The End Game

FOREWORD

Hi Rex: Just wanted to thank you for the tremendous job that you did with the XXXX case. I can't begin to explain how much you assisted me throughout the whole process. I learned more from you in a couple of weeks than spending a couple of years in graduate courses. You saved our students from an unsafe environment just as I am sure you have saved other students all-across the state from similar conditions. (E-mail, May 22, 2001)

I wrote that e-mail to Rex Schultze over eighteen years ago following a due process hearing to end the employment of a twenty-year teacher in my first year as an elementary principal. I will not go into the details other than to say Rex first became involved when observations and an evaluation of a veteran teacher revealed substantial issues with classroom management and thereby instruction. Through his philosophy about teacher evaluation, Rex supported me to fully understand the importance of teacher supervision that focuses on growth instead of merely compliance. We worked together to develop a strategy and plan to help improve the teacher's performance and, when the teacher rejected such efforts, worked with me to prepare for the due process hearing that ensued.

Rex Schultze is the trusted expert in the teacher evaluation process for the purpose of improving learning for all students. First and foremost, Rex cares deeply about every student in each classroom. As a former teacher himself, Rex puts himself in the position of the student and teacher while empowering school administrators to develop teacher evaluation policies and procedures that are transparent and tightly aligned to support the academic, cognitive, social, emotional, and behavioral development of all students.

Rex offers more than a system, but rather an approach that allows administrators to support each staff member by stretching their unique talents and supporting their needs to reach district goals and beliefs about effective teaching. Rex supports the school district to clearly define what effective teaching and learning looks like based on the instructional goals that are agreed upon and approved in school board policy.

Every district has differing beliefs about what effective teaching is. Some districts emphasize mastery of basic skills, others value the development of problem-solving skills and inquiry-based learning strategies, and others believe in developing cooperative learning strategies. Rex's philosophy about teacher evaluation and supervision can be applied to work with any instructional goals about learning a school district might have.

When instructional goals about learning drives the school's purpose, teachers and school administrators become more motivated, confident, and connected to the mission of the school district. Psychologist Mihaly Csikszentmihalyi found that people are much more likely to reach their flow state at work than in leisure due to the structure of clear goals, immediate feedback, and challenges matched to abilities. According to Csikszentmihalyi, "the single greatest motivator is making progress at work."

A cornerstone of Rex's philosophy is establishing effective collaboration between the teacher and administrator built on trust and a sincere purpose to improve learning for all students. It is important for the teacher and principal to work together to establish crystal clear goals and expectations that will be reinforced through support by the principal. Rex encourages principals to provide time and support for every teacher. A scheduled plan of action is essential for ensuring progress. Rex challenges principals to provide ongoing direct observations of teachers while they are performing their goals. Through these observations, the principal develops anecdotal notes to describe the teacher's actions taken toward their goals. The principal will also record the effects these actions had on students.

Anecdotal notes are used to provide feedback to the teacher. The teacher begins by reflecting back about how they planned, what actions they took, and what was the result. The principal then shares anecdotal notes to retrace teacher actions and to promote reflective inquiry about what teacher strategies are working and what new strategies might be implemented in the future. Together, the principal and teacher choose researched-based instructional strategies to support the needs of the teacher and instructional goals of the district. This is a cycle that continues throughout a school year and across multiple years promoting incremental improvement by the teacher.

Having this knowledge has been pivotal to how I have supported teaching and learning throughout my career. I used his approach in every school district I have been. As a director of human resources and now superintendent, I have guided principals to implement Rex's philosophy and have had Rex work with them directly as well. His philosophy has worked in the best and most difficult situations.

Improving instruction just like teaching is complex. Sometimes teachers are really motivated to make incremental improvements, and sometimes they would rather settle with their current skills and abilities. I have found Rex's philosophy to support all teachers because it connects them to the larger purpose of the school district and motivates them to get started. The approach keeps the principal persistent in supporting the teacher through direct observations and reflective dialogue. I have applied Rex's philosophy every single time even during some of the grimmest of situations. His approach has never failed me or our school district, and most importantly, it has always propelled me to take the necessary action to improve instruction to provide students the best of learning opportunities.

I have believed in Rex Schultze's approach so much, I have shared it with other administrators, educational experts, and even educational attorneys.

Through this book, you, too, can learn Rex's approach. It will make you a better administrator and educator, which is the goal for all of us in the profession.

Dr. Randall Gilson, Superintendent of Schools,
Blair Public Schools, Blair, Nebraska

PREFACE

The book that follows incorporates a philosophy that the school lawyers in our firm—the Perry Law Firm in Lincoln, Nebraska—have recognized and encouraged for over twenty-five years the concept that *"by changing nothing but the ability of the teacher to teach, we can bring about a more dramatic change in the success of a child in learning than through the manipulation of any other factor"* (James B. Gessford, JD).

INTRODUCTION

"Who are you who are so wise in the science of teaching?"
"The expert [by knowledge, skill, experience, training, or education]!"[1]

So, Mr. M'Choakumchild began in his best manner. He and some one hundred and forty other school masters had been lately turned at the same time, in the same factory, on the same principles, like so many pianoforte legs. He had been put through an immense variety of paces, and had answered volumes of head-breaking questions. Orthography, etymology, syntax, and prosody, biography, astronomy, geography, and general cosmography, the sciences of compound proportion, algebra, land-surveying and leveling, vocal music, and drawing from models, were all at the ends of his ten chilled fingers. He had worked his stony way into Her Majesty's most Honourable Privy Council's Schedule B, and had taken the bloom off the higher branches of mathematics and physical science, French, German, Latin and Greek. He knew all about all the Water Sheds of all the world (whatever they are), all the histories of all the peoples, and all the names of all the rivers and mountains, and all the productions, manners, and customs of all the countries, all their boundaries and bearings on the two-and-thirty points of the compass. Ah, rather overdone, M'Choakumchild. If he had only learnt a little less, how infinitely better he might have taught much more! (Charles Dickens, *Hard Times*)

Over nearly forty (40) years of practicing school law, I have seen the focus on student outcomes and learning steadily increase. Yet, at the same time, there has not been a corresponding improvement in the application of approaches to the science of teaching to assist teachers to improve their performance and thereby student outcomes (e.g., learning). As school lawyers, we are called upon to read hundreds of teacher evaluations and the background documentation provided by school administrators, in most cases for purposes non-renewing or terminating (or at times canceling) the employment contracts of teachers under their supervision based upon competency.

---

[1] *Federal Rules of Evidence* Rule 702, "Testimony by Expert Witnesses," and Neb. Rev. Stat. §27-702.

Generally, the quality of the evaluation documentation, application of the evaluation instrument,[2] and particularly the writing of narratives to support the evaluation ratings have been found to be wanting at best. Further, there is little knowledge of, and/or emphasis on the meeting of the statutory requirements for teacher evaluation in our state—Nebraska.

Throughout this book, you will read some references to Nebraska law, regulations, and case law—since that is where I am from and have practiced. That said, the themes herein are universal to education in any state.

Recently, the executive director of the state teacher's union in Nebraska stated to me *that most principals do not know how to teach and move up into administration to avoid the classroom; that they are not qualified to evaluate teachers; and, that schools do not do enough to train their administrators in what is good teaching*, e.g., the science of teaching. Or to paraphrase Dickens's quote above, had they learnt a little less administering and more about teaching, *how infinitely better they might have taught much more!*

Such feelings are common among teachers. One teacher commented as follows:

> Just how many administrators are master teachers? In my 43 years of experience, I have had exactly one. That is not to say that many of the others were not decent people, they just did not have any idea how to teach, which is why they became administrators in the first place. At one point, two of our key administrators had a combined total of five years total classroom experience and neither one of them was an exemplary teacher. Not that either of them could not become one. Becoming a master teacher takes time and it takes the coaching and mentoring of a good administrator to help make an exemplary teacher. *The bottom line is time…you just don't jump from degree to master teacher in a couple of years.* They were then entrusted with evaluation teachers by virtue of their degrees, not any mastery of the multiple facets of effective teaching. An effective administrator has to be a coach with ideas for improvement rather than a laundry list of things the teacher did wrong, coupled with demands that they be addressed all the while reading and reporting on a bunch of books.[3] (Emphasis added)

There is a clear need for a focused course on the foundation needed by school administrators to (1) be effective at guiding and coaching their staff and, as part thereof, (2) have the skills for the writing of effective teacher formative and summative evaluations to assist in the improvement of instruction. A course for administrators (i.e., building principals) designed to provide a structured approach to the teaching, support, and assistance to your teachers in

---

[2]   And the underlying instructional framework—Madeline Hunter's Instructional Theory in Practice (ITIP), and educational model/standards—Marzano, Danielson. Note: there is a difference between ITIP and Marzano and Danielson. See below.

[3]   Anonymous, June 2020.

the science of teaching is needed to develop, maintain, and excel at their craft—great and committed teachers. To this end, school administrators (through their boards of education) must establish the district standards of performance that teachers consistently meet, standards set forth in the school district's evaluation instrument (on file with NDE in Nebraska). Where teachers meet the district's standards of performance, student learning will improve.

Expert in the Science of Teaching

Note the key words here, "the science of teaching." Based upon my experience over five decades (5—really—ouch!), there is a needed level of emphasis on preparing perspective administrators (or existing administrators) in the writing of effective teacher evaluations. An emphasis on the science of teaching is not a new concept. Some twenty-five years ago, my partner, Jim Gessford, pointed to the need for teacher evaluation to embrace and incorporate the science of teaching to improve student outcomes. In an article for school lawyers and presented to school lawyers at the conference for the National Association of School Boards—School Law in Review Law in 1995, Jim wrote with outside citations:

> While it was once thought that teaching was simply an "art form,"…modern theory refers to teaching as more of a "science" that can be learned and improved.[4]

Teaching models, methods and strategies become even more useful if they are utilized by administrators in the process and incorporated into a school's evaluation system and documents. While "there is no panacea, no magic formula, and no definitive evaluation system or mode," the use of "performance criteria" that have been shown to indicate the teaching-learning relationship within the classroom will strengthen a schools position.[5]

Despite increased judicial scrutiny by some courts, an evaluation system or document using research-based models, methods and strategies, administered by a properly trained professional is a nearly perfect weapon in the school's arsenal of defense. Attorneys and administrators would do well to become more familiar with, or revisit, the educational literature available

---

[4] James B. Gessford, JD, National Association of School Boards—School Law in Review Law in 1995, 6-1. See perrylawfirm. com to view the entire article. Note: Jim's article was originally written in 1995. Since that time additional scholars have published their "scientific teaching works" (e.g., Charlotte Danielson, Thomas McGreal, Robert Marzano, Debra Pickering, Jane Pollock, and Elaine McEwan and the CCSSO's) and additional case law has been decided. Nevertheless, the article and its theoretical underpinnings continue to remain the stalwart in effective teacher evaluation. Both Rex and Jim present annually on teacher evaluations and supplement the article with the latest case law and academic and scientific research. For ease of reference, however, the comments herein reference Jim's original work.

[5] Gessford, 6-2.

and draw on its precepts and theoretical underpinnings. There can be no doubt that by doing so, the "implementation lag" will be narrowed, the attorney will be a more effective advisor and advocate, and the administrator will be a better supervisor and witness.[6]

The primary legal significance of teacher evaluations is their value in adverse employment matters, for the well-documented teacher evaluation is a critical piece of evidence in teacher termination proceedings. The documentation system becomes an essential ingredient in preparing the district's principal not only for a hearing before the board of education, but for appeals and lawsuits filed with a state commissioner of education, an arbitrator or a court. *In a termination proceeding, teacher evaluations and supporting evaluator testimony are considered to be expert evidence of teacher effectiveness.* Hence, in addition to the written evaluations, *the attorney must also demonstrate how the evaluator, which in most cases is the principal, trained and competent in the area of teacher evaluation and diagnosis. Evaluators must be familiar with teaching models, methods and strategies and have appropriate training to be able to explain how a teacher's performance is hindering the learning environment in the classroom.* Overall, it must be demonstrated that the teacher's performance did not meet the required level or standard of performance for teachers within the school system.[7] (Emphasis added, citations and footnotes omitted)

Finally, Jim notes the damaging effect on our education system of the failure to evaluate staff objectively and based upon the science of what is effective classroom instruction as behooves any profession.

It should also be noted that experts recognize the high rate of a phenomenon known as evaluation inflation that occurs within our nation's school systems. Evaluation inflation refers to the overall human tendency to avoid harshly criticizing another. In addition, a similar phenomenon known as the "halo effect" can also account for some inadequate teachers receiving positive evaluations. The halo effect occurs when a below average teacher receives positive evaluations because the teacher is well liked or generally a pleasant person. Both attorneys and administrators must be aware of and guard against these phenomena. In exceptional cases, an attorney may even

---

[6] Gessford, 6-2.
[7] Gessford, 6-3 to 6-4.

be forced to use them to attempt to discount existing evaluation documents[8] (citations and footnotes omitted).

Over the years since Jim's article, our firm has worked with countless school districts to incorporate his concept of the science of teaching in the evaluations of their professional instructional staff. As school attorneys, we are asked to be involved only when an administrator has identified a teacher that is having difficulties in the classroom (many times because parents have complained, not because of evaluative efforts by the principal) and to assist the school district administration to develop the documentation to end the teacher's employment, thus Jim's focus on supporting expert evaluator testimony. As will be discussed later in this book, if the school district has engaged in training their administrator effective evaluation, the ending of employment efforts will take care of themselves. Alas, as we have worked with school districts of various sizes in student enrollment, the use of the science of teaching in improving instruction in the classroom, and evaluation thereof, that instruction has been uneven at best.

Despite the long-standing principle of incorporating the science of teaching in teacher evaluation, while some in the education field may dispute it, at a teacher level, there appears to be little emphasis on teaching would-be administrators the application of the science to teaching in the classroom, so they can ascertain good teaching from poor teaching, and how to use that knowledge to help teachers teach and students to learn. It is one thing to have a nice state-of-the-art evaluation model (see infra). It is another to teach your principals how it applies to the day-to-day classroom. We see this disconnect in reviewing the evaluative work of building principals too often. The foregoing may sound harsh, but the intent here is to identify the problem and do something about it. Ergo, this book.

Unfortunately, it is difficult to find graduate coursework on developing the foundation (you are going to read that word a lot) that administrators need to effectively apply their professional expertise to assist teachers and thereby provide students with the master teachers they deserve. While most universities offering graduate programs in school administration have appraisal classes, there does not appear to be any that provides the in-depth focus on the "in the field" preparation of these rising school administrators for effective evaluation, the importance of such preparation, and the application of such preparation to the teacher evaluation process.

Having been a classroom teacher, and knowing the challenges teachers must meet every day, their need for support, guidance, evaluation, which includes areas for improvement and affirmation of areas of strength, I have structured a course to provide the foundation and the application of that foundation to the final product—the effective evaluation of each teacher with the overriding goal of improved teaching and thereby student learning.

---

8   Gessford, 6-4.

The course is structured in five subparts with the following headings, and underlying chapters (with "anticipatory set" descriptions. There is an "anticipatory set" at the beginning of each chapter as an example of this essential part of each lesson engaging students in the learning process; see Madeline Hunter's ITIP lesson structure, infra. The subparts and chapters are as follows:

- Part 1: The Preparation
    - Chapter 1: The Elephant in the Room—What Does a Lawyer Know about Evaluating Teachers?
    - Chapter 2: The Assets—The Intangible and Essential Component
    - Chapter 3: The Master Teacher—How Long Do You Think It Takes to Really Get Good at Teaching?
    - Chapter 4: The Expert—Wise in the Science of Teaching
- Part 2: The Foundation
    - Chapter 5: The Foundation—Building a Base from Which to Lead Your Staff
    - Chapter 6: The Tools and Setup—Notice, Notice, and Notice
    - Chapter 7: The Instrument—The Measuring Device
    - Chapter 8: The Key Component or the Kiss of Death (or the Lifeline)
- Part 3: The Teaching
    - Chapter 9: The Communication—A Two-Way Street
    - Chapter 10: The Documentation—Being There and MBWA
    - Chapter 11: The Assistance—"Teach, Don't Tell"
- Part 4: The Skills
    - Chapter 12: The Composition—The Art of Painting, Drawing a Picture of Observations, Guidance, Support, Directives, Expectations, and Results
    - Chapter 13: The Summative—The Delivery of the Results of Your Joint Efforts
    - Chapter 14: The Closure—Where the Rubber Meets the Road
- Part 5: The End Game
    - Chapter 15: The Testimony—A Time to Shine
    - Chapter 16: The Hearing—A Long Day's Journey into Night
- Conclusion

While part 2 is titled "The Foundation," the term "foundation" will be found in all parts and chapters of this book because it is the essential base component to all learning, and thereby teaching.

"Part 1: The Preparation" sets forth the foundation that all administrators must have to (1) be effective in learning, teaching, and evaluating their professional teaching staff; and (2) to be recognized as an expert by your staff and community and, God forbid, at a hearing before a board of education or before a judge. You must have the foundation of the "knowledge, skill, experience, training and education" to be able to render an opinion on whether a teacher meets the district standard of performance under *Federal Rules of Evidence* Rule 702.[9]

"Part 2: The Foundation" sets forth the foundation you must give your teachers to identify the scope of their duties and provide them the basic structure of the educational process and the standard of performance expected as adopted by your board of education and implemented by the administration through you—the building principal.

"Part 3: The Teaching" sets forth the foundational tasks necessary for you as a building administrator to instruct, guide, and lead your staff (not tell/dictate unless absolutely necessary, e.g., some folks have to be "told"). Those tasks include the observation (formal and informal), determinations of performance (exemplary, okay, needs improvement, unsatisfactory), identifications of deficiencies, assistance in overcoming deficiencies, follow-up assistance, and evaluation to provide direct guidance and directives to improve performance.

"Part 4: The Skills" sets forth the foundational skills you must have as an administrator to communicate effectively with your staff to provide the information and data on the performance of your teaching staff, and the guidance needed for improvement of performance. These skills involve basic composition and writing, the management of time, and prioritizing the constant improvement of your staff. Even the best can get better. The knowledge and skill outlined in Chapters 1 through 14 provide the foundation for your expert testimony to the decider regarding the competency or other conduct of a teacher, and whether that teacher meets the standard of performance expected of other teachers performing the same or similar duties.

"Part 5: The End Game" sets forth the foundation in the law and the knowledge of the overall legal process relating to the continuing contract rights of certificated employees (teachers, counselors, administrators, superintendents) and the legal requirements for you as an administrator to use and express to a decider of fact (the board of education and, possibly down the road, a judge), the knowledge and skill outlined in parts 1 to 4 as the foundation for your expert testimony to that decider regarding the competency or other conduct of a teacher, and whether that teacher meets the standard of performance expected of other teachers performing the same or similar duties.

Lawyers for both the school district, the teacher, and the board love the term "foundation" in the legal sense. In many ways, that is what this book is about. However, underlying the legal stuff, is, as noted above, the concept of a foundation upon which to build a great teaching staff is essential to opening the world to students!

A good example is Bloom's Taxonomy, a road map for helping students learn, moving from a foundation to higher levels of thinking. The base of that critical thinking pyramid is knowledge—the foundation upon which Bloom's elements of comprehension, application, analysis, synthesis, and evaluation are built. As will be discussed in detail later, there is a new

---

[9]   In Nebraska, this is found in Neb. Rev. Stat. §27-702.

version of Bloom's Taxonomy that turns it to a less scientific and more academic approach, e.g., remembering, understanding, applying, analyzing, evaluating, and creating.

The sum of the parts will hopefully be useful to you in using teacher evaluation to improve your school's assets and thereby student learning—the unique product produced by your assets (your teachers).

Throughout this book you will hear from my partner, James B. Gessford, and administrators, educational experts and leaders like Dr. Nick Pace, professor chair, University of Nebraska–Lincoln Department of Educational Administration,[10] and Dr. Kevin Riley, a retired superintendent for the Gretna Public Schools in Gretna, Nebraska,[11] whose contributions to this effort provide the perspective of one who has had your job—the building principal.

There will be reading and writing assignments for each session. Sorry, but there must be some assessment of student learning.

Finally, this book is meant for you, and is intentionally written as conversation between you and me—exactly in the manner you should communicate with your teaching staff.

So, welcome to the course, and hopefully you will have people asking, "Who are you who are so wise in the science of teaching?"[12]

PS. As you will surmise quickly in reading this book, I have had the fortunate circumstance of being immersed in public education my entire life from 1951 to the present—as a teacher's and administrator's kid; as a high school teacher; as the brother of an elementary school teacher and administrator; and as a lawyer with a practice focused on public education, both K–12 and recently community college levels. As such, I bring a lifetime of perspective on the value of an education, and particularly public education, the most important equalizer of the citizens of our country.

PSS. I am a boomer—as in baby boomer[13]—an early version of that generation that grew up in the fifties and sixties, so you will find references to the movies and music of those days throughout this effort. Thus, I will apologize in advance, and you can google the references. It will be my contribution to your personal history journey.

Let's get to work and bridge that gap! Nuff said!

---

[10] Dr. Nick Pace, EdD, educational leadership, University of Northern Iowa, 2005.
MSE, educational administration, Drake University, 1997.
BA, sociology, University of Northern Iowa, 1992.
[11] Dr. Kevin Riley, EdD, educational leadership, University of Nebraska—Lincoln, 1991.
MSE, educational administration, University of Nebraska—Omaha, 1981.
BEd, University of Nebraska—Omaha, 1977.
[12] From the witch scene in *Monty Python and the Holy Grail*, 1974.
[13] Baby boomers were born between 1944 and 1964. They're currently between fifty-five to seventy-five years old as of this writing in 2019 (seventy-six million in the United States).

PART 1
The Preparation

CHAPTER 1

The Elephant in the Room—What Does a Lawyer Know About Evaluating Teachers?

> Ignorance is no excuse! Why weren't you aware of the sign-in policy?
> You went through orientation. Why out of all the first year teachers
> were you the only one who didn't know to sign in yesterday?
> —Assistant Principal DeNaples to Tony Danza[14]

The Elephant in the Room

So, why is a *lawyer* writing to you about effectively observing, monitoring, assisting, nurturing, and evaluating teachers? Well, for two reasons. First, the legal process that mandates the evaluation of teachers and the due process required to end employment of a certificated teacher. Second, to address the role of an effective evaluation process to improve student learning, a process that, if done correctly with knowledge, effort, and integrity, takes care of the legal process.

I Have Your Back!

A word here about "school lawyers." Obviously, as a lawyer who has dedicated his career to advising school districts on a myriad of topics, I think such attorneys are an essential part of the school district team. Dealing with personnel issues is a part of every business. That is why there are human resources departments. The difference for schools is that unlike businesses, schools have statutory requirements that govern the hiring, contracting, supervising, evaluating, terminating, and the retirement of their instructional staff. The school lawyer is there to provide you with the legal guidance and counseling based upon vast experience in personnel matters. We have all heard the admonition "Ignorance of the law is no excuse." The school lawyer is there to educate you in the law, and have your back when involved in a legal process—a personnel matter or otherwise. So, make sure you have one on your side!

---

[14] Tony Danza, *I'd Like to Apologize to Every Teacher I Ever Had: My Year as a Rookie Teacher at Northeast High*, 23.

Specially, with regard to personnel matters, the assistance of a school attorney can be career saving, helping you to:

1. Avoid due process hearings. *One of the most difficult events in any school administrator's career is going through a formal or informal due process hearing.* No one wants to be there. A person's job is on the line. And the administrator's performance in appropriately and competently evaluating the teacher is on display, and subject to criticism, before the ultimate judge, the board of education—the administrator's employer. Such events are like a car wreck. Everyone wants to come watch, and they can be damaging to the teacher, administrator, and the community. If you seek and follow legal advice early, and conduct the evaluation process well, you have a 99 percent chance of not having a hearing.

2. Win due process hearings. If you are going to go through with a teacher due process hearing, you will want legal counsel to prepare you for the hearing—to help you shine, demonstrating your knowledge and skill in assuring student learning is occurring in your school through effective evaluation and removing incompetent staff.

3. Avoid or win court cases. And you will need knowledge of the proper procedures to be followed—maintaining a testimonial and documentary record, assurance that all time lines and required actions have been met and/or followed, and other procedural matters to avoid technicalities that could potentially set aside the decision of the board of education.

4. Improve student learning. *But the most important aspect of the evaluation process is to improve instruction and thereby ensure improved and improving student learning and achievement.*

So, get someone to have your back! It is worth every penny!

All that said, this book is not about school attorneys or the legal process.[15] Rather, our focus is on the educational process of training, teaching, assisting, and evaluation of your teachers and support certificated staff—guidance counselors, etc.

---

[15] The process to evaluate teachers, the application of that process, and the due process requirements for non-renewing, terminating or canceling the continuing contract of a certificated employee of a Nebraska public school district. Because of the continuing contract laws, teachers have what is called a property interest in their job, which cannot be ended without following the statutory due process requirements. As such, school administrators evaluating staff should have a good working knowledge of the

- statutes,
- regulations, and
- case law.

Educational Process

Teachers are every school district's most important asset (see Chapter 2); they produce the product—educated students. As such, school districts must provide professional development to enhance each teacher's skills in lesson planning, instruction, classroom management, and personal and professional performance. Such professional development establishes the foundation for assuring effective instruction and student learning, including the following elements, many of which are developed in conjunction with legal counsel for the school district:

- Job descriptions and employment contracts
- Board and administrative policies and regulations
- Instructional framework and educational models
- Evaluation tools
- Teacher training

An effective educational process with your staff has very real benefits in the real world.

Objective

As stated above, the objective of this book is to provide building administrators, principals and (when applicable) assistant principals, practical educator-driven approaches to the development and implementation of a proactive administrator and teacher evaluation process focused with the administrator (principal) being an expert in teaching.

Essential to this objective are leadership, commitment, and accountability within the entire school community: the board of education, the superintendent, the principal, the teachers, and the students and their parents.

The *goal* is to improve the overall instructional performance of your school district's administrative and instructional staff and thereby improve *student learning*.

We will explore how to prepare you as an administrator to be an effective evaluator of your staff to improve student learning through the evaluation instrument and procedure—on file with the state department of education if required by regulation or statute, as is the case in Nebraska.

Basis: Commitment to the Profession or "Kids First, Adults Second"[16]

The first step in preparing administrators in effective evaluation is identifying in them a commitment to students (and by extension their parents and the community as a whole) and

---

[16] Dr. Riley, former superintendent of Gretna Public Schools in Gretna, Nebraska, explains his philosophy and culture of the expectation of his instructional and support staff.

a passion for helping young persons grow—people who heard the call and answered it. The following is a personal example of two people who heard that call.

The Cubicle

My brother and I are the children of what Tom Brokaw calls the Greatest Generation, and as such, we are Baby Boomers. Our parents were part of what is now called the Greatest Generation because they grew up during the Great Depression in an isolated and mostly rural society, took up the call to action and service in World War II, and with the help of the United States government, they created the greatest economic boom and largest middle class in the history of the world. My dad and mom, Robert and Barbara Schultze, epitomized their generation. Both grew up on farms in Northeast Nebraska.

My mom was from a relatively prosperous farm family through her mother's side. She was raised by a stern mother and quiet father. Significantly, her mother was a college graduate, something extremely rare in rural Nebraska in the early part of the twentieth century. As such, it is not surprising that my mom was encouraged to go, and did attend college, first at her mother's alma mater, Peru State College, and after two years, she enrolled at the University of Nebraska. There she earned a degree in home economics and vocational education, graduating in the spring of 1948. While at Nebraska, she lived in a boarding house, as the concept of dormitories had not hit the hinterlands of Nebraska at that time. Next door just to the east, my dad and his brother rented a room while getting back in college after the war. One day, Barbara was walking back to her house from campus when this boy, or young man, hung from a tree limb in front of her residence. He said hi. She, after recovering from her shock of this evident monkey hanging from a tree, decided he was worth a look.

My father, Robert Schultze, was from near Norfolk, Nebraska. Unlike Barbara, his family was hit extremely hard by the Depression. His father, his grandfather, and his uncle lost their farms in the early thirties and ended up renting those farms for the balance of their farming careers, and there were times when money was nonexistent and food scarce. Mouths were so hard to feed that the summer my father was fourteen, he was loaned out as a farmhand to a distant cousin of my grandfather, with the sole payment at the end of the summer being a runt pig—but, he had a roof over his head and he had a meal every day. By the time Bob graduated from high school in 1941, it was clear that he would have to find a profession outside of farming. So, he worked all summer and scraped up enough money to attend college in the fall of 1941 at the University of Nebraska. His education plan was to go to school one semester, work one semester, with a seven-year plan to graduate from college. That plan was in place until December 7, 1941, with the attack on

Pearl Harbor and the declaration of war by the United States against Japan and Germany. He was drafted in the spring of 1942 and entered the service, eventually becoming a clerk typist and moving up in rank to a staff sergeant by the end of the war. He received his basic training in Fort Sam Houston, Texas, and eventually was assigned to an army surgical unit (MASH) unit as their Radar O'Reilly. In 1943, he shipped out to England to begin preparations for what was eventually the invasion of Europe in Normandy in June of 1944. Like many World War II veterans, my father never discussed his experiences during the war. When asked, he would say, "Those are things I would like to forget."

Bob reentered the University of Nebraska in January of 1946 under the GI Bill and, as discussed previously, moved into his sister's house on Holdrege Street. As things happened, eventually Bob and Barb fell in love and were married on August 5, 1948. Barbara, having graduated from the University of Nebraska, took a teaching job in Louisville, Nebraska, some thirty miles east of Lincoln. The couple lived in an upstairs apartment at Twenty-Seventh and A Streets in Lincoln, and Bob continued his studies to obtain an accounting degree and bookkeeping degree. By the spring of 1949, Bob was on the cusp of graduating and had been offered a job with Bausch and Lomb Optical Company in Kansas City, Missouri, to serve as a bookkeeper. One day, the superintendent at Louisville Public Schools approached Barbara and said, "Barb, our bookkeeping and accounting teacher just resigned. You don't suppose Bob would like to come here and teach bookkeeping and accounting, do you?" My mom responded, "Oh, of course not. He has a job with Bausch and Lomb in Kansas City." Later, it was determined that Mr. Pickerel made that suggestion because he did not want to lose my mom as a teacher at Louisville, whom he knew would soon resign and head to Kansas City. So, Barbara went home, saw her husband that night, and said, "You know, Bob, Glen [the superintendent] made the silliest suggestion today. He asked whether or not you would like to come teach accounting and business at Louisville High School next year. I told him we were moving to Kansas City so you could work at Bausch and Lomb." Bob paused, thought for a minute, and said, "You know, I think I'd like to do that. I'd rather be working with people and helping kids than sitting in a cubicle in an office building in Kansas City." And with that chance suggestion, my father became a lifelong educator. He took summer classes to obtain his teaching certificate and began teaching school at Louisville Public Schools in the fall of 1949. He would go on to receive his master's degree in educational administration and his doctorate degree in elementary education and spend the next thirty-six years dedicated to public education in the state of Nebraska.

Equally significant, my mother, who had been told by her father when she announced her engagement that she had just wasted four years of an expensive college education, also taught the next thirty-six years, taking only one year off to work on her master's degree in home economics, which she received in 1963.

For those administrators that have made the commitment to students, such commitment involves assuring that a student's time in school is honored with quality instruction and guidance as the basis for their life's journey. Why else are students in our schools from age four through eighteen or nineteen? These students and their parents are investing the time to learn the skills upon which they will base their futures. We all owe them a return on their investment.

Which brings us to the quality assurance aspect of school administration. It is the hard part of the job. But, as Jimmy Duggan (Tom Hanks) says in the movie *A League of Their Own*, referring to baseball, "It's supposed to be hard. If it wasn't hard, everyone would do it. The hard is what makes it great."[17] Being a leader of your professional faculty is often hard, but the rewards of helping teachers and thereby students grow in knowledge and skill, and discovering new and exciting knowledge and opportunities is the great. As with my dad and mom, education of young people is what gets inside you; it needs to be what lights you up.

The point of this book is the challenge to school administrators to build the foundation for your teaching staff (and yourself) for an eventual determination (judgment, if you will) as to the quality of instruction provided by a program, and the professional teaching staff that guides the learning of students through an evaluation process. A process that should be ongoing every day.

Obviously, from a personnel management standpoint, evaluation is a form of quality assurance, an effort at due diligence to determine if teachers are performing to district standards of performance set forth in board policy and procedure. Note, we did not use the words "quality control"—as the word "control" evokes a negative connotation.

The difficulty of effective evaluation of a professional is the establishment of objective standards to measure what at times is a very subjective determination or at least in the eyes of some people—particularly the teacher being evaluated. Education generally suffers from the concept that a teacher is a teacher is a teacher—with no differentiation, which in the human experience, generally, is impossible, as we are all different and approach our work with our own personality and work ethic. This overriding concept is supported by our method of compensating teachers on a grid based solely upon years of experience and degrees and hours of postgraduate attainment without any merit-based measure of compensation.

---

[17] In one of my all-time favorite sports films, *A League of Their Own*, Tom Hanks plays Jimmy, a battle-tested baseball manager charged with the task of coaching a team in the women's major leagues during World War II. Opposite Jimmy is Dottie, played with tortured passion by Geena Davis, the reluctant star player on the team and the linchpin of the fledgling league. After a particularly challenging stretch of games and just before the championships, Dottie tells Jimmy that she's had enough and is quitting.

Jimmy, in a fit of frustration, gives Dottie a piece of his mind. "Sneaking out like this…quitting…you'll regret it for the rest of your life. Baseball is what gets inside you. It's what lights you up. You can't deny that."

Dottie doesn't pause, and with tears in her eyes, she says, "It just got too hard."

Jimmy's response is poignant and priceless, "It's supposed to be hard. If it wasn't hard, everyone would do it. The hard is what makes it great" (https://www.irunfar.com/2018/07/the-hard-is-what-makes-it-great.html).

As such, from a practical point of view, there is no real monetary incentive to improve instructional performance. We are left with two alternatives to encourage improved performance:

- A negative approach: The job retention motivation
- *A positive kid-centered approach*: The commitment to improve student learning, a commitment that must be school- and/or district-wide so teachers do not feel that their efforts are not supported by others or valued by the principal, superintendent, board of education or community at-large—the persons to whom their students are eventually entrusted

This course is based upon the positive kid-centered approach (hereinafter PKCA). The idea of building the best teaching staff collectively through consistent, fair, and thoughtful evaluation process that has a sound base from which to construct that staff.

The Training of Evaluators

Effective teacher evaluation is a "big deal" and should be done well with integrity.[18] (Mary Beth Lehmanowsky Bakewell, April 12, 2019)

Anticipatory Set[19]

Question: What is a principal's most important job?
Answer: To assure that students are learning in the classroom—everything else is ancillary!
Question: How does a principal accomplish this most important job?
Answer: By effectively observing, monitoring, assisting, nurturing, and evaluating the persons who deliver the product of students who are learning and learning how to learn, the principal's greatest asset—their teachers.

Objective

The first step in building our PKCA is to train (teach!) the administrators responsible for the evaluation of staff, and subsequently evaluate the administrator's skill and effort in conducting teacher evaluations. If the administrators are NOT taught how to improve instruction and are NOT all-in on that goal, your school district and its students have lost already.

---

[18] E-mail from Mary Beth Lehmanowsky Bakewell, April 12, 2019:
"Hi Rex and Happy Friday, April 12, 2019
Thank YOU for presenting. We had a debrief after you left, and *I think the big rock they took away from your presentation is that this is a big deal and should be done well with integrity.* That is perfect. Yes, they learned a ton and I shared your power point with them. I greatly appreciate your time and expertise—you gave us lots to think about."
[19] From the ITIP lesson structure of Madeline Hunter. See infra.

Thus, your school district must be committed to teaching and then evaluating the evaluators. This instruction and learning by building is the principal's first step toward the end focus of this book—effective teaching, assistance, and evaluation of instructional staff.

Input

The framework for training and evaluating administrators includes the following elements:

First, evaluators must have the knowledge and skill to recognize the evaluative criteria in action.

Second, evaluators must have the skills to interpret the performance of a teacher based upon the evaluative criteria. Ideally, such interpretations should be based upon more than one observation or event.

Third, the evaluator must make a judgment about the teacher's performance, linking the interpretations to performance criteria. In reaching a determination (conclusion), the administrators must use an evidence-based process for the application of the evaluative criteria to the teacher's performance.

Fourth, and most important, the evaluator must effectively communicate the judgment about the teacher's performance using the performance criteria.

   A.   *Teaching as science*: The premise for all of what has gone before and what follows is the fact that effective teaching is, in part, based upon science. For many years, teaching was considered an art, e.g., "I know it when I see it." And, there is much merit to the innate talent to teach—those that have the creative minds and ability to communicate with people. People who just love to teach. So, as we discuss below the science of teaching and the concept that effective teaching can be taught, the art of teaching should not be dismissed or lost.

   Over the past forty years since Madeline Hunter authored the ITIP (Instructional Theory in Practice) model of the mastery of learning,[20] the fact that teaching is indeed a science has been universally accepted by educators at all levels—elementary, secondary, and postsecondary. The leading proffers of the science of teaching after Hunter have been Charlotte Danielson through her

---

[20] "Planning for Effective Lesson Design Los Angeles, California, Seeds Elementary School," 1976. Dr. Hunter's research showed effective teachers have a methodology when planning and presenting a lesson. Dr. Hunter found that no matter what the teacher's style, grade level, subject matter, or economic background of the students, a properly taught lesson contained eight elements that enhanced and maximize learning. The elements referred to as lesson design, target teaching, or critical teaching, have stood the test of time.

Framework for Teaching[21] and Robert Marzano, Debra J. Pickering, and Jane E. Pollack in *Classroom Instruction that Works.*[22]

The magic of good principalship is provide the structure of the science of teaching, while assisting your teachers to gain skills in the art of teaching to allow them to take their technical knowledge and be great (rather than abhorrent in front of their jury—their students. A sometimes difficult task, but one that has infinite rewards.

Dr. Riley's comment: When we think of the work of Madeline Hunter, Charlotte Danielson, and Robert Marzano, we should always pay respect to the researchers that came before them. For example, researchers from the late 1960s and early 1970s, such as Barak Rosenshine and Norma Furst, come to mind. Their research determined that teacher behavior directly affects student achievement. Although common knowledge today, such was not the case prior to their research. In fact, teacher evaluation in that time period primarily focused on items such as teacher dress, bulletin board displays, cleanliness of room, etc.

B. *Administrator's duty*: The administrator's duty is to assure that his/her staff has learned, understands, and can apply the elements of the science of teaching on a consistent basis in their lesson planning and instruction. All the elements of the ITIP framework are equally applicable to teaching the teachers. In fact, administrators should take the opportunity when providing an in-service to the teaching staff to model the science of teaching in the framework and educational model adopted by the school district. In other words, practice what you preach.

C. *Students > master teachers*: Students deserve and need master teachers that can guide them to learn how to learn, to understand concepts and ideas, and to engage in higher levels of thinking. All of this learning, exploring, and discovering must occur in a safe and nurturing learning environment that values every student.

D. *Competency*: While our focus is on improving teacher competency, such competency is measured on the basis of a just cause standard. Generally, "just cause" is defined as follows:

---

[21] Charlotte Danielson, *Enhancing Professional Practice: A Framework for Teaching*, 1996.

[22] Robert Marzano, Debra J. Pickering, and Jane E. Pollack, *Classroom Instruction that Works: Research-Based Strategies for Increasing Student Achievement*, 2001.

(4) Just cause means: (a) Incompetency, which includes, but is not limited to, demonstrated deficiencies or shortcomings in knowledge of subject matter or teaching or administrative skills; (b) neglect of duty; (c) unprofessional conduct; (d) insubordination; (e) immorality; (f) physical or mental incapacity;...or (h) other conduct which interferes substantially with the continued performance of duties.[23]

See Appendix A for similar statutes in other states.

Considering all of that discussed above, the result of the entire process is a measurement of teacher competency. It sounds harsh. No one wants to be called incompetent.

Dr. Pace's comment: And an administrator who has conducted or allowed drive-by evaluations that say "meets expectations" with little or nothing more is just as incompetent and shares in the blame.

An administrator with whom I was working on an evaluation document once told me that stating the just cause elements in an evaluation was soul crushing. And in part she was right. Those words can apply hurt to a person. In part, however, she did not appreciate the realities of the legal process. Those words carry weight and are required by statute. That said, if you are going to use those "soul crushing" words, you had better have the evidence set forth in documentation to back it up! Your credibility with your entire staff is on the line.

For our purposes here, we are focused for the most part on incompetency in the delivery of instruction in the classroom, and management of the classroom (e.g., the learning environment). Certainly, administrators must evaluate a teacher's personal and professional conduct that goes to the other elements of just cause that may affect student learning, but we are focused here on the quality of instruction and the learning going on in those classrooms.

In upcoming chapters, we will explore how to measure teacher competency, i.e., does a teacher meet the standard of performance expected of teachers in your school district.

E. *Process and the law.* We are not going to discuss herein specific statutes with regard to teacher competency or the measuring of same under laws established by state legislators that govern teacher contracts, evaluation, or termination or

---

[23] Neb. Rev. Stat. §79-824(4). Nearly all states have a similar definition of just cause. See Appendix A for a listing of each state and a link to their respective statutes on teacher tenure.

cancellation of contract. Every state has specific statutory schemes and case law interpreting same, setting forth the continuing contract rights of teachers (if any), required evaluation procedures and time lines, and the process and procedure governing the cancellation or termination of teacher contracts. The teacher tenure statutes of all fifty (50) states are listed in Appendix A attached hereto. *You should consult with your school attorney about the content and application of these statutes and case law.*

It is essential to the job of a school principal to know the law, because the failure to know and follow the law or your attorney's teaching or advice can be career ending.

Could You Send Us the Nonrenewal Letter?

The call was scheduled at eight thirty, April 13. On the line was the assistant superintendent, the middle school principal, and the assistant principal. On the other end was the school attorney.

The assistant superintendent said, "We have a third-year probationary teacher. He teaches pre-algebra. We have concerns about his treatment of students—too much touching, being too familiar, nothing really serious, but since we can non-renew for any reason, we think he is not a good fit for our district."

The middle school principal chimed in, "He knows math, but I just think we can do better. Can you send us the nonrenewal letter?"

The attorney paused, and said, "Well, before we can send you the letter, we need to see the teacher's entire personnel file, including all of your observations and evaluations of the teacher for each of his three years of employment."

The middle school principal said, "That should not be a problem, Mr. Assistant Principal has evaluated the teacher. Can you send the letter?"

There was no comment during the conversation from the assistant principal.

The attorney said, "No. Not until we see the file."

The middle school principal said, "Well, okay. I will scan it in and send it to you."

The scanned file arrived later in the afternoon. A cursory examination of the file revealed that the teacher had been evaluated only once in each of his three years of service to the school district, in March of each year, including the current year on March 10. And, he was rated as meeting school district expectations and standards in virtually every rubric under that school district evaluation instrument, including teacher-student relations. Obviously, the middle school principal and the assistant principal had not met the statutory requirements

---

mandating the observation and summative evaluation of probationary teachers once each semester for each of the three-year probationary period.

The attorney called the assistant superintendent back and said, "I have examined the file your principal provided. It is clear that your middle school administrative staff, both the principal and the assistant principal, have not met the minimum requirements for the evaluation of the teacher—a probationary teacher—under your evaluation procedure and state statute. Yes, you can non-renew a probationary contract for any reason you deem sufficient, but our Supreme Court has held that in order to do so, you must comply with the statutory requirements for teacher evaluation, and your team is not even close."

The assistant superintendent said, "I looked at the file too. I can see that we have not done a good job."

The attorney said, "Obviously you can go forward with nonrenewal if you want and see if the NSEA raises the lack of evaluations. It is pretty obvious, and as we say in the law, 'Bad facts make bad law,' and these are bad facts. So, I would advise against it."

The attorney further advised, "Termination is a remedy available if you have not complied with Section 79-828, but not here. Unfortunately, not only are you not in a position to non-renew, but you do not have just cause to terminate the teacher's contract. The teacher's evaluations that were done rate him as exemplary and give no indication of the issue you identified yesterday. So, your only option is to see if you can counsel the teacher out without threat of nonrenewal or termination."

The assistant superintendent asked, "Any other advice?"

The attorney said, "Yes. It would seem the evaluations of the principal and assistant principal should reflect the failure to meet the minimum standards of your evaluation procedure and state statute. Both were at the workshop we [the school attorney] presented last year, and yet they failed to meet the minimum statutory standards."

In the end, the teacher was counseled out, the assistant principal left the school district, and the middle school principal hopefully will make sure that the assistant principals she delegates the duty to evaluate staff do so.

The moral of the story:

1. *Do your evaluations when required by your evaluation process and the law!* The failure to do so is neglect of duty, unprofessional conduct, insubordination, and substantially interferes with the continued performance of a principal's duties.

2. *Listen to your school attorney!* He/she does this all the time, knows the law and the application of same by practice and the courts, and most importantly, has experienced most personnel situations and can guide you to a result that is best for students, staff, the school and community, and—to be sure—you.

Jim Gessford notes the legal peril of not following the rules in statute, state regulation, or the school district's own policies.

James B. Gessford: Strict compliance. Many courts will require strict compliance with all source requirements, and with the evaluation model, even the slightest variation may be cause for reinstatement. For example, the Ohio Supreme Court recently held that if a board of education fails to strictly comply with the evaluation procedures mandated by statute, a teacher is entitled to back pay and reinstatement. In *Farmer*,[24] each written evaluation was to be based upon two classroom observations. Since the school principal only observed one class before giving his written evaluation, the statute had been violated, and the teacher was reinstated with an award of back pay. In some states, the failure to follow state department of education policies with respect to teacher evaluations prohibits the "board from discharging, demoting, or transferring an employee for reasons having to do with prior misconduct or incompetency that has not been called to the attention of the employee through evaluation and which is correctable." *The court noted that school personnel regulations and evaluation policies should be strictly construed in favor of the teacher. Therefore, when the principal failed to have a post-observation evaluation conference, the teacher was entitled to be "reinstated and given an open and fair opportunity to prove her professional competency as a teacher"*[25] (emphasis added, citations omitted except as footnoted).

Dr. Riley's comment: These problems can be avoided by knowing your teachers, knowing the law, and having a solid relationship with your school district attorney. Building administrators should have a relatively good feel for the strengths and weaknesses of every staff member. Furthermore, a building administrator should know the abilities and areas for improvement of each probationary staff member within the first two weeks of such staff members' tenure. Proper communications with new and probationary staff through the utilization of the district evaluation and supervision model are essential. Once it is determined that there is a viable concern, the district legal counsel should be brought into the conversation. Administrators cannot make mistakes when it comes to contract renewal or contract nonrenewal of teaching personnel.

---

[24] *Farmer v. Kelleys Island Bd. of Educ.*, 630 N.E.2d 721 (Ohio 1994).

[25] James B. Gessford, JD, National School Boards Associations, The School Law Review 1995, 6-5. See also *Lapan v. Board of Educ. County of Hancock*, 295 S.E.2d 44 (W.Va. 1982), and *Cox v. York Cty. Sch. Dist. No. 083*, 560 N.W.2d 138 (1997) (holding that the school district could not terminate/non-renew the teacher's contract because the first semester evaluation based on actual classroom observations for an entire instructional period as required by Neb. Rev. Stat. § 79-12, 111 [now § 79-828] did not occur until the second semester of the school year).

Check for Understanding

So, where do we start? We start where every successful human endeavor begins, with laying down a solid foundation! To check your understanding of the concept we have been discussing, you need to answer the following questions:

- How does your school district train evaluators of teachers to competently and effectively evaluate their teaching staff?
- How do effective administrators view and treat the teachers under their care and supervision?
- How do effective administrators teach and lead (rather than tell and dictate) the teachers (the basic and the distinguished) under their care and supervise the science of teaching?
- How do effective administrators go about using the science of teaching in their schools to support and increase student learning?
- How do you engage teachers through education, guiding, supporting, and nurturing their skill to maintain or develop the master teachers that students, parents, and communities deserve?
- How do you communicate to teachers the job duties and expectations and standards of performance expected of your teaching staff in a positive collaborative manner?
- How do you effectively assist teachers in clear and direct language through well-written communications through formative and summative evaluation?

Our goal is to encourage a philosophy of administration that develops teacher skills and provides the tools and develop skills for you to effectively write evaluations of teachers.

Guided Practice and Independent Study

Your assignment:

1. Please obtain through Barnes and Noble or other online service the following books:
   - *I'd Like to Apologize to Every Teacher I Ever Had: My Year as a Rookie Teacher at Northeast High* by Tony Danza, 2012.
   - *Teach Like a PIRATE: Increase Student Engagement, Boost Your Creativity, and Transform Your Life as an Educator* by Dave Burgess, 2012.

   Reading will be assigned from both books throughout the course.
2. Obtain a copy of Nebraska Department of Education, Rule 10, Section 0007, or your state's regulations on teacher evaluation.
3. Download Neb. Rev. Stat. §79-824 through 79-848, or your corresponding state statutes, at https://nebraskalegislature.gov/laws/statutes.php?statute.

CHAPTER 2

The Assets—The Intangible and Essential Component

In that classroom my life makes sense.[26]

—Erin, *Freedom Writers*

In our society, each endeavor, whether charitable, nonprofit, or for profit, is intended to produce a certain result or has a certain goal. Schools, colleges, and universities, whether public or private or religious in financial support and philosophy, all seek the same result and goal—to effectively educate the students entrusted to them. To put it in business terms—the well-educated student is the product produced by the endeavor.

The Assets and the Product

To carry our analogy further, every business endeavor needs assets to produce the product.[27] The assets needed to accomplish the result or goal of producing the product of a well-educated student obviously can include writings. If fact, it is often said that the basis for modern society was the invention of the printing press (thank you, Guttenberg)—the vehicle that allowed the spread of ideas and the refinement of those ideas, which became the building block of technological and learning advancement. While books may appear to be old school, the writing down of ideas remains the basis for learning and advancement in whatever form.

In addition to books, today education relies on other assets and equipment. We live in the Information Age. Through computers (now old school) and the use of the Internet through various devices and platforms (new school)—we literally have the total of the human experience from time immemorial in our hands every day; that does not mean it is a good thing! Everywhere you go, people are looking at their devices (phones, iPads, computers, etc.) rather than talking to one another—leading to a society that lacks the ability to communicate

---

[26] *Freedom Writers* is a 2007 American drama film written and directed by Richard LaGravenese and starring Hilary Swank, Scott Glenn, Imelda Staunton, Patrick Dempsey, and Mario. In the film, Swank's character, Erin, is arguing with her husband, who just does not understand her all-consuming zeal for teaching. Erin turns to him and says, "I don't know, but in that classroom my life makes sense."

[27] Dr. Pace's comment: Some will, rightly in my view, push back on the factory-product analogy, but I'm not sharing anything new there.

on an interpersonal level, a challenge we must address going forward, a challenge that educational institutions are now called upon to address.

Whether old school or new school, the essential element to learning has always been, and continues to be, effective teachers to teach the skills students need to learn and learn how to learn *and* the social and societal skills and responsibilities to effectively communicate and be positive and productive members of society and citizens who are knowledgeable and capable of higher levels of thinking.

Thus, the essential asset of any educational institution, preschool, elementary schools, middle school, high school, college, or university are the *teachers, instructors, and professors.*

Merriam-Webster Dictionary's definition of asset:[28]
noun
    1: a valuable person or thing
    2: something that is owned by a person, company, etc.

Craftsman

Unlike most businesses, however, the product produced by these assets—the well-educated student who has been taught and learned the basic skills of how to learn—is not mass-produced in the Henry Ford manner. Each student (the product) is different, just as every original painting is different. The assets referred to here—our teachers—are craftsmen.[29] These craftsmen recognize that every student is different—different in learning style, different in background and home life, different in interests, each one unique. A teacher that develops his/her craft can have a profound effect on the lives of students. As one commentator encouraging a career in elementary education so succinctly noted, "*Elementary school can shape a child's view of education. If you can spark an interest in learning in the children of your class, you can have a positive effect on the rest of their education career. Through creative learning techniques and inventive ways of approaching the curriculum, you can ensure your students will appreciate the job of discovery and have a lifelong interest in learning*" (emphasis added).[30]

---

[28] https://www.merriam-webster.com/dictionary/asset#synonyms.
[29] *Merriam-Webster Dictionary*'s definition of craftsman:
noun
    1: a worker who practices a trade or handicraft
    2: one who creates or performs with skill or dexterity especially in the manual arts jewelry made by European craftsmen
Merriam-Webster Learner's Dictionary's definition:
    a person (especially a man) who makes beautiful objects by hand
[30] http://www.jobs.net/article/cb-224-talent-network-hospitality-molding-minds-6-reasons-to-become-a-grade-school-teacher.

Mrs. Crosspatch vs. Mrs. Columbus

There once was a little boy who loved school. He smiled easily, and he loved to learn. His kindergarten picture shows a little boy with a sunny personality and an ease of being. He graduated into the first grade and was assigned to the classroom of Mrs. Crosspatch (the name has been changed, but not much). As her name sounds, Mrs. Crosspatch was not a craftsman teacher. Her approach was the mass production approach of Henry Ford—a rigid, regulated, and demanding environment. She was not nurturing her students. She was not empathetic. She was stern and demeaning toward first graders! The little boy lost this love for school and came to think he could not learn, that learning was hard and not fun. In short, he lost confidence in himself at the age of six. A loss of confidence that he struggled with his entire life. Through sheer will and perseverance, he became an excellent educator and eventually a school administrator—dedicated to never having a Mrs. Crosspatch in his school.

There was another little boy who had the privilege (yes, privilege) of having Mrs. Columbus in the sixth grade (Columbus after Christopher, get it?). Mrs. Columbus saw every student as unique and laid before each a challenge that fit their interests. If she saw a student bored or off task, the student was given a learning opportunity, something fun and engaging. She oozed excellence and gave students the opportunity to achieve it without demanding a level of performance. It was up to the student. There was pressure, but only self-imposed to meet the standard set in the classroom—a bit of a competitive environment. But as noted above, Mrs. Columbus sparked an interest in learning for the little boy in the sixth grade that carried over for the rest of his educational career and his chosen career thereafter. Mrs. Columbus was a craftsman who had mastered the art of giving her students the experience of discovery and engendered a lifelong interest in learning. Mrs. Columbus went on to become a superintendent of schools in a very large district, and eventually a college professor—teaching the next generation of craftsmen.

As the adage goes, teachers have the opportunity to mold the minds of students—not just in learning but as persons in our society. As one teacher stated, "Cheesy as it may sound, my past and present students are always my inspiration in teaching. I want to use the time they spend in my class to mold them to become better individuals someday."[31]

---

[31] https://lifestyle.inquirer.net/277230/teacher-molds-students-minds-clay/#ixzz69hR00kdB.

Developing and Maintaining the Assets (Craftsmen)

So how do businesses seek to improve their human assets—their employees? The answer for businesses is effective appraisal of an employee's performance, and assistance in improving that performance. The long-held purposes of employee appraisal really have not changed over the past forty years.

Dr. Pace's comment: Reminds me of the old wisdom that says, "Don't tell me your priorities. Show me your budget (or your calendar) and I will be able to tell." Despite the competing demands on the principal's time, the way we spend our time is telling.

As stated the *Harvard Business Review* in a 1976 article by Harry Levinson:

> Performance appraisal has three basic functions: (1) to provide adequate feedback to each person on his or her performance; (2) to serve as a basis for modifying or changing behavior toward more effective working habits; and (3) to provide data to managers with which they may judge future job assignments and compensation. The performance appraisal concept is central to effective management. Much hard and imaginative work has gone into developing and refining it. In fact, there is a great deal of evidence to indicate how useful and effective performance appraisal is. Yet present systems of performance appraisal do not serve any of these functions well.[32]

The modern approach to the effective use of appraisal for businesses (and by analogy for schools) has been stated as follows:

> If you're a small business owner and haven't gotten around to offering employee performance appraisals, now is the time to start. Performance appraisals can benefit employees and organizations by clarifying goals and

---

[32] https://hbr.org/1976/07/appraisal-of-what-performance.

"As it is customarily defined and used, performance appraisal focuses not on behavior but on outcomes of behavior. But even though the executive in the example achieved his objective, he was evaluated on how he attained it. Thus, while the system purports to appraise results, in practice, people are really appraised on how they do things—which is not formally described in the setting of objectives, and for which there are rarely data on record.

"In my experience, the crucial aspect of any manager's job and the source of most failures, which is practically never described, is the 'how.' As long as managers appraise the ends yet actually give greater weight to the means, employ a static job description base which does not describe the 'how,' and do not have support mechanisms for the appraisal process, widespread dissatisfaction with performance appraisal is bound to continue. In fact, one personal authority speaks of performance appraisal as 'the Achilles heel of our profession.'"

expectations and creating an environment of open communication. The best performance appraisals offer positive feedback and advice for improvement, and typically consist of a conversation between management and the employee.

Function

Performance appraisals help supervisors and employees to identify strengths and weaknesses of employee performance. They offer an opportunity for supervisors and employees to discuss the employee's goals for himself, the supervisor's goals for the larger department or organization and ways that the employee and the supervisor can work together by further developing skills and strengths necessary to reach these goals.

Significance

The best performance appraisals create a link between individual employee expectations and how the employee's work contributes to the larger organization's success. They clarify expectations that the supervisor has for the employee and help the employee prioritize his duties. Ideally, performance appraisals open the lines of communication between supervisors and employees.

Benefits

Performance appraisals benefit the company as well as individual employees. They increase rapport between management and employees, increase job satisfaction and improve employees' sense of loyalty toward the company. Performance appraisals assist the employee in seeing how her role in the organization contributes to the company's overall success, thus increasing employee morale. All of these lead to higher productivity among employees, which improves organizational productivity.

Considerations

Performance appraisals should not be used as substitutes for consistent, open communication.

According to Carter McNamara of Authenticity Consulting LLC, "Nothing should be surprising to the employee during the appraisal meeting. Any performance issues should have been addressed as soon as those issues occurred." After a performance appraisal, make sure to check in with the employee consistently to discuss his progress toward the goals set during the meeting. This will help keep employees motivated.

Expert Insight

McNamara recommends starting the performance appraisal meeting by making it clear that the goal of the appraisal is to exchange ideas and work together to come up with an action plan for meeting the employee's and the organization's goals. He suggests allowing the employee to offer input first, responding with your own input and then discussing any areas of disagreement. "Attempt to avoid defensiveness... Discuss behaviors, not personalities," says McNamara. He also recommends trying to end the meeting on a positive note. ("How Performance Appraisal is Helpful for Business Improvement" by Megan Martin)[33]

Effective teacher evaluation can have the same effect as for businesses, and "lead to higher productivity among employees, which improves organizational productivity." As stated by commentators on teacher evaluation:

We find that teachers are more productive during the school year when they are being evaluated, but even more productive in the years after evaluation. A student taught by a teacher after that teacher has been through the Cincinnati evaluation will score about 10 percent of a standard deviation higher in math than a similar student taught by the same teacher before the teacher was evaluated. ("The Effect of Evaluation on Teacher Performance by Eric S. Taylor and John H. Tyler).[34]

As noted by Megan Martin above, in each of her elements of effective appraisal, the key word is "communication." Logically, a first step in our consideration of effective teacher evaluation is asking those "who are so wise in the ways of science" are evaluating, "What do teachers want out of the evaluation process?"

Teacher buy-in to the use of a teaching framework and educational model and the attendant evaluation process is essential. I asked Maddie Fennel, executive director of the Nebraska State Education Association, this exact question; she responded as follows:

"Teachers want a process that is:
- Realistic—don't expect them to be 100% perfect nor are they 100% deficient.

---

[33] https://smallbusiness.chron.com/performance-appraisal-helpful-business-improvement-3073.html.
[34] https://scholar.harvard.edu/files/evaluation-performance-tt.pdf.

- "Focused on growth—be clear about how a teacher *has* grown and provide concrete examples if you need to see more growth.
    - What does [the administration] want you to see?
    - By when?
    - What is evidence of that?
- "NOT that everything must be proficient by next year; set realistic expectations.
    - How will the district support that growth? What are they offering to help?
    - "Help EVERY teacher grow. I hear from so many exemplary teachers who are disappointed when an administrator just says how great they are but doesn't offer ANY way for them to grow or change."
    - "Support by facts—be clear about when you were in the classroom, what you saw and how that is contributing to the evaluation. Don't be vague or make statements you can't support with concrete evidence and examples."
- Be honest about WHY someone isn't advancing.
    - Give them suggestions about what they could do to enhance their prospects, even if that means suggesting they go to another district (I know that's easy to say but hard for an admin/employer)."
    - "And, if a performance improvement plan is needed, make it should be:
        - Concrete.
        - Time bound.
        - Realistic—they still have a full-time job!
        - Focused only on 2-3 necessary changes at a time."
        - "Clear about what the evidence of improvement is (not—"Your attitude is better")."
        - "Clear in saying what time or resources the district is committing to help the individual achieve the needed result."
    - Control of curriculum (involved in development).
    - Opportunity to advance.

Fairly and constructively evaluated as to quality of teaching by caring administrators who are master teachers, e.g. qualified."

A veteran master teacher agreed with Ms. Fennel's analysis of what teachers want from the evaluation process, and added that a principal should consider what he called an audience analysis when evaluating the effectiveness of a teacher's performance, stating, "At some point administrators need to use what my high school speech teacher used to call 'audience analysis.' Give a teacher a class filled with students on IEPs and a bunch of 'normal' kids who are on academic probation and expect Rhodes Scholars is just a bit outside of the realm of possibility."[35]

To this point, principals need to know the students in their school and recognize the challenges presented to a teacher. As public educators, we all understand that we are committed to teach every student that enrolls in our schools. The measurement of a teacher's success in the classroom cannot be test scores per se, but the level of preparation and instructional skills demonstrated in an attempt to reach students. A good teacher will not reach all students, but more than if the effort is not being made. That should be the measure.

Investing

While communication with your teaching staff is essential, it is equally essential that you consider those teachers as an investment that has been made by (1) you personally if you were involved in the hiring of this person or, indirectly, (2) a person hired by the school district prior to your tenure as an administrator. Investors want a return on their investments. That is why there are so many advertisements on trading strategies—TD Ameritrade, Schwab, etc.

School districts in hiring a teacher want a return on investment—excellent teaching. Your job is to teach (not tell) your staff the science of teaching to assure that return on investment.

A failure to teach your staff to the standard of performance expected of teachers in your school district results in a loss on the school district's investment with ramifications much more critical than a loss of dollars on a stock. It is a loss for the students being taught by a failing teacher. It is a possible loss for the teacher of self-confidence and possibly a career in education (and we cannot afford these days to lose these professionals) and a loss to the school district's overall mission.

Two and Out!

She was a twenty-four-year-old second-year teacher. Her first teaching job. She taught high school students Algebra I and Algebra II. She knew her subject. But she struggled conveying her knowledge to her students. In her second year, only 25 percent of her students received a passing grade in her classes on average.[36] Halfway through the second semester, the same ratio was playing out. As a result, the administration of the school district recommended that her probationary contract not be renewed at the end of her

---

[35] Gary Largo, master teacher, Scottsbluff High School in Scottsbluff, Nebraska.

[36] Dr. Pace's comment: And I know some teachers who would view that as a badge of honor and indication of the rigor of their class. And teachers would be reflecting deeply on how they failed. I've always liked Dr. Tony Wagner's definition of rigor, which is that which students are able to do as the result of a learning experience. Far too often what some call rigor is actually tedious busy work. And that's a shame.

second year. She requested a hearing before the board of education—arguing that she should be given another year and that she would improve with administrative assistance.

The following is the opening statement to the board of education by school district counsel at the hearing:

Good evening. I will keep this short. We are here to address the administration's recommendation to non-renew the probationary teaching contract of Ms. Smith.

The evidence you will see and hear from the administration and Ms. Smith supports that recommendation. Ms. Smith began teaching at the School District during the 2012–2013 school year. Her evaluations during that year raised some concerns. Specifically, she did not utilize "learning targets" and relied too much upon lecturing—talking at students instead of engaging them in learning.

The evidence will show that Ms. Smith's method of teaching did not and does not lead to student success. Ms. Smith's struggles persisted in 2013-2014.

She once again did not engage students in learning. Students did not understand what was expected of them. Ms. Smith again relied too heavily on a lecture style of teaching.

Ms. Smith did not communicate effectively with students or with parents.

In many ways, she had significant problems in that she left students behind. That is really why we're here tonight—Ms. Smith's inability to effectively engage students in the learning process. As a result of this inability, students did not learn the subject matter that Ms. Smith was to teach as established by the grades reflecting student learning issued to students by Ms. Smith.

These problems persisted despite advice from administrators and monthly PLC meetings.

In sum, the evidence will show that despite assistance, Ms. Smith is simply not an effective classroom teacher. She has not competently planned and prepared lessons, has not delivered instruction in a manner that effectively engages students, has not differentiated instruction, and has not created an environment that is conducive to student learning, and as a result, the students in her class are consistently falling behind. As you listen to the evidence, the primary thought to keep in the forefront is that this hearing is not about Mrs. Smith, this hearing is about student learning as we go forward into the 2014–2015 school year and future years.

At the end of the hearing we believe you will find that students have not learned mathematics effectively in Ms. Smith's classroom and that Ms. Smith's probationary teaching contract with the district should not be renewed. Thank you.

Unfortunately, as Paul Harvey always said (maybe too old for most of you), we need to consider the rest of the story. The facts as brought out in the hearing were that while Ms. Smith was provided PLC[37] training in classroom management, she was not provided any individual assistance by the building principal. The principal was in her classroom for observations one time during each semester and based the semester evaluation (as required by law) upon that observation and student failure records. While Ms. Smith had been struggling her first year, and student assessments indicated the students' overall difficulty in grasping the subject matter, there was no assistance from the administration in lesson planning, presentation, teaching to understanding, or preparing assessments of student learning—nothing. In other words, there was no investment in Ms. Smith. The message or approach—sink or swim with the measure being only student achievement.

In the end, Ms. Smith's contract was not renewed. The board based its decision on assuring student learning in future years—not taking the risk on Ms. Smith going forward.

The students lost, Ms. Smith lost, and the school district lost a potentially talented teacher who just needed a bit of nurturing and support in the science of teaching. In short, an investment lost.

PS. Shortly after, the principal left the school district.

So how do you invest in your assets? *By laying the foundation for effective teacher improvement and thereby student learning!*

In part 2 of this book, we will address the foundation to be laid for your teachers, but first, we must consider the foundation that administrators must have to teach and lead their professional staff in the science of teaching.

Your assignment:
1. Write a paragraph of what you learned from reading "Two and Out!" In your paragraph, answer the following questions:

---

[37] A professional learning community, or PLC, is a group of educators that meets regularly, shares expertise, and works collaboratively to improve teaching skills and the academic performance of students. An ongoing process in which educators work collaboratively in recurring cycles of collective inquiry and action research to achieve better results for the students they serve.

- o The supposed expert in teaching did nothing to help her improve, so what is the principal's role in that failure?
- o What would you have done?
2. Read Chapters 1 to 3 of *I'd Like to Apologize to Every Teacher I Ever Had.*
3. Read part 1, "Teach Like a Pirate!" of *Teach Like a PIRATE.*
4. Draft a memorandum answering the following questions:
    - o What courses in undergraduate or graduate school have you taken that focus on the elements of effective teaching?
    - o Are you a master teacher?
    - o What do you need to do to be a master teacher?
    - o Did you learn an instructional framework and education model in your undergraduate or graduate classes? If so, which one?
    - o Do you know the elements of that instructional framework and education model?
    - o Has your school district adopted an instructional framework and education model, and if so, which one?
    - o Is your instructional framework and education model embedded in your evaluation instrument?
    - o Have you been trained on your school district's instructional framework and education model? If so, does that training occur every year?
    - o Is your training on your instructional framework and education model documented? If so, how?

CHAPTER 3

The Master Teacher—How Long Do You Think It Takes to Really Get Good at Teaching?

It's when they get it. It takes some time for sure, but you can tell the ones who'll be great teachers. They are the ones with the passion. The ones who try things and watch other teachers, and network with teachers even outside their subject areas… You've got to be able to excite the kids with a story or an action and then get them to bite on what you want them to learn.

—Bobby responding to Tony's question[38]

Recently a longtime elementary principal said to me, "You must be a master teacher to lead and train master teachers."[39]

What does it mean for an administrator to be a master teacher? While one can get a certification as a master teacher, the master teaching we are discussing is an administrator's skills and attributes of *being a master teacher who can teach teachers* the skill of the science of teaching to get students to learn and learn how to learn. (Wow! That was a mouthful! Your assignment is to say that three times really fast and see how you do).

You as an administrator need to be a master teacher to fill four essential aspects of leadership in your school. First, be able to recognize all elements of good teaching in the classroom, effective planning, effective (and varied) delivery of instruction, effective student assessment, effective intervention/reteaching, enrichment, effective classroom management, and appropriate personal and professional conduct. Second, have the skills to provide effective assistance to these skills of effective teaching. Third, demonstrate master teaching skills in leading your staff, either individually or in groups. Collectively these three elements can be summed up in three words: "teach, don't tell."[40] And fourth, create a standard as a basis for a culture of excellence for and with your instructional staff.

What is a master teacher? Is it in the eyes of the beholder? Or, again, are there scientifically established elements to the skill? Obviously for our purposes it is the later.

What then are the characteristics of a master teacher?

---

[38] Danza, *I'd Like to Apologize to Every Teacher I Ever Had*, 75.
[39] Mark M. Schultze, principal, Disney Elementary, Millard Public Schools in Omaha, Nebraska.
[40] Dr. Todd Whitaker, keynote speaker, Nebraska Counsel of School Administrators—Administrator Days, August 11, 2019.

A commentator has described a master teacher as one who has mastered the basics of teaching, goes above and beyond to ensure a positive learning experience for each student, and shares his or her knowledge with the broader learning community.[41]

Most experts agree that master teachers are those who clearly demonstrate competency in five (5) specific areas.

- Focus on student learning
- Fair and effective classroom management
- Experts in their practice as a teacher
- Active participation in ongoing professional development
- Leaders in the educational community

Let's discuss each of these areas.

1. First, a master teacher is focused on student learning; believes that all students can learn; is committed to the success of their students; possesses a deep understanding of how students learn and develop; and strives to create positive learning environments for all students, regardless of current skills or ability levels. A master teacher is focused on creating a learning environment that is consistent, fair, and effective; has an organized and pleasant environment that is conducive to learning and academic risk-taking; and is a place where students feel valued, encouraged, and safe.

2. Second, master teachers are experts in their practice. They use research-based teaching methods to design, plan, and deliver effective lessons; they understand and use the most current and effective teaching strategies to engage students in their learning. Most importantly, they think outside the box, *moving beyond worksheets and textbooks* to provide the most *meaningful learning experiences possible for their students*.

3. Third, master teachers are experts in their content areas. They know their subjects and not only understand the history, content, and real-world applications of their subjects, but they also possess a deep understanding of how students with diverse sets of skills and background knowledge can learn. They anticipate gaps in understanding and can predict the skills or concepts with which students will most likely struggle and take measures to prevent or fill those gaps. They offer clear paths to learning by balancing structure, flexibility, and opportunities for students to practice and develop over time.

4. Fourth, master teachers actively participate in ongoing professional development and are lifelong learners and are never satisfied with the knowledge and skills they have already gained. They continually seek out opportunities to develop as practitioners in their content areas, studying the latest research and literature on their subjects and

---

[41] https://study.com/academy/lesson/master-teacher-definition-and-examples.html.

stretching their skill sets and strategies in the classroom, and critically examine their methods and practice and adjust their techniques as they learn more.[42]

5. Fifth, the most important part of being a master teacher is helping students to feel good about themselves. Taking an answer that is not quite there and helping the student to gain the rest of it and feel good about the process. And you have to have a genuine love of kids and a willingness to let them *struggle* and not hold that against them. *If that works for teachers and students, why not with administrators and teachers. You would be amazed at how far a positive statement or supportive comment goes, especially when so few are ever heard or even dreamed of.*[43]

Dr. Riley's comment: In my opinion, the best definition of a master teacher was given by a professor at the University of Nebraska at Lincoln. His name escapes me. Regardless, he stated there are four types of teachers:

1. The task master: This teacher starts class on time and is extremely prepared. There are high behavioral and academic expectations for the students and the teacher. No class time is wasted.
2. The social connector: This teacher knows the students by name. This teacher knows the student's likes and dislikes, knows their family, knows their activities. This teacher attends student activities, games, concerts, and performances.
3. The creative dynamo: This teacher is constantly finding new and innovative ways to teach a concept in a manner in which students never forget. This might be a chemistry teacher that teaches the chemical compounds of ice cream and then applies that knowledge by making the delectable dessert, with students, during class time.
4. The master teacher: This teacher knows how and when to move in and out of the first three categories.

We discussed above how you as an administrator would apply the skill of being a master teacher to leading your instructional staff.

Your next question may be, am I a master teacher? If the answer is yes, great! But do not sit on your laurels. Always strive to get better, learn more, and share that knowledge with your staff.

If the answer is no or there is self-doubt, e.g., what if I do not feel I have those skills?

Not to despair! As noted above, you need to be a lifelong learner. No matter what we do as a professional, we are all a work in progress—or hopefully so. If you do not feel you are a

---

[42] https://study.com/academy/lesson/master-teacher-definition-and-examples.html
[43] Gary Largo.

master teacher at this point, work to make yourself one. Read books on great administration and teaching skills. The numerous works of Dr. Todd Whitaker (he of "teach, don't tell") are an excellent source for administrators. Work at modeling master teaching skills every day. Your teachers are your students.

In education today, is the foregoing pep talk realistic? Yes, it is what all school administrators (principals) should strive to attain, but does the lay of the land in American education structure to promote master teaching? Dr. Pace poses the following question:

> What percentage of teachers would label their principals as master teachers? This has probably been studied. I suspect it is a small percentage and that leads me to think of the problems with teaching as a profession. It is so hard to move up or advance or stay fresh or earn more, unless one leaves the classroom to become an administrator. That is a systemic problem and one that deprofessionalizes teaching. In my view, the all too frequent lack of professional pathways for expert teachers is an indictment of how we view education, teachers, and investing in professional growth.

Dr. Pace has hit on a key to improving educational results in our country—raising the compensation for the teaching profession to allow master teachers to stay in the classroom at a level commensurate with their education, skill, and dedication to student learning, and while that is a battle for another day,[44] an effective evaluation process and principals who understand what constitutes good teacher and coaches to it, and can recognize good teaching, will be an essential component to improving teacher compensation.

---

[44] In Nebraska, teachers are literally paid by the day at a per diem rate based upon their step on the indexed salary schedule, a salary schedule that is totally objective—year of experiences down and level of education across, with no adjustment for merit or achievement. The teacher's association has roundly rejected any effort to distinguish between Mrs. Jones and Mrs. Anderson in relation to their effectiveness as a teacher. A first step would be to change that culture, with the salary schedule being the floor of compensation and merit pay added. Which brings us full circle back to our topic: effective evaluation of teacher performance. If a good evaluation would result in increased pay, the evaluation process takes on an entirely new perspective for both the administrators (we all like to regard good performance) and the teacher (we all like to see something for our efforts—a pat on the back is just not enough, dollars talk).

So how could this be done? Well, it is a subject for another possible book, but in short, with today's technology and the fact that studies show students regress in their learning over the three-month summer, a move to fewer teachers through more efficient use of staff even in remote areas and year-round school with teachers paid at their per diem base rate plus performance stipends or bonuses can raise teacher salaries by no less than 30 percent. Assuming a 240-day school year, a teacher with a master's degree making $60,000 a year for a typical 185-day contract would make a base pay of around $78,000 on a 240-day school year, with possible merit pay bonuses. Some will say that teachers need the summer months to get postgraduate hours to move across the salary schedule. In fact, over the past ten years, statistics show that teachers achieve graduate hours throughout a calendar year though online coursework from accredited colleges and universities, so this excuse is a misnomer.

As a society, we would have to give up the agrarian time off for planting and harvest and accept that we are a society that is more homogenous through technology wherever we live. *It will also require teachers as a whole to have faith in the evaluation process and integrity.*

Obviously, such a sea of change would involve significant political issues, both financial and social, the impact on local control of schools, and a change in family schedules. Change is hard but, in this case, necessary. But I digress.

A Culture of Excellence

In being a master teacher to your teachers, you have an essential tool to create a culture of excellence. A culture of excellence is a habit. A habit that can be a result in subconsciously adopted behaviors that generate excellent outcomes. A culture of excellence is here defined as "an organizational context encouraging behaviors that, when deployed, continuously improve task performance."[45]

The term "culture of excellence" combines the well-established concept of organizational culture with the notion of excellence as a moral category, i.e., it is our moral/professional obligation to use combined (organized) efforts to teach students concepts and then apply those concepts so the student can learn and learn how to learn.

Five Tall Women

In the spring of 1975, I was asked by two female students in my seventh-hour class if I would be interested in coming to their basketball game that afternoon. It was the first year of interscholastic basketball for girls in the Omaha Public Schools, thanks to Title IX. So, I went down to the gym at 4:00 p.m. (girls did not yet play in the evening and had second choice of gym time in any event). The opponent for the Bryan Bears was the South High Packers. South High had a very quick little guard who could dribble with both hands and make a layup, and the Bryan girls had no such talents or an organized defense. Our team lost 73–8. Yes, 73–8. Not being particularly bright, I commented that even I, one who never played organized basketball, could do a better job of coaching than that. Having uttered those ill-conceived words, I felt a tap on my shoulder. It was our athletic director, Joe York, a rather gruff man of whom I was deathly afraid. He said, "Schultze—the job's yours!" *Yeah right, Mr. York*, I thought. Sure enough, the next fall, I came to school on the first day, and there in my staff mailbox were my assignments for the year, including head girls' basketball coach.

Well, as all basketball coaches know, 90 percent of winning games is the talent on the floor, and I got lucky. We had five good players. One, a guard named Carol who enrolled at Bryan in the fall of 1975, could hit from the outside (too bad there was no three-point line in those days). The best athlete in the school (boy or girl), whom the coach the prior year had cut, came out for basketball. Her name was Cindy, and she was six feet tall (big for those days), could run like a deer, and with a bit of coaching, she became a force around the basket both on offense and defense. As a senior, Cindy averaged sixteen points and nineteen rebounds a game. We lost our first game to the best team in the city

---

[45] https://www.tandfonline.com/doi/full/10.1080/2331186X.2014.934084.

(Benson), and then beat the second-best team (Burke) the next game. We were off and running, finishing 9–3, and headed in the right direction for a new program.

It was after that season that I got a call from a man named Forest Roper,[46] who was the coach of one of the best girls' AAU basketball teams in the Midwest centered out of North Omaha (Amateur Athletic Union, very big in the sixties and seventies for what we now call club sports). Mr. Roper was one of the legendary coaches in Omaha's African American community, along with Bob Rose and Josh Gibson (Bob Gibson's older brother).[47] Forest was a strict disciplinarian and required his girls to work hard at school and play hard in games. He was a father figure and mentor to those kids. He established a culture of excellence. He called and asked if Cindy would play for his team, the Hawkettes, in the summer of 1976. Cindy did, had a great time, and learned a lot from Coach Roper.

At the end of the summer of 1976, an Eighth Circuit Court of Appeals decision required the Omaha Public Schools to desegregate their K–12 schools, and as a result, African American students from all over the city could elect to go to any school they liked. Forest decided to send one of his players to Bryan. She was very tall (five feet, eleven inches), a skilled player, and a very good student. With Cindy back for her senior year, we did well again. The next year, with Cindy's graduation, Forest sent another player our way, also a very good student but not as tall (five feet, eight inches). Then in the spring of 1978, Forest asked me to come watch a group of five players he wanted to keep together (five feet, ten inches to six feet, two inches), any basketball coach's dream. They turned out to be marvelous players and, most of all, wonderful young women. They enrolled at Bryan and, as seniors, won the state's highest classification Nebraska state championship. Every one of those girls that Forest coached and taught went on to college. Some played college basketball, some did not. But all graduated and went on to professional careers. All the result of the mentoring, life coaching, and a culture of excellence demanded by their coach, a volunteer at that, Forest Roper.

Years later, a beloved teacher and avid supporter of the Bryan girls' program passed away. As the church was silent, awaiting the beginning of the funeral service, five very tall poised and professional women entered the church and walked to a front alcove. They were the young women of Bryan's only state championship team, again showing the character and the culture that made them successful in their youth and in adulthood. They were there to honor a beloved teacher and friend. For a teacher and coach, it does not get any better than that!

---

[46] For a complete story of the gift of leadership and guidance of Forest Roper to young girls, African American and others, during the 1960s, '70s, and '80s, see "Roper Saw a Dynasty Grow" by Chris Heady, *Omaha World Herald*, April 26, 2020.

[47] See *24th & Glory: The Intersection of Civil Rights and Omaha's Greatest Generation of Athletes*. Award-winning journalist Dirk Chatelain uncovers the mystery of Omaha's greatest generation of athletes. They rose out of segregation as racial tensions in North Omaha boiled hotter and hotter. During the civil rights era, they ascended to national prominence—Bob Boozer, Gale and Roger Sayers, Marlin Briscoe, Ron Boone, Johnny Rodgers, and Bob Gibson.

Establishing a culture of excellence has its base in Dr. Whitaker's theme "teach, don't tell" (I keep repeating this theme because it is the key to effectively leading your staff).

As the master teacher in your building, you can and should lead your staff in the creation of a culture that supports a collective effort by the entire school to assure that students have the best educational experience as we prepare them for hopefully productive lives.

Dr. Riley, describes his approach to establishing a culture of excellence in his schools, both as a principal and superintendent.

Dr. Riley's comment: Throughout my university preparation for the principalship and the superintendency, I was taught that the number one responsibility of the principal was to be an instructional leader. As a classroom teacher, assistant principal, principal, and super-intendent, I quietly questioned this. There is no doubt that the principal needs to fully understand the process of teaching, learning, and assessment and be able to lead a staff accordingly. However, in my opinion, an important priority is missing. *The principal's primary responsibility is to develop a building culture that promotes the importance of teaching, learning, and assessment* [emphasis added]. A skilled instructional leader has limited effect if the desired culture is not in place.

School building cultures are built upon the foundation of a collaborative student-centered vision. A student-centered vision is the result of countless conversations among the principal and building staff. A properly crafted student-centered vision becomes the rallying force for the principal and staff when problems arise and decisions need to be made. All solutions start and end with the collaborative student-centered vision.

A student-centered vision should lead to a culture of high behavioral and academic expectations for students and principal/staff. I place high behavioral expectations in front of high academic expectations because if the behavioral issues are not effectively addressed within a school, academic achievement suffers for all. Teachers need to be able to run their classrooms without disruption. No child has the right to disrupt the education of others or their own. Properly and effectively addressing the misbehavior of students and helping classroom teachers manage classrooms may be the most important responsibility of the building principal.

This leads to the importance of teacher evaluations in the development of an effective school culture. Dr. Al Kilgore, a longtime professor at the University of Nebraska at Lincoln and a personal mentor, conducted a teacher morale survey across the state, each summer, for decades. *The same three results appeared each time the survey was conducted: (1) Teachers want to have some say in what is to be taught, (2) teachers want to have opportunities to improve and advance, and (3) teachers want to be evaluated. As a young administrator, number three surprised me. It no longer does* [emphasis added].

Establishing a high standard of teaching and learning within a school's student-centered culture becomes the responsibility of the principal and staff. It starts with teaching expectations that are research based, collaboratively developed, and communicated to and expected of each staff member on a daily basis. *Effective principals formally evaluate all of their teachers every year. They conduct regular (preferably daily) walk-throughs of each classroom and conduct formal and informal evaluations throughout the year* [emphasis added]. This constant attention to the teaching and learning process sends a clear message to the staff. This attention also allows a principal to identify possible teaching concerns early and address as needed. The courage and skills needed by a principal to address teaching concerns is a matter for another time.

The ongoing effectiveness of a school's culture always returns to the collaboratively developed student-centered vision. Cultures suffer when student-centered visions morph into adult-centered priorities. In our profession, this occurs more than it should. David Kirp, in his book *Improbable Scholars*, states that effective schools "*put the needs of students, not the preferences of staff, at the center of decision making*" [emphasis added]. A good reminder for us all.

David Kirp, *Improbable Scholars: The Rebirth of a Great American School System and a Strategy for America's Schools* (Oxford Press, 2013).

Mark Schultze,[48] former principal in Millard Public Schools, provides a personnel director and building principal viewpoint to building a successful and effective school culture for teachers.

Building A Successful/Effective School Culture: A Practitioner's Viewpoint

This comment is based upon twenty-three years of practical experience as a district- and school-level administrator and thus will not be citing any theorists or providing any research data as support. However, if any principal enacts the approaches as described, they will enhance the climate and student achievement within their building.

Team first: Consider for a moment characteristics/attributes all championship football teams possess and/or demonstrate (think time). *You may have considered some of the following: prepared and talented players, goal-oriented players, focused task oriented at practice as well as on game day, effective daily and situational communication, trust in one another*

---

[48] Mark M. Schultze was a teacher, central office administrator in the personnel office, and a very successful building principal at Disney Elementary in Millard Public Schools in Omaha, Nebraska, for over thirty years. While he has suffered for over sixty-five years for being my brother, he has been an invaluable resource to me in answering questions and consulting with me on school administration issues throughout my career. Many thanks to Mark for his contribution to this book.

to do assigned jobs, and a consistently demonstrated "team first" attitude. Weaker or more unsuccessful football teams may demonstrate some of these attributes but not as consistently as successful teams. For example, it is not an accident (like them or not) that the New England Patriots have been in and won so many championships in the last twenty years! *They have had the same coach and quarterback, but all other personnel has changed over and over. The results, however, have been very consistent.* Successful schools are just the same as championship football teams, and it is not an accident. It is intentional.

Considerations for developing an effective school culture: The development of effective school culture requires important considerations for a principal new to his/her school as well as for an experienced principal who knows some adjustments are needed. The following are some of those considerations. While the listed ideas may not be the "be-all and end-all" list of to-dos, if sincerely implemented, these strategies will enhance your school climate.

- *Personnel selection*: One of the most important tasks a school administrator has is staff selection. Not just teachers but every staff member (secretary, para, custodian, cook, etc.). This task may take a few school years to fully achieve but should be a priority from day one on the job. Remember, you may have to live with your choices for a long time. As it is said, "One spoiled apple can spoil the bunch." Here are some fundamental considerations when selecting staff:
  1. Consider what skills and characteristics you need in a new staff member. Do you need experience, or are you willing to spend the time to mold a rookie with great potential?
  2. Review candidate applications with these skills and characteristics in mind.
  3. Select and interview at least three (3) candidates for each position.
  4. Interviews should include other selected staff as part of the interview team (e.g., for a fourth-grade classroom opening, the team might include the following: principal (you), a fourth-grade team member, another grade-level teacher, a building specialist, and a parent.) These stakeholders should understand up front that they are providing you input but that you will make the ultimate staff selection.
  5. Develop/adopt a set of questions specific to the position available prior to the interviews. Each team member should select or be assigned specific questions to ask during each interview. Any member should feel free to ask an appropriate follow-up question. Doing this ensures a fair, focused, and consistent evaluation of the interviewed candidates.
  6. After the team has given their input, you (the principal) should consider if the appropriate candidate has been found or if further interviews should be considered. Interview team members should be told to hold all

information about the interview process in confidence before and after interviews are complete. The principal should be sure to contact some of the applicants' references to confirm their skills and abilities. Be a good listener on these calls. Not all good references are equal.

7. Communicate with your team about the result of your interview process, then share the news with your remaining staff.

- *Mission, belief, goals, and objectives*: All schools / school districts have established their mission statement, belief statements, and have created goals and objectives to achieve their mission and beliefs. The most effective/successful schools live their mission/beliefs and overtly work toward the achievement of their stated goals and objectives every day. The following are some ideas to keep this going in your school:

  1. Review the beliefs, mission, goals, and objectives with your entire staff each year on the first day.
  2. Every few years, take the time, with a representative number of all stakeholders (staff, parents, and community), to reestablish that the belief statements, mission, and goals are still valid, making any appropriate adjustments.[49]
  3. Place emphasis and/or appropriately declare goals and objectives possibly with the greatest need for work/achievement during a specific school year.
  4. Display your beliefs, mission, goals, and objectives prominently in public spaces.
  5. Display your mission prominently on websites, newsletters, letterhead, etc.
  6. Gather data annually to demonstrate that the established goals have been met or not met. Being honest about goal achievement is very important!

- *Building trust*: Establishing trust of performance and expectation among school staff (family) takes time and takes clear intent on the part of the principal. *Establishing a trusting environment is key to success within a school.* Think about your favorite teacher during your K–12 experience. Consider all the qualities that person displayed that made them your favorite (think time). Knowledge and clarity were probably on your list. Students thrive in an environment where they trust the instructor's knowledge and are comforted by the clear expectations for performance each day. *It is essential for effective/successful principals to also*

---

[49] Dr. Pace's comment: And I would say that if no one can repeat these, there is work to do. Most of those statements are elegantly worded PR statements that look good on letterhead and the sign the booster club purchased out front. The great ones live it, like Dr. Riley's time at Gretna Public Schools. Those statements have to guide what we do on a Tuesday afternoon.

demonstrate appropriate knowledge and clarity for their staff every day of their profes-sional lives. The following are a few ways to enhance trust within your building:

1. Make it a priority to ensure that staff has everything (supplies, equipment, time, etc.) that they need to be successful.

2. Be a collaborative decision maker on important building issues. *Allow staff the opportunity to provide input on major change initiatives with the knowledge that the principal has the final decision-making responsibility.* For example, staff members have expressed concern about the comportment of students as they walk down the hall to specials. Seems like a small issue, but how this is dealt with by the principal can make a big difference in how happy/successful their building functions. Suggested solution: have a representative portion of staff get together (including the principal) to work out what the expectation should be for all students as they move in the hallway. Present this plan to the entire staff, make any changes, and then get consensus on the new hallway procedure.

3. *Learners/learning should always be the focus* when making change initiatives for the building or the individual student. The decision-making stance should always be *do what is best for learners, not what is most expedient/easy for adults (e.g., "is your school/classroom mostly about teaching or learning?")*[50]

- *Communication: The daily messaging from the principal to his/her staff should be direct, consistent, honest, and frequent.* Staff will see very quickly if the daily messaging and the overall stated mission are not congruent. *The ability for a principal to "talk the talk and walk the walk" is essential for success in all ways.*

A principal does not need to know everything, and when they don't know, effective principals say, "I will find out" and then follow through. If it is important to the achievement of goals within a building, the principal must model, model, model the desired behavior—always. Ineffective communication (written, spoken, demonstrated) to stakeholders (students, staff, and parents) within a school community will ensure failure of trust for a principal!

When building the most effective/successful school culture, the best principals, like the best football coaches, *stress the importance of nurturing the "we" mentality within a school stakeholder group rather than the "me" focus of "I am the principal, so do as I say"* [emphasis added]. Inclusiveness and collaboration are key components to a healthy and productive school environment that has student learning success at the forefront.

---

[50] Dr. Pace.

Dr. Riley's comment: From my experience and from the words of a trusted colleague from the Gallup team in Omaha, "When selecting personnel…talent trumps fit."

As a lawyer representing school districts, in laying the foundation when assisting principals to address circumstances when teachers are not meeting district standards, I inquire with regard to their knowledge of teaching and their application of that knowledge to assist the teachers under their charge to improve their instructional and classroom management skills. Ideally, a principal can demonstrate the characteristics and skills of a master teacher, one who has established a collective culture of excellence. The application of the instructional model and framework for evaluating staff becomes more objective, supportable, and constructive for improvement of teaching or, if unsuccessful, future employment decisions. That said, no one is perfect, and all of us need to continue to hone our skills to be master teachers and master principals (and master lawyers—note that we lawyers are always "practicing"). So, keep practicing your profession and improve every day. As discussed above, it is a process, but with the consistent goal of improving instruction and student learning.

Your assignment:
1. Write a paragraph on what you learned from Dr. Riley's comment.
2. Write a paragraph on what you learned from Mr. Mark Schultze's comment.
3. Reread the "Passion" section of *Teach Like a PIRATE* on pages 3–12.
4. Draft a memorandum answering the following questions:
    o What courses in undergraduate or graduate school have you taken that focus on the elements of effective teaching? Find the instructional materials in your attic or basement! Review them!
    o Does your school district have a mission statement? If so, describe how it is implemented in your school's culture. If a mission statement does not exist or is not currently implemented into your school culture, describe how you would go about developing and adopting a mission statement and the importance of doing so.
    o Does your school district have established goals? If so, how are those goals communicated to your staff and how is the achievement of those goals measured each year? If your school does not currently have established goals for school achievement, describe how you would go about creating and implementing such goals and measuring success in achieving same.

CHAPTER 4

The Expert—Wise in the Science of Teaching

Less of you, more of them. Focus on your lesson plans, spend more time on less information, be specific, and stick to the topic. Let them read—and do—their own work... You can't learn for them [students]. [T]eaching is not a popularity contest. It about getting them [students] involved in their own education.
—David Cohn, administrator, to Tony Danza[51]

You as an administrator are special. Special as a dedicated educator. But even more special in the eyes of the law. As Daffy Duck once said, "I'm not just your ordinary, meat-on-the-table duck. I'm gifted. I'm just slopping over with talent."[52]

Talent? Yes, talent as a leader of your teaching staff, students, parents, and the community. As Dr. Pace notes, "I often say to students that there is a difference between being an administrator and a leader. The administrator balances the books, moves some paper, etc. The old beans, balls, and busses stuff. *A leader improves instruction. Inspires. Includes. Impacts. Has conversations that need to happen.* Big difference" (emphasis added).

Such talent is recognized in the law. Under the *Federal Rules of Evidence*, which have been adopted in most states in some form,[53] witnesses who are not experts are often called fact witnesses, and their ability to render an opinion that is relevant to the decider of fact is limited.

Federal Rule of Evidence §701. Opinion Testimony by Lay Witnesses
If a witness is not testifying as an expert, testimony in the form of an opinion is limited to one that is:
(a) rationally based on the witness's perception;
(b) helpful to clearly understanding the witness's testimony or to determining a fact in issue; and

---

[51] Danza, *I'd Like to Apologize to Every Teacher I Ever Had*, 45.

[52] Again, Daffy Duck may predate some of you. My guess is that you need to be over forty-five. See https://www.google.com/search?q=daffy+duck+cartoon&rlz=1C1GCEU_enUS836US836&oq=daffy+duck+cartoon&aqs=chrome..0j69i-57j0l4.9569j0j7&sourceid=chrome&ie=UTF-8.

[53] *Hollingsworth v. Bd. of Educ.*, 208 Neb. 350, 360, 303 N.W.2d 506, 512 (1981). "Although strict adherence to the rules of evidence cannot be demanded or even expected at a hearing before a school board, when a teacher's career hangs in the balance, the basic principles of due process demand that hearsay statements of students be given little, if any, weight. Certainly, this is true with respect to the hearsay comment of an unidentified female student to her physical education teacher."

(c) not based on scientific, technical, or other specialized knowledge within the scope of Rule 702.[54]

On the other hand, as an expert witness, *you, once qualified as an educational expert, are not so limited.*

> Federal Rule of Evidence §702. Testimony by Expert Witnesses
> A witness who is qualified as an expert by knowledge, skill, experience, training, or education may testify in the form of an opinion or otherwise if:
> (a) the expert's scientific, technical, or other specialized knowledge will help the trier of fact to understand the evidence or to determine a fact in issue;
> (b) the testimony is based on sufficient facts or data;
> (c) the testimony is the product of reliable principles and methods; and
> (d) the expert has reliably applied the principles and methods to the facts of the case.

Thus, once it is established that you have special "knowledge, skill, experience, training, or education" that will help the trier of fact (the board in due process hearings), you are an expert. To use Daffy's point of view, you are gifted and just slopping over with talent.

Mere mortals—the rest of us—can only be fact witnesses. We may ask of you as a school administrator the essential question of this book, *Who are you who are so wise in the science of teaching?* "the expert [by knowledge, skill, experience, training, or education]!"[55]

As we discussed in the introduction, courts have held that teaching is a science. In a termination proceeding, teacher evaluations and supporting evaluator testimony are considered to be *expert* evidence of teacher effectiveness (*Eshom v. Board of Education of School Dist. No. 54*, 364 N.W.2d 7, Nebraska, 1985).

"To determine whether conduct is unbecoming, even though not in violation of an explicit rule or ethical code, we look to the opinions of educational professionals" (*Shea v. Board of Medical Examiners*, 81 Cal. App. 3d 564, 576, 146 Cal. Rptr. 653, 660 [1978], citing *Morrison v. State Board of Education*, 1 Cal. 3d 214, 461 P.2d 375, 82 Cal. Rptr. 175 [1969]. See also *Sanders v. Board of Education*, 200 Neb. 282, 263 N.W.2d 461 [1978]).

In "light of their professional expertise, schoolteachers are normally expected to be able to determine the type of conduct which constitutes unfitness to teach" (*Johansson v. the Board of Education of Lincoln County School District No. 1, also known as North Platte Public Schools*, 256 Neb. 239, 254; 589 N.W.2d 815, 825 [1999]).

---

54 See also Neb. Rev. Stat. §27-701.
55 Federal Rule of Evidence 702

So, how do we establish you as an expert witness with the requisite knowledge, skill, experience, training, or education? Well, we begin by establishing that teaching is the science that the foregoing cases recognize, and that you have the qualifications to perform teacher evaluations and give supporting evaluator testimony sufficient to provide expert evidence of teacher effectiveness.

The Science of Teaching

Due to the work of Madeline Hunter and others in the 1970s and 1980s, professional educators began to research the characteristics and habits of effective teachers. As a result of this research, several teaching models, methods, and strategies have been developed to ensure that learning is occurring in the classroom:

- Madeline Hunter's Instructional Theory into Practice (ITIP) and lesson design model
- Charlotte Danielson's *Enhancing Professional Practice: A Framework for Teaching*
- Robert J. Marzano, Debra J. Pickering, and Jane E. Pollack's *Classroom Instruction that Works: Research Based Strategies for Increasing Student Achievement.*

Teaching models, methods, and strategies become even more useful when administrators use them in the process and incorporated them into a school's evaluation system and documents. While there is no panacea, no magic formula, and no definitive evaluation system or mode, the use of performance criteria that have been shown to indicate the teaching-learning relationship within the classroom will strengthen a school's position in any personnel matter—whether instructing your entire staff, working to improve a teacher's performance and developing improvement plans, or, in the end, recommending the ending of a teacher's employment with the school district.

You Must Be an Expert in the Science of Teaching

NDE Rule 10, Section 007.06A1f requires the school district policy to *describe the district plan of training administrators.* Section 007.06B requires that all evaluators possess a valid Nebraska Administrative Certificate and to be *trained to use the evaluation system adopted by the district.*

Trained in the use of the system means not only training in how to fill in the blanks, but also training in the educational theory behind the criteria in the instrument and the performance of a teacher that meets those criteria. This training should be both formal and informal and be documented by the school district and the administrator on an annual basis.

Following Rule 10 provides a structure for the foundation for the veracity of the evaluation of a teacher and the basis for accepting the opinion of a principal by

- in the first instance, the teacher;

- the superintendent in deciding what action to recommend to the board;
- the lawyer representing the administration in evaluating the case;
- the board of education in a hearing; and
- the judge on an appeal.

To be confident in your assessment of a teacher's performance, you must be and continue to make yourself an expert in the science of teaching. This must and should be an ongoing process. To do so, you must draw on your coursework in undergraduate and graduate school on all the elements of good instruction—knowledge of the subject matter, lesson planning, lesson presentation, assessment of student learning, etc. In your case, as a building principal, you must have the knowledge of the subject matter of what constitutes good teaching practice so you can teach your staff. It is this knowledge that makes you the expert!

Hopefully you already have this knowledge. That said, as the saying goes, we should all be lifelong learners—continuing to enhance our knowledge, learning and accepting new ideas and approaches to teaching and student learning, and making changes as required to meet new challenges and apply new knowledge. Being an effective principal requires acceptance of change. It is a mutable job.

Thus, to be an effective expert for your staff (and for your school attorney as an effective expert witness), you must have, demonstrate, and use your expertise in all instructional areas identified above.

- *Knowledge of how to teach*: There are several well-accepted instructional models and frameworks for effective classroom instruction. We are going to focus on the Instructional Theory in Practice (ITIP) framework for instruction as incorporated into the model lesson plan template (Appendix B), which incorporates the hybrid instructional model derived in part from Charlotte Danielson's *Enhancing Professional Practice* (EPP) and from Madeline Hunter's ITIP model. The ITIP model in particular provides a time-tested structure for planning and delivering effective lessons, and the Danielson instructional model is the predominant measuring tool for establishing the domains (or components) of teaching responsibility—planning and preparation, the classroom environments, instruction, and professional responsibilities.[56] A commentator has said that evaluators must be familiar with teaching models, methods, and strategies and must have appropriate training to be able to explain how a teacher's performance is hindering the learning environment in the classroom.[57]

  If your school district uses these, you must study, understand, and be able to apply in the field the underlying basis for both the ITIP structure and the EPP domains. Having this knowledge and these abilities, you must think of yourself an expert and present yourself accordingly. The next step is for your staff to consider

---

[56] Danielson, *Enhancing Professional Practice* (1996), 61.
[57] M. L. Cogan, *Clinical Supervision*; J. Millman, *The New Handbook of Teacher Evaluation*.

you an expert. The hard work is having them buy in and accept you as such. From that point, you are positioned to lead your staff in incorporating the best teaching practices into their classrooms with the goal of meeting the highest level of performance that a teacher in your system can achieve—not that all will get there. That highest level under the Danielson model is "distinguished," which describes a level of teacher performance where "classrooms operate at a qualitatively different level, consisting of a community of learners, with students highly motivated and engaged *and assuming considerable responsibility for their own learning*" (emphasis added). With this as a stated goal, and professional development directed toward this goal, your status as the educational leader and expert will be golden!

Part of establishing your expertise is prioritizing and emphasizing the basic elements of good teaching in the classroom—lesson planning, classroom instruction, and assessment of student learning.

- *Knowledge of and leading on lesson planning*: In my youth, there was a television sportscaster named Howard Cosell who was a former lawyer turned commentator. He was made famous by his interviews in defense of Muhammed Ali,[58] who was suspended from boxing for refusing to enter the armed forces. When asked why he left the legal field and went into broadcasting, Cosell's response was telling. He said that being a lawyer was too hard. It took six hours of preparation for one hour in court. Those of us who have taught know that Cosell's statement is equally applicable to teaching. The key to good teaching is good preparation.

  While we will discuss planning in detail in Chapter 8, it is critical that you as the expert have the foundational knowledge of effective lesson planning and can lead your staff to develop those skills. If lesson planning or the understanding of the elements of lesson planning is an area of weakness for you, this is a "teach thyself" moment.

- *Knowledge of and leading on lesson presentation and assessment of student learning*: You are relying upon your education and training in the skills necessary for effective classroom instruction. Your knowledge may be specialized regarding the application of fundamental components elementary and/or secondary instruction, but most evaluation instruments do not distinguish between the components of good teaching on that basis. In other words, teaching is teaching, whether you are teaching a five-year-old or a sixty-year-old. In fact, as I began practicing law and trying cases, it dawned on me that I was using my teaching skills in preparing, presenting, and arguing cases to a judge or a jury. "What are those 'teaching skills,' a myriad of interpersonal means of communicating—some planned, and some in the moment—persuasion,

---

[58] Muhammed Ali, the three-time world heavyweight boxing champion, who was a dominant public figure in the 1960s and 1970s, and an icon to the boomer generation.

empathy, eye contact, social cues, humor, toughness, and a million other things… this is the art."[59]

We will discuss the application of the elements or domains, the underlying components thereof, and the performance of a teacher evaluated based thereon in Chapters 13 and 14. For purposes of establishing you as an expert for your staff on classroom instruction and assessment (and for your board, if necessary down the road), you should focus on those experiences that show that you have been in the trenches (so to speak). You were a classroom teacher, have planned instruction, have delivered instruction, and have assessed student learning. You have worked to become a master teacher (see Chapter 3), and have made the effort to "make a contribution to your teaching field" or focus during your teaching days, "both in and outside your school."[60] As noted above, a longtime elementary principal said to me, "To evaluate and assist teachers effectively you must consider yourself to be a 'Master Teacher' and convey that to your staff."[61]

Maybe your experience was in a differing discipline or subject matter, but the basic elements (domains) of teaching are the same, and the subcomponents of each are present in every classroom. Further, you should have taken coursework on those basic elements of teaching and have an understanding of the scope of the duties of a teacher at the classroom level. You have reviewed the job descriptions for a teacher (elementary and secondary), have in fact performed those job duties, and have observed successful teaching in the classroom.

James B. Gessford: Preparation for evaluations. You must prepare yourself for the evaluation of each teacher. This preparation is particularly important for those teachers that have specialized disciplines or students, i.e., students with disabilities or other special needs for whom the teacher is expected to prepare individual plan lessons and adjust instruction as required in the student's IEP. One court has held that expert testimony was admissible to the effect that a principal's evaluation of a special education teacher was improper and possibly invalid because the principal failed to review the IEPs of the students in a teacher's class so that the evaluator had sufficient knowledge to accurately and objectively evaluate the teacher's performance.[62]

---

[59] Dr. Nick Pace.
[60] Danielson, *Enhancing Professional Practice* (1996), 37.
[61] Mark M. Schultze, June 2019.
[62] *Powell v. Valdosta City Sch. Dist.*, Civil Action No. 7:13-CV-53 (HL), 2014 U.S. Dist. LEXIS 157158, (M.D. Ga. Nov. 6, 2014). In *Powell*, the school district required principals to appraise both regular and special education teachers. *Before observing a teacher, an administrator was required to be fully informed and prepared so that the teaching performance could be fairly critiqued in light of the teacher's objectives.* One aspect of assessing special education instructors was determining whether their students

- *A mentor and resource*: Significantly, you need to let your teachers know of your experience, knowledge, and skill as a teacher—not in a bragging way, but in a mentoring/resource manner. Be confident! Be convincing! Your teachers will gain respect for you, and courts will not second-guess you!

You now have been qualified as an expert. Congratulations! That status gives you special privileges under the *Rules of Evidence*. (As noted before, the *Rules of Evidence* do not strictly apply to termination and cancellation hearings under the Teacher Tenure Act, but courts and lawyers still like them to be followed as much as possible to protect the veracity of the evidence adduced in the proceedings). One of those special privileges is that as an expert, you are allowed to rely upon hearsay evidence in reaching your expert opinion. The legal definition of hearsay is provided:

27-801. Definitions; statement, declarant, hearsay; statements which are not hearsay.
The following definitions apply under this article:
  (1) A statement is (a) an oral or written assertion or (b) nonverbal conduct of a person, if it is intended by him as an assertion.
  (2) A declarant is a person who makes a statement.
  (3) Hearsay is a statement, other than one made by the declarant while testifying at the trial or hearing, offered in evidence to prove the truth of the matter asserted.

Your special status comes from the exceptions to Hearsay Rule 27-803(17), "Statements contained in published treatises, periodicals, or pamphlets on a subject of history, medicine,

---

were progressing in the students' individual education programs, or IEPs. To ensure a fair outcome under the school district's evaluation process, teachers had the right to unbiased observations and evaluations. In *Powell*, the principal conducted a formal, unannounced observation of Powell's teaching. Prior to observing Powell, *the principal did not review all of the IEPs for Powell's students, so the assistant principal did not know what the goals and objectives of Powell's teaching were on the day of the observation.* Out of the eleven categories on the evaluation form used by the principal for the observation, Powell was rated as needing improvement in three areas: instructional level, building for transfer, and use of time (id., 6-7).

The case involved summary judgment motions prior to trial on an appeal of the dismissal of Powell. At issue was the calling of an expert witness with prior teacher evaluation experience to opine in part on the evaluation process and the adherence to that process procedurally and substantively by the administration.

The expert was prepared to testify that (1) the school district's administrators did not properly administer the observations of Powell because they were not familiar with the students' IEPs or the challenges created by their particular needs; (2) a special education teacher should be evaluated in terms of the progress her students are making in their IEPs, and Powell's students demonstrated such progress; (3) the "needs improvement" ratings assigned to Powell were based on expectations for how a class with nondisabled students functioned, rather than a special education class like Powell's, and therefore, the "needs improvement" ratings Powell received do not accurately describe her teaching performance (id., 13).

The appellate court allowed this testimony to go to the jury, stating the expert opinions were relevant as to *"how the evaluation tools were implemented, how the Defendants may have ignored the clear guidelines of the School District's evaluation policy, and whether Plaintiff's students showed progress in their IEPs"* (id., 15).

or other science or art, established as a reliable authority by the testimony or admission of the witness or by other expert testimony…relied upon by the expert witness in direct examination. If admitted, the statements may be read into evidence but may not be received as exhibits."

What does this exalted position mean to you as a school administrator/principal?

Well, it allows you to gather information and reach conclusions that includes statements of others, observations of others, or documents prepared by others, as long as you can establish the same as credible and as the type of information you usually rely upon in the performance of your duties. We will discuss what these hearsay-type documents may be in Chapter 11, "The Assistance," where we will explore the practice and the art of collecting meaningful data that allows for an objective and expert analysis of a teacher's performance in the classroom in support of student learning.

As we leave this chapter, I hope you feel like an expert or, if not, that you have an idea of the steps to be taken to get there.

Your assignment:
1. Reread the "Immersion" section of *Teach Like a PIRATE* on pages 13–18.
2. Collect your school district's:
    o   board policies and job descriptions
    o   evaluation procedure filed with NDE by your school district
    o   teacher handbook
    o   walk-through observations form
    o   the code of ethics for teachers in your state
    o   teacher's contract
    o   extra-duty contract or assignment document
    o   teaching certificate
    o   teacher staff development and in-service materials
3. Please write a memorandum with your analysis of how you use or would propose to use each of these tools of the trade in your work in preparing for the school year and guiding your teaching staff during the school year.

PART 2
The Foundation

CHAPTER 5

The Foundation—Building a Base from Which to Lead Your Staff

Above the blackboard, I've glued big letters to spell out:
TAKE PART IN YOUR OWN EDUCATION.[63]

—Tony Danza

The word "foundation" has many meanings.[64] As stated in the Introduction, for our purposes, the term "foundation" has two distinct applications. The first use of "foundation" that which all administrators must have to be effective in informing, teaching, and evaluating their professional teaching staff. The second use is the foundation (through education, training and experience) sufficient for the administrator to be recognized as an expert with the "knowledge, skill, experience, training and education" to enable him/her to render an opinion on whether a teacher meets the district standard of performance under *Federal Rules of Evidence* Rule 702.

Here in Chapter 5 we are focused on the "first" use of "foundation"; in Chapter 15 we will consider the elements and necessity of the second use of the term "foundation". Both uses of "foundation" should be apparent and recognized by your professional and support staff, the community, the board of education and a court sufficient to establish you as an expert in the science of teaching.[65] In both uses of the term "foundation" the legal concept of "laying a foundation" is used. Think here of this as a term of art—"laying a foundation—literally as the foundation for a building.

So how to make sense of the "laying of foundation" for your staff and its applicability to the teacher evaluation process. To assist you in the beginning the journey consider the following synonyms for the term "foundation".

- a starting point
- a base

---

[63] Danza, *I'd Like to Apologize to Every Teacher I Ever Had*, 4.

[64] *Merriam-Webster Dictionary's* definition:
noun
  1. The lowest load-bearing part of a building typically below ground level
  2. An underlying basis or principle
  3. An intellectual basis—reason, justification, grounds
  4. A physical basis.

[65] In Nebraska, this is found in Neb. Rev. Stat. §27–702.

- a point of departure or beginning
- a premise
- a fundamental point/principle
- a main ingredient
- principles
- as fundamentals
- rudiments
- the cornerstone
- the core
- the heart
- the essence
- a kernel
- the underpinning,
- *(most important) the groundwork*

Now, pause here for a moment and review the foregoing list of terms or phrases. Consider how these alternative terms for the concept of "laying" a foundation could be applied to your work with your staff, collectively and individually. It is here where you can start your journey toward preparing meaningful and valuable informal and formal evaluations of your staff—evaluations that help teachers teach better and assist them in have a more fulfilling and regarding career. You start by using the hierarchy of Bloom's Taxonomy, taking these synonyms for foundation, and incorporating them through "*remembering, understanding, applying, analyzing, evaluating, and creating*"—moving from basic knowledge to higher levels of thinking—to your teaching and leading of your staff. [*Note—As we proceed the rest of the way, keep the Bloom's hierarchy close at hand, and use it to take your thinking process all the way through each element culminating in "creating".*]

James B. Gessford: Sources. While legislative and administrative regulations may form the primary basis or source for teacher evaluation requirements, the careful practitioner must also consult all other secondary sources and documents. Secondary sources and documents include, without limitation, collective bargaining agreements, board policies, employee handbooks, individual employment contracts, etc. It is common for schools, even in many highly regulated states, to have at least some teacher evaluation standards, procedures, or instruments in these secondary documents. Secondary document requirements or procedures may be more stringent than primary legislative or administrative regulations and constitute traps for the unwary. One must never forget to consult and review all applicable primary and secondary materials in the evaluation area.[66]

---

[66] Gessford, "Termination of School Employees: Legal Issues and Techniques," Evaluation, 1995, 2-2.

Laying the Foundation

Laying a solid foundation for instruction is the single most important aspect to assuring that student learning is occurring in the classroom. Without a foundation, teachers are left to their own devices—sinking or swimming (some are Olympians like Michael Phelps, and some never rising above a dog paddle).

Sinking or Swimming

Close to fifty years ago (in 1974—wow, am I old), I was a newly minted history teacher at Omaha Bryan High School. "Green behind the ears" hardly describes my entry into the teaching profession. I had student taught the previous year, but nothing really prepared me for 160 students every day. Some of whom were just 4 or 5 years younger than I was. I had received virtually no advance training in an instructional framework or educational models. (There were no such things in 1974. Madeline Hunter did not really come along in college education departments until the late seventies.) I was blessed with a great principal, Dr. John McQuinn, who visited my class and provided some helpful hints, and told me at one time, "You could teach anything" (which I think related to my basketball coaching, and taking an 0–12 team to a 9–3 record, but that is another story involving a tight zone defense and talent). Anyway, as with any new teacher, I tried to prepare lesson plans (we had a lesson plan book) based upon the textbook and covering the material. However, I soon realized that most of my students were never going to college.

The packing houses of old (Armor, Cudahy, Swift) were fading, but some were still in full operation in South Omaha, and for purposes of learning (and classroom management), I needed to make world history relevant to them. I did have a good grasp on resources—my room was across the hall from the library—like all the *Life* magazines from 1940 to 1946 (great for World War II) and the Omaha Public Schools film library (yes, we used projectors, and the film would break). But having no framework to work with, I flew by the seat of my pants, so to speak, and did an adequate job by 1974 standards. I even tried to teach American history backward once. Enough said.

But, upon reflection, my preparation and presentation were, overall, pretty poor. I certainly did not meet all the ITIP framework elements, or adjust my instruction to the Danielson or Marzano characteristics of the age group and different learning styles—visual, auditory, manipulative, etc. I tried to use knowledge of cultural heritage and interests and make it relevant to the students, but on an inconsistent basis. Significantly, I do not recall ever having any specific goals to meet for a week, a quarter, a semester, or a year. As they said at the time, it was a bit of throwing the grade book in the classroom and following it in, and survival from there. As with anyone, I wish I knew then what I know now, and realize how much I still do not know. I do know that had I been provided a good foundation in the science of teaching, I would have been a better teacher, and my students would have benefited from that knowledge.

Laying a good foundation begins with a step-by-step process: putting the pieces together in an orderly fashion, all with a reminder to staff at every step that each piece is part of the description of their duties as a professional educator in your school district. The duties should not be presented as a "do this or else" model, but as an essential part of the effort to support and improve the instruction of students, and thereby teacher competency through effective training and leading of staff. The following are the foundational elements that should be communicated to your teaching staff *every year* prior to the beginning of the school year through specific training:

- training your teachers on their duties and responsibilities
- training your teachers on the instructional framework and educational model adopted by your board of education
- giving your teachers notice of the standard of performance expected of them in your school district through in-services and review of the evaluation instrument and process.

See Chapter 6, "The Tools and Setup."

Communication is *the* essential element to laying a solid foundation. As will be discussed later, a key to any personnel matter is notice to an employee (teacher or otherwise) of the rules and expectations of the job. Thus, you must communicate with your staff on a regular and continuing basis through meetings with teachers as staff, group, or individuals. You as an expert and master teacher must provide your staff with information, ideas, and resources on ways to meet expectations in a manner that will improve instruction in their classroom.

Challenge to Administrators

Preparing and prioritizing each year to lay the foundation upon which teachers can build their skills and understand the applicability of the educational model set forth in the evaluation instrument and supporting documentation is essential. Such an effort will make them better teachers and, in the end, make their job easier on a daily and annual basis.

- *Foundational sources*:
  - *Base documents*: As will be discussed in detail in Chapter 6, you will use certain base documents to establish the culture of learning in your school:
    - Teacher job description
    - Teacher contract
    - Teacher handbook
    - Evaluation instrument and process
    - Student handbook
    - Lesson plan template

    You should provide all these base documents to your staff either directly on paper (the old-fashioned way) or by electronic means or on the school district's website. No matter where they are located, they *should not be lost or ignored* by you or your staff.

The *job description* is a critical document to let your teachers know that their job is to teach children how to learn. It is shocking to observe that when asked, most principals had never looked at their job description or those of their teachers. As a principal, the job description is a critical piece of information for many employee issues, including employee illness or disability (and resulting Family and Medical Leave Act [FMLA] and Americans with Disability Act [ADA] issues).

The *teacher contract* sets out teachers' essential obligations and duties. It requires teachers to hold a valid and appropriate certificate to act as a teacher of schools in the state with such endorsements as are required by accreditation regulations (where required) or board policy for the teacher's assignment. It states that teachers will be governed by the policies of the board of education and that their teaching duties are subject to assignment by the superintendent with the approval of the board. They are obligated to devote full time during days of school and days of assigned duties to the teacher's position. They must diligently and faithfully perform the assigned duties to the best of the teacher's professional ability, and their dependable attendance is an essential function of their position.

The *teacher handbook* is the means of communicating information to your staff in a single source. Having an effective teacher handbook has many advantages. By communicating information about your district and its policies, teachers are made aware of the district's mission and the expectations they are to meet. On the one hand, this makes teachers more comfortable as they are not left guessing as to what they are to do and not do. On the other hand, should a teacher fail to meet your district's expectations, the teacher cannot claim they did not know what those expectations were. Further, teacher handbooks reduce legal exposure. There are numerous circumstances where a district may avoid liability if and when it has provided notice to teachers of expected conduct. Teacher handbooks also serve the purpose of giving the various legal notices which must be given to employees.

The *evaluation instrument and procedure* provides the road map for proper and complete instructional practices. Further, the evaluation process will be of interest to your staff, probationary and permanent alike. It will inform them if and when you are coming into their classrooms and how you are going to appraise their work. Remember, like everyone else, teachers want feedback. They prefer the positive kind but will accept negative comments if they are founded in fact.

Dr. Riley's comment: Although these base document recommendations seem trivial, they are a primary professional responsibility of every principal and superintendent. For the superintendent, it is imperative that these base document requirements are communicated to the building principals and administrative team prior to the start of the school year. It then becomes the responsibility of the building principal to share and communicate these base documents with staff. Proof of base document receipt cannot be underestimated.

Public school districts in Nebraska are now legally required to have a *student handbook*. This requirement was imposed in a somewhat back-door fashion via adoption of the student fees law in the 2002 legislative session. The student fees law requires that schools adopt a student fees policy, publish the policy in the student handbook, and provide a copy of it to all students. Implicit in meeting these requirements is that the school actually has a student handbook. While the mandatory nature of student handbooks is of recent origin, most public schools in Nebraska have used student handbooks for decades. Schools primarily use student handbooks to meet their legal obligation to communicate the school's student discipline rules to students and their parents. In addition, student handbooks are used to give official legal notices required by state and federal laws. The legal importance of student handbooks has been recognized in recent published articles. These commentators emphasize that student handbooks can be a double-edged sword in the battle to minimize the school's liability. Well-drafted student handbooks can serve to reduce the school's exposure to liability, while poorly drafted student handbooks may create legal liability or add legal complications.[67]

Finally, the *lesson plan template* is the *key* to success in the process of teaching and learning. All of us who have taught know that a teacher who is prepared is well on his/her way to a successful instructional experience. The lesson plan template is so important, it deserves its own chapter. See Chapter 8.

- *Regulatory requirements*: You will also need to remind your staff of the regulatory requirements established by the Nebraska Department of Education, the most important of which is NDE Rule 10, which provides that teachers are to be evaluated on the basis of
  - instruction (planning and delivery, assessment, and reteaching);
  - classroom management;
  - professional conduct; and
  - personal conduct

---

[67] https://www.halpernadvisors.com/importance-student-handbooks/

o *Ethical standards*: Teacher ethics should also be addressed. You should have a copy of NDE Rule 27, "Professional Practices Criteria," and the board of education policy on professional ethics which often mirrors Rule 27. (For those of you in other states, you should reference the code of ethics and conduct for teachers and administrators in your state.) Equally important is NDE Rule 27, the ethics standards for you and your teachers established by your board of education. There will be instances—hopefully not often—when a teacher's conduct will rise to the level where you will be required to report unethical behavior. The failure to do so places your administrative certificate at risk.

All of this information should be specifically discussed with your staff. You should identify and discuss your evaluation instruments and educational models that address these specific areas of professional responsibility. As Tony Danza told his students, your teachers must *take part in their own education* on these essential documents as they constitute the *foundation* of their job as professional educators and they are responsible for knowing the contents thereof.

Your assignment:
1. Write a paragraph recounting your experience similar to the "Sinking or Swimming" experience, with all the flowers and warts!
2. Read Chapters 1, 2, and 3 of *I'd Like to Apologize to Every Teacher I Ever Had.*
3. Answer the following questions:
   o Have you been trained on the educational model your instruments are based?
      ▪ As a classroom teacher?
      ▪ As part of your masters program?
      ▪ As part of staff development by your school district?
      ▪ As part of self-study and improvement?
      ▪ Or not at all?
   o How would you rate your knowledge of the educational model use in your school district?
      ▪ Rank yourself from 1 (no knowledge and understanding) to 10 (expert knowledge and understanding).
   o Are you an expert educator?
      ▪ If your answer is yes, what are your areas of strength?
         • Lesson planning?
         • Instruction?
         • Classroom management?
         • Employee supervision?
         • People skills?
         • All the above?

- o "The expert [by knowledge, skill, experience, training, or education]"?
  - Go on YouTube and watch the witch scene from *Monty Python and the Holy Grail.*
    - https://www.youtube.com/watch?v=I8ZWgrf6Qds
    - http://www.montypython.net/scripts/HG-witchscene.php

CHAPTER 6

The Tools and Setup—Notice, Notice, and Notice

You can't learn for them… It's about getting them involved in their own education.[68]

—Tony Danza

The Tools of Ignorance

> Baseball Players call the catcher's armor the "tools of ignorance." Outfielders contend that no one in their senses would clutter themselves up with a mask, a heavy chest protector and weigh down their legs with shin guards. All of this when the mercury is trying to climb out of the top of the tube, and those outfielders are on vacation, waiting for something to happen. (*The Sporting News*, April 4, 1944)

The Tools of Knowledge

What the ballplayers were really saying is that a catcher is involved in every play and does the hard work—the dirty work.

By analogy, a school administrator is involved in whether learning is occurring in every classroom every day, does the hard work—the dirty work—using the tools of knowledge to mentor, guide, and evaluate the teachers under his/her care as the foundation for instruction for the upcoming school year!

- First, you are committed to conveying your knowledge to your assets/teachers. See Chapter 2, "The Assets."
- Second, the most essential tool of knowledge is your own learning and knowledge on how to be a master teacher. See Chapter 3, "The Master Teacher."
- Third, you are an expert and are committed to conveying that knowledge to your staff. See Chapter 4, "The Expert."
- Fourth, you will have provided your assets/teachers with the essential functions of their job, and the resources where they can find those essential functions. See Chapter 5, "The Foundation."

---

[68] Danza, *I'd Like to Apologize to Every Teacher I Ever Had*, 45.

Now that you have the foundation laid with the standards of performance expected of your assets/teachers through these tools of knowledge, the next step is to assure that this staff understands how the tools of knowledge will be implemented in their day-to-day efforts in the classroom, during the quarter, semester, school year, and so on. To use another baseball analogy, your staff needs to know who's on first, what's on second or third base. "I don't know!" Bud Abbott and Lou Costello.[69] *You want to avoid "I don't know"!*

To avoid the "I don't know," you need to use teacher staff development and in-service materials to provide notice of the essential functions to your assets/teachers through the use of the tools of knowledge. Here, however, the focus must not be a punitive or dictatorial approach to the tools. Rather, the key is creation and maintenance of the culture of excellence and professionalism described by Dr. Riley and Principal Schultze in Chapter 3, "The Master Teacher." The establishment of a culture where the job duties and the evaluation process are one of collaboration to a common goal to answer the student's question: *How do you learn how to learn? Stated another way, we are all in this together to a common goal!*

The Setup

We will call this process the setup. That does not mean that the setup is only a beginning-of-the-year process. Obviously, there should be a focus at the beginning of the year to prepare and set the stage for the upcoming school year, but there must be a continuum of staff development, one-on-one interaction with you as the administrators, and other supplementary nurturing, counseling, guiding, observing, and evaluating—formally and informally.

- Things to do *at the beginning of every school year*
    - Receive training on the evaluation instrument and process! (A reminder again, this is *very important* as the base for everything else.)
    - Prepare staff development presentations (PowerPoints are very good for this purpose) to review all the tools of knowledge.
    - Inform all teachers of the evaluation process.
    - Identify each teacher's evaluator.
    - Initiate system of providing ongoing instructional support to all staff, e.g., staff development calendar.
- Things to do *as the school year begins and continues*
    - Conduct brief observations in *all* classrooms to communicate, "I am around. I care. I am here to help."
    - Set up a computer filing system to accumulate various forms of documentation that reflect the performance of each teacher.

---

[69] https://www.google.com/search?rlz=1C2GCEU_enUS836US847&source=hp&ei=uPXaXKbHAZLr-wTv9IywCw&q=abbott+and+costello+baseball&oq=ABBOT+AND+COSTE%3BLLO&gs_l=psy-ab.1.5.0i13l10.2094.6269..9801...0.0..0.131.2140.3j17......0....1..gws-wiz.....0..0i131j0j0i10j0i22i30.Y4ac1WxpHY4.

o Use staff development to
- draw on in-house expertise, providing mentoring and demonstration opportunities with emphasis on differing degrees of teacher experience and skill, not always based upon years of teaching, but on effectiveness of instruction;
- provide enough time for follow-up support with marginal or less-experienced teachers to help them master new ideas, content, and strategies and integrate them into the classroom;
- focus initially on formative evaluation to support teacher growth and development;
- allow good and marginal teachers to interact and provide opportunities to explore, question, and debate new ideas about classroom practice; and
- offer intellectual, social, and emotional engagement with ideas, materials, and colleagues.

The First Witness

Our purpose in this book is the training and support of teachers by expert administrators to improve instruction, and thereby student learning. That said, to illustrate the importance of the setup, the following portion of the testimony of the person who is usually the first witness called in a personal hearing is instructive.

Who is the first witness, you ask? The teacher whose contract has been recommended for termination or cancellation and for whom the hearing is being held.

Why would you call the teacher who is the subject of the hearing be called as the first witness? The answer may be surprising to you. You do it to lay the foundation for the expert testimony of the principal, which will follow.

Why wouldn't the principal be the best person to lay that foundation? Well, the principal will have to qualify himself or herself as an opinion expert during testimony, but the teacher can testify to the tools of knowledge that he/she was provided by the principal [70] and the school district setting forth the standards of performance expected of teachers performing the same or similar duties in the school district.

The following is a Q&A from a hearing showing how the setup practices of the principal and the administration provide the foundation for building the case to the fact finder—the board of education. The hearing is for a Mr. Jones, a science teacher in the Anywhere Public Schools. The administration's attorney has already asked the preliminary

---

[70] Federal Rule of Evidence 702.

questions of the witness, e.g., name, business address, employment with the Anywhere district, years of employment, and teaching assignment.

Q. Mr. Jones, were you present at your assigned school on August 15, 20__?
A. Yes.
Q. And did you attend the in-service for all teachers in your school on that date?
A. Yes.
Q. Could you tell the board the subject matter of the in-service at your school on August 15, 20__?
A. I don't know if I recall exactly, but I believe Principal Williams reviewed some practices and procedures that we needed to know for the upcoming school year.
Q. Did the practices and procedures reviewed by Principal Williams include the Job Description for the position of teacher in your school district?
A. Yes, I think she did.
Q. Mr. Jones, I hand you what has been marked as Exhibit No. 11, is that the Job Description that Principal Williams reviewed with you on August 15th?
A. Yes.
Q. Mr. Jones, did Principal Williams also review the school district evaluation instrument and procedure at the August 15th in-service?
A. Yes.
Q. And did Principal Williams provide each teacher, including yourself, with a copy of the evaluation instrument and procedure?
A. Yes.
Q. I now hand you what has been marked as Exhibit No. 12, is that the evaluation instrument and procedure that Principal Williams reviewed with you on August 15th?
A. Yes.
Q. And did Principal Williams also provide the staff with a PowerPoint that went through each domain of the evaluation instrument and the components thereof.
A. Yes.
Q. At the in-service, were you provided a copy of the PowerPoint so you could follow along with Principal Williams' presentation?
A. Yes.
Q. Here is what has been marked as Exhibit No. 13. Is Exhibit No. 13 the PowerPoint that went through each domain of the evaluation instrument and the components thereof that Principal Williams reviewed with you on August 15th?
A. Yes.

Q. What other material did you review at the in-service on August 15th?

A. We did a general review of the Teacher Contract we all signed. We also were provided the new Teacher Handbook for this year and went over the calendar for the year, and the requirements for planning, grading, safety and student discipline. And the Student Handbook.

Q. I have marked as exhibits, Exhibit 14—a copy of your Teacher Contract, Exhibit No. 15—the Teacher Handbook for the 20__–20__ school years, and Exhibit No. 16—the Student Handbook for the 20__–20__ school year. Are each of these documents true and correct copies of your Teacher Contract, the Teacher Handbook, and the Student Handbook.

A. Yes.

Q. Mr. Jones do you know that educational model the board of education has adopted as the basis for classroom instruction?

A. I think it is stated in the PowerPoint you just handed me.

Q. Do you need the PowerPoint, Exhibit 13, to assist you in your answer as to the educational model this board of education has adopted as the basis for classroom instruction?

A. No. It is based upon the Danielson model.

Q. You mean the Charlotte Danielson—Enhancing Professional Practice?

A. Yes.

Q. And have you received training on the Danielson educational model and the four Domains therein—Planning and Preparation, The Classroom Environment, Instruction and Professional Responsibilities.

A. Yes.

Q. When?

A. Well, at the in-service. She went through all four of those Domains with us.

Q. Have you had any prior training on the Danielson model, and the four Domains and components thereof?

A. Yes. We have had two all day in-services on the Danielson model last year and the year before.

Q. With regard to the in-service on August 15th, did you review all four Domains of the Danielson model, and all of the underlying components of each.

A. Yes.

Q. In fact, Principal Williams had the teachers break into groups, and discuss each domain, and the components of thereof, then reconvened the whole group and reviewed the expectation of the level of performance expected for each component?

A. Yes.

Q. And what was the level of performance expected?

A. Proficient.

Q. So, you understood that the level of performance that was the standard that teachers in the Anywhere Public School District should meet was the Proficient level.

A. Yes.

Q. Can you tell me what constitutes Proficient performance?

A. Well, I can't quote it verbatim, but it is where a teacher understands the concept being taught and can convey those concepts to our students well.

Q. As part of your review of the Planning and Preparation domain, did you review any other documents?

A. Yes. We reviewed the Danielson Lesson Plan Template.

Q. Is this document, Exhibit No. 17, that Danielson Lesson Plan Template?

A. Yes.

Q. And were you provided a copy at the in-service at the time of the review?

A. Yes.

Q. And were you further provided a Word version for your use in preparing lesson plans for the upcoming school year.

A. Yes.

Q. And did you understand that you were to prepared lesson plans on the Danielson Lesson Plan Template.

A. Yes, but…

Q. Mr. Jones, did you use the Danielson Lesson Plan Template as required?

A. At the beginning of the year for the first unit, but after that, well it took too much time. So, I guess the answer is "No."

Q. And you understood the Danielson Planning and Preparation domain and underlying components or rubrics were all incorporated into the template—so by not using the template, you did not meet even the Basic level of performance.

A. Well, that is what Principal Williams decided.

Q. Did Principal Williams work with you to help you use the lesson plan template?

A. Yes. She tried to get me to use it, but I preferred my own methods of planning.

Note this line of questioning continued into the substance of the evaluation, but the setup showed Mr. Jones had been given the information and provided the foundation to get to the issue of the teacher's performance.

The administration's attorney to the attorney representing the board:

Mr. Osborn and the board: "I would offer Exhibits 11, 12, 13, 14, 15, 16 and 17 into the record.

Mr. Osborn to the teacher's attorney: "Is there any objection?"

Teacher's attorney: "No objection."
Mr. Osborn: "Exhibits 11, 12, 13, 14, 15, 16 and 17 are received."

From an evidentiary standpoint through the teacher, the administration has laid foundation and established the relevance of the exhibits which will allow the principal to base her testimony thereon.

Ancillary to the evidentiary process, but equally important, the teacher's testimony established the credibility of Principal Williams, established that she had done her job of providing her teachers with the base documents upon which they were to perform their job and the standard of performance expected of them, all without saying a word!

Of course, we want the foregoing to be the exception and not the rule. We want our teachers to learn from what the principal has taught them in the setup and perform accordingly. As will be discussed later, we all understand that no one is perfect, neither the teacher nor you, but aspiring and striving for that standard is easier if you know what it is!

The Setup as the Resource

We lawyers often refer to what we do as the practice of law.[71] Practice in the legal profession generally means giving folks advice in some form, guiding clients through the legal process. However, I have always considered the term to mean the generic form of "practice," the concept of constantly working to get better within the foundational and ethical standards of the profession. In other words, practice in the sense of "perform (an activity) or exercise (a skill) repeatedly or regularly in order to improve or maintain one's proficiency."[72]

While the first witness is part of the end game when efforts to improve the performance of a teacher have failed, the resources you provide your staff as part of the setup are essential to overall professional practice of teaching. The teacher job description, teacher contract, teacher handbook, student handbook, evaluation instrument (with the education model set forth therein), and lesson plan template should be referred to in assisting teachers. It is their base upon which to build their teaching. From these setup documents, teachers can and should be encouraged to build their instructional practice. Surprisingly, these setup documents are often forgotten in the overall teacher improvement process. Here is a lawyer's advice to you: *do not forget them*! See Appendix F, "Who's on First—Tasks and Responsibilities."

---

[71] In its most general sense, the practice of law involves giving legal advice to clients, drafting legal documents for clients, and representing clients in legal negotiations and court proceedings such as lawsuits, and is applied to the professional services of a lawyer or attorney at law, barrister, solicitor, or civil law notary. However, there is a substantial amount of overlap between the practice of law and various other professions where clients are represented by agents.

[72] https://www.merriam-webster.com/dictionary/practice.

You Are the Instructional Leader throughout the School Year

The setup also provides you the opportunity to establish yourself as the educational leader with your assets/teachers. Here are ten factors that can serve as a springboard to success for anyone occupying a leadership role.

- Transparency. Leaders who are transparent are challenged less by those they oversee.
- Listening. When a leader listens to those they oversee, they are learning what is needed and can guide their charges to a desired result.
- Trust. When you develop a relationship with your staff that they truly know you are there to help, not to judge.
- Confidence. When you exhibit confidence in your own knowledge of the science of teaching, teachers become confident in your assistance, that it is honest and without arrogance, based upon best practices that are supported by resources, and you are there to make them better.
- Commitment. When you show that you will stay the course in working with a teacher to improve performance, they feel that you value them as an asset to the school, staff, students, and parents—and, by extension, the community.
- Decisiveness. When you make the hard call and do not waffle or wring your hands, call it as it is but without knee jerks and then work to address the issue in a positive and meaningful manner. You will not always be right, but leaders have to take those risks after thoughtful consideration (sometimes you have to sleep on it!).
- Humility. When you work with your staff, seek their input, consider it, and incorporate what is good—collectively or individually. You do not always have to be right; you just need to listen, learn, research, and decide a direction, and admit mistakes when appropriate.
- Integrity. When you deal with staff, always consider all sides and do what is right. If teachers have the perception that you favor someone or are just out to get them (though you will have those folks no matter what if they are not doing their job and you call them on it), then you have already lost. To be effective and produce results, your evaluation of teachers requires a belief by your staff that you are knowledgeable, thorough, *and fair*.
- Creativity. When you have a teacher who is stuck, either with an approach to planning, delivery of instruction or classroom management, the art of being a principal involves taking into account the teacher's skills, personality, approach to teaching, and arriving at a plan that fits them and the student and subject matter they are teaching. It may be a process of trial and error, but it is also part of the fun of education.

Dr. Riley's comment: I would add "inclusive" to this list. Including your staff in the decisions that affect them and their daily work promotes a positive, productive, and enjoyable working environment. That doesn't mean you can or will make everyone happy. You won't. But if you take staff suggestions into account and share the reasons for your final decision, your staff will be appreciative. This applies to teacher evaluation. Teacher evaluation is a profoundly personal experience. When you include the staff member in the research, best-practice teaching techniques, goal-setting and reflection activities, you become a team.

Your assignment:
1. Write a paragraph about what you learned from reading "The First Witness."
2. Read Chapters 4 and 5 of *I'd Like to Apologize to Every Teacher I Ever Had*.
3. Reread the "Rapport" section of *Teach Like a PIRATE* on pages 19–32.
4. Create your own PowerPoint show to in-service your staff on the tools and the setup for the ensuing school year.

CHAPTER 7

The Instrument—The Measuring Device

Teaching is different today. Teachers don't just stand at the board and lecture while kids take notes. What we're ultimately teaching them is to teach themselves.[73]

—Tony Danza

Over the past half century since teaching has been recognized as a science rather than an art, educators have struggled to figure out how to measure good teaching. And some education professionals have been reticent (administrators and teachers alike) to actually apply the measurement theories and their resulting written form. Administrators are not comfortable applying those theories either because they do not understand the practical application thereof, or it is just too hard. That is a harsh statement, but it is true in many cases. And teachers, well, they do not think anyone should tell them how to teach. Kind of a conundrum, don't you agree?

> James B. Gessford: Legal significance of teacher evaluations. The primary legal significance of teacher evaluations is their value in adverse employment matters, for the well-documented teacher evaluation is a critical piece of evidence in teacher termination proceedings. *"The documentation system becomes an essential ingredient in preparing the district's principal not only for a hearing before the board of education, but for appeals and lawsuits filed with a state commissioner of education, an arbitrator or a court."* In a termination proceeding, teacher evaluations and supporting evaluator testimony are considered to be expert evidence of teacher effectiveness. Hence, in addition to the written evaluations, the attorney must also demonstrate how the evaluator, which in most cases is the principal, is trained and competent in the area of teacher evaluation and diagnosis. Evaluators must be familiar with teaching models, methods, and strategies and have appropriate training to be able to explain how a teacher's performance is hindering the learning environment in the classroom. Overall, it must be demonstrated that the teacher's performance did not meet the required level or standard of performance for teachers within the school system[74] (emphasis added, citations omitted).

---

[73] Tony Danza, *I'd Like to Apologize to Every Teacher I Ever Had*, 46.
[74] Gessford, National School Boards Association, School Law Review, 1995, 6-2.

Nonetheless, as noted before, both statute[75] and regulation[76] in most states require the evaluation of your teachers. And notwithstanding the foregoing comment on how administrators and teachers view the evaluation process, teachers want and need help. The evaluation process must be about *help*! There is a wonderful quote from the foreword of Charlotte Danielson's *Enhancing Professional Practice: A Framework for Teaching* that captures the concept of teaching students to teach themselves and the want/need of a teacher for help to get better.

> I walked into the classroom, hands trembling, knees knocking. I tried to look composed and sophisticated (which can be difficult for a young, short person). The class waited expectantly. That's all I remember from my first day of teaching… Sometime later, in a different classroom, I introduced a lesson on creative writing by reading the beginning of a short story… I stopped reading at a critical moment in the plot and asked each student to write an ending. Their papers were fascinating, showing imagination and logic, and giving me insight into their thinking. They clearly had been engaged in learning—and I was thrilled. *I wish I'd had a forum where I could have shared my experiences and received some tips to improve the lesson.*[77] (Emphasis added)

That is what the *help* should mean, dialogue, discussion, sharing, guidance, and resources to improve, what the evaluation process should be. If both administrators and teachers look at the evaluation process in that way, administrators will not fear it and teachers will embrace it. That really is the essential challenge of the evaluation process and the incorporation of the educational model in the evaluation instrument into the day-to-day effort of educating students. The key is the development of an evaluation instrument that is understandable to both the principal and teacher and that is easy to use.

As we explore the content, organization, and use of the evaluation instrument and process, we will again reference throughout our discussion the hybrid of the Danielson instructional model set forth in Appendix C, its four domains of teaching responsibility and its components and its rating levels—unsatisfactory, basic, proficient, and distinguished—as a starting point. *However, we endorse and will not endeavor here to provide instruction to you on the Danielson (literal or hybrid) or any other education model. That is left to you, your school district, and/or your graduate programs.*

Nor have we used Danielson's forms or templates. The model lesson plan template (Appendix B) was created by me utilizing the ideas of Charlotte Danielson and the Madeline Hunter ITIP lesson structure, and mirrors the performance model (summative evaluation form,

---

[75] Neb. Rev. Stat. §79-828.
[76] Nebraska Department of Education Rule 10.
[77] Danielson, *Enhancing Professional Practice: A Framework for Teaching*, vi.

Appendix C), which is an original evaluation instrument developed by a Nebraska school district based in part on Danielson and in part on ITIP and used herein with permission. The teacher-classroom observation form, Appendix D, was also created by me based upon Appendix C.

The Evaluation Process and Instrument

From an academic standpoint, the evaluation instrument is the document used to communicate with a teacher about his/her overall level of performance under the standards established by the board of education. There are generally two forms used in applying the evaluation instrument, the formative evaluation process and the summative evaluation instrument. Both are a means of communicating with your staff to provide the results of your observations of a teacher's performance in the planning and execution of classroom instruction. It provides a rating in each domain/rubric/element or criterion to be measured in the school district's evaluation process, which incorporates the required evaluation of performance in lesson planning, instruction, classroom management, professional conduct, and personal conduct.

The Formative and Summative Portions of the Evaluation Process

Formative assessment is used to monitor a teacher's performance to provide *ongoing feedback* that can be used by the principal and teacher to improve instruction and by students to improve their learning. Summative assessment is *used to evaluate teacher's performance at the end of a specified period* either in the process or at times deemed necessary by the principal by comparing it against the standard of performance expected of teachers performing the same or similar duties.

Formative[78] Process

The formative portion of the evaluation process is where the teaching by the principal occurs. The Nebraska Department of Education's "Nebraska Model Evaluation Project: Teacher/Educational Specialist Evaluation Policy"[79] defines the formative evaluation process

---

[78] *Merriam-Webster Dictionary's* definition of formative:
　　adjective
　　　　1a: giving or capable of giving form: *constructive*—a formative influence
　　　　b: used in word formation or inflection
　　　　2: capable of alteration by growth and development
　　　　also: producing new cells and tissues
　　　　3: of, relating to, or characterized by formative effects or formation
[79] https://www.education.ne.gov/wp-content/uploads/2017/07/TeacherEducationalSpecialistEvaluationPolicy.pdf.

as follows: "Formative evaluation takes place at specified points within the evaluation cycle prior to the summative evaluation and includes the rating of some components of the evaluation process and may include a non-summative review of other components."

As we have discussed (and will discuss further), using the "teach, don't tell" approach to leading our staff, the formative process is where you observe, collect, apply, reflect, analyze, synthesize, and also evaluate, conclude, communicate, and assist. In sum, it is everything that you do with your staff collectively and individually to guide your teachers up to the writing of the formal summative evaluation. The documentation of this process is discussed in Chapter 11. It is the most important part of your overall effort to evaluate and assist your staff.

Summative[80] Evaluation Instrument

The Nebraska Department of Education's "Nebraska Model Evaluation Project: Teacher/Educational Specialist Evaluation Policy"[81] defines the formative evaluation process as follows: "Summative evaluation takes place at the end of the evaluation cycle and includes the assessment of all components of the evaluation process."

The basic components identified in all educational models apply fully to pre-K through twelfth grades. Certainly, the components of each such model are nuanced to allow them to be conformed to the age and maturity of the students begin taught, but the essential elements should be present in each classroom regardless of grade level. It's your challenge to match the components to the classroom, the teacher, and the students to arrive at a valid evaluation of the teacher's performance through the application of the components, individually and collectively, to reach an overall conclusion on the teacher's performance.

Levels of Performance

Of course, before endeavoring to apply a component, you must be informed, instructed, and have a good understanding of the level of performance used in rating whether a teacher meets district standards. Using Danielson's educational model as an example, you have therein four rating levels defined as follows:[82]

[80] *Merriam-Webster Dictionary*'s definition of summative:
adjective
additive, cumulative
[81] https://www.education.ne.gov/wp-content/uploads/2017/07/TeacherEducationalSpecialistEvaluationPolicy.pdf.
[82] Danielson, *Enhancing Professional Practice* (1996), 36–37.

Level	Description
Unsatisfactory	The teacher does not yet appear to understand the concepts underlying the component. Working on the fundamental practices associated with the elements will enable the teacher to grow and develop in this area.
Basic	The teacher appears to understand the concepts underlying the component and attempts to implement its elements. But implementation is sporadic, intermittent, or otherwise not entirely successful. *Additional reading, discussion, visiting classrooms of other teachers, and experience (particularly supported by a mentor) will enable the teacher to become proficient in this area.* For supervision or evaluation, this level is minimally competent. *Improvement is likely with experience, and little or no actual harm is done to students.* [Emphasis added]
Proficient	The teacher clearly understands the concept underlying the component and implements it well. Most experienced, capable Teachers will regard themselves and are regarded by others as performing at this level.
Distinguished	Teachers at this level are master teachers and make a contribution to the field, both in and outside their school. Their classrooms operate at a qualitatively different level, consisting of a community of learners, with students highly motivated and engaged and assuming considerable responsibility for their own learning.

Note that the levels of performance:
1. Identify proficient as the standard of performance expected.
2. Set out the type of assistance that should be provided to help a teacher improve from unsatisfactory or basic to proficient. (Note: This is an important point, as the indicator indirectly sets out the performance expected of the principal! E.g., "Additional

reading, discussion, visiting classrooms of other teachers, and experience [particularly supported by a mentor] will enable the teacher to become proficient in this area.")

3. Provide that to be rated as basic, there must be some hope that the teacher will improve. Otherwise the rating should be unsatisfactory. (Note: The recalcitrant or simply incompetent veteran teacher could have difficulty getting to the basic stage *if* [a] they do not accept or participate in the "additional reading, discussion, visiting classrooms of other teachers, and experience [particularly supported by a mentor] will enable the teacher to become proficient in this area"; [b] improvement is unlikely with experience; and/or [c] *actual harm will be done to students and their learning*.)

Domains, Rubrics, Components, and Elements: What You Are Rating?

The ratings of performance are to be applied to each of the components of each domain in the Danielson model effectively. And, there are elements within each component. To use the Danielson-based evaluation model, your evaluation instrument must allow you and the teacher to consider each element in determining the teacher's level of performance for the component. What does that look like?

The following is an example of an evaluation instrument based in part on Danielson that breaks the component down to the elements. Remember, the purpose is to communicate clearly and concisely so the teacher understands why you rated his/her level of performance as you did, and what is needed to improve, continue. Remember that you need to note teaching that is exemplary. And, also remember to identify the good, great, and fantastic as well as the deficient performance, and they can be all be in one evaluation.

Dr. Riley's comment: We need to be careful as to how we communicate performance levels to teachers. As stated previously, evaluation of a teacher is profoundly personal. One of the phenomena that I have observed over the last few years is the negative reaction from teachers to the categorical labeling under a new evaluation model adopted by their district. Quite often, teachers who had been placed at the highest level of the scale in the previous model are now subject to being at a lower level on the newly adopted scale. They are often told, "Very few teachers reach the highest level." Really? I know this wasn't the intention of the model researchers/developers, but this is how it plays out in the reality of teacher perception. This can be demoralizing to the best people in our profession and an unintended consequence of adopting a model carte blanche.

Performance Rating Key:

Level of Performance	Numerical Rating
Unsatisfactory	1
Basic	2
Proficient (Standard of Performance)	*3*
Distinguished	4

PLANNING:

Component 1: Lesson Planning, Alignment with State Standards, Curriculum, and Instructional Materials Prepared.

Proficient Level:

There is evidence of consistent planning of daily instructional goals, strategies, and methods of assessment. The teacher can provide a clear rationale for the design and sequence of units. Evidence indicates that instructional content is consistently aligned with the local or state standards. Plans indicate that the instructional goals of the curriculum are met. There is evidence of that the lesson plan provides opportunities to accommodate individual student needs. The teacher is prepared for class with all necessary materials and equipment readily accessible.

Standard of Performance and Comment:
- There is evidence of consistent planning of daily instructional goals, strategies, and methods of assessment.
  - o Comment:
- The teacher can provide a clear rationale for the design and sequence of units.
  - o Comment:
- ITIP design consistently followed.
  - o Comment:

- Evidence indicates that instructional content is consistently aligned with the local or state standards.
  - o Comment:
- Plans indicate that the instructional goals of the curriculum are met.
  - o Comment:
- There is evidence that the lesson plan provides opportunities to accommodate individual student needs.
  - o Comment:
- The teacher is prepared for class with all necessary materials and equipment readily accessible.
  - o Comment:

Overall Comment:

Level of Performance	Numerical Rating

See Appendix C for complete summative evaluation form.

You as the principal have the opportunity to separate each portion of the element; discuss the level of performance in the comments, noting deficient, acceptable, or exemplary performance; and provide suggestions, resources, and a means of follow-up. It seems like a lot, but actually this separation of elements provides an organized and focused means of considering the teacher's performance. At the end, combine the sum of the parts to a closing comment and then the rating. Again and again, this is about improvement and the means of communication to achieve the desired improvement. As Charlotte Danielson said, it is that "forum where [the teacher can] have shared…experiences and received some tips on how to improve the lesson."[83]

---

[83] Danielson, vi.

James B. Gessford: Remediation. Many courts have construed source[84] requirements or common law principles of good faith as requiring the school district to allow a deficient teacher time for remediation. Along these lines, it has been held that if the state evaluation statute requires that a teacher be given a specific recommendation for improvement and a means that a teacher can obtain assistance to improve, a failure to provide either of these will entitle the teacher to reinstatement. In addition, state statutes have been read as to require school districts to provide notice of deficiencies and to allow sufficient time for the teacher to show improvement before any adverse employment action is taken[85] (citations omitted).

Courts have held that "in light of their professional expertise, schoolteachers were normally expected to be able to determine the type of conduct that constituted unfitness to teach."[86] Teachers know good teaching from bad. They either see it, hear it, or observe it from the progress of students in their class. As such, principals should listen to the comments of their teachers—have their "ear to the ground"—as the principal's staff often knows what is really going on. While teachers are reticent to rat out another colleague, the vast majority of teachers care particularly about their students (past and present), and all students generally. Should you get the feeling that something is not right in a teacher's classroom—instructionally or by reason of in appropriate conduct—you may (and should) ask other staff members. Of course, this only works if you have developed the trust of your staff, and their confidence in you that you will do something about the problem. And, if all staff knows that you are so connected, a teacher who might stray may think twice about their performance or personal actions. The following is an example of a principal who gained the trust of his staff.

---

[84] Source: State statute or state regulations or board policies which set out the requirements of teacher evaluation.

[85] Gessford, National Association of School Boards, School Law Review 1995, 6-6.

[86] *Johanson v. The Board of Education of Lincoln County School District No. 1*, also known as North Platte Public Schools, 256 Neb. 239; 589 N.W.2d 815 (1999).

The Judgment of Peers

Teachers know good teaching from bad. They see it, hear it, or observe it from the progress of students in their class. Yet, they are reticent to say anything to the administration *unless* they have confidence in the administration and believe that the administration will take action to address incompetent teaching.

One such case involved a veteran teacher of more than twenty years, Mrs. Brown, who taught elementary physical education and mathematics. The principal, in his first year, had a staff of ten elementary teachers, one half of which were probationary. At the beginning of the school year, he reviewed in detail the new evaluation instrument and procedure adopted by the board of education that summer. At the first teachers' meeting, he told the veteran (permanent) teachers that he would get to their classrooms later in the first semester as he was focused on working with and guiding the probationary staff (a mistake on his part, but those were the facts).

The principal finally got to the veteran teachers, including Mrs. Brown, and informed them he would be formally evaluating them in November and told them the exact date for such evaluation. On the appointed date he observed Mrs. Brown in her first-grade PE class. It went off like clockwork, perfect in every way. The students were orderly, followed instructions, and had a successful activity, and Mrs. Brown reviewed the concept taught and did an assessment exercise to measure student learning of the concept taught. It was an exemplary performance. The next day, a fellow teacher whose daughter was in the class told the principal that the students had been doing the same lesson and activity every day of the past week in preparation for the formal observation.

About that time, a parent visited the principal and voiced a concern that her daughter in Mrs. Brown's fifth-grade class was failing math, her favorite subject, and that her daughter did not want to come to school or at least to Mrs. Brown's class.

So alerted, the principal began listening outside the door of Mrs. Brown's classroom. He heard Mrs. Brown use a shrill negative voice with students and demeaning and belittling comments. He then began walking into the classroom and standing in the back. He noted upon entry that Mrs. Brown's demeanor changed and that she was clearly uncomfortable with his presence. The principal talked with other staff members about their observations of the students in Mrs. Brown's class and about Mrs. Brown's teaching, seeking facts upon which to determine the issues and seek solutions to assist Mrs. Brown.

After a week or so, he met with Mrs. Brown and discussed the need to change her classroom management from a negative and controlling approach to that called for in the newly adopted evaluation instrument, "use of classroom management skills that create a classroom environment which is positive, nurturing, friendly, and overall conducive to student learning, and deals with student performance and disciplinary matters in a manner which encourages and stimulates positive interaction between student and teacher." The principal provided Mrs. Brown with an improvement plan that included mentoring, counseled her on techniques to improve classroom management, and gave her resource materials to provide for self-reflection and an opportunity to improve. Notwithstanding continued observation and positive assistance, Mrs. Brown's performance deteriorated, and she returned to her controlling approach to instruction and classroom management. Other teachers, now aware of the principal's efforts, reported their observations.

In March, as the principal was meeting with Mrs. Brown to review her improvement plan and discuss needed improvements heading into the ensuing school year, Mrs. Brown told the principal that he was wasting his time, that he did not know what he was talking about, and that she was simply jumping through the hoops until the statutory deadline for notifying a teacher of the possible termination of employment.

The principal and superintendent called legal counsel to determine whether under these facts they had sufficient basis to recommend to the board of education the termination or cancellation of Mrs. Brown's contract based upon the insubordination and incompetency elements of just cause elements set by statute. On advice of counsel, the superintendent decided to make the recommendation for the termination of Mrs. Brown's contract, but not without some trepidation. Mrs. Brown was a twenty-year teacher who was established in the community and had a family member on the board of education. The principal was in his first year; the superintendent was a relatively new superintendent, and both were from outside the community.

The administration needed to have a solid case. Legal counsel and the principal turned to the other staff members for foundational support for the principal's expert determination that Mrs. Brown did not meet the standard of performance established by the evaluation instrument adopted by the board just that summer. The principal asked Mrs. Brown's fellow teachers who had come forward to warn and advise him of their observations during the school year and prior years whether they would agree to testify. In the end, five of the teachers agreed to do so. One teacher was very reticent to testify and told the principal and counsel, "If I am going to do this you need to make sure Mrs. Brown does not return, as she is not good for kids, and it will be very difficult for her and the rest of the staff." It was an extremely tough situation for any fellow employee anywhere.

Courts have held that under the formal due process requirements of most teacher tenure statutes, the teacher subject to a recommendation of dismissal must be advised of the names and the nature of the testimony of witnesses against him or her.[87] So, the

---

[87] See *Johansson v. Bd. of Educ.*, 256 Neb. 239, 240, 589 N.W.2d 815, 817 (1999). "When a teacher whose contract is to be terminated for cause opposes the termination, minimum procedural due process requires that (1) the teacher be advised of the cause or causes for the termination in sufficient detail to fairly enable him or her to show any error that may exist, *(2) the teacher*

administration had to provide the substance of each fellow teacher's testimony and did so through sworn affidavits. The following is that of the aforementioned concerned teacher in Mrs. Brown' case:

[Fellow Teacher], being first duly sworn upon oath, deposes and states:

1. I have been employed as an elementary teacher at the Anywhere Public Schools elementary school attendance center for eleven years. I currently teach third and fourth grade. I have worked in the same building with Mrs. Brown for seven years and care about her. My classroom was next to Mrs. Brown's for three years, from the 2014–2015 school year through the 2016–2017 school year. This year, 2017–2018, Mrs. Brown is the Title I teacher in my classroom for two classes per week.

2. During the course of my employment for Anywhere Public Schools, I have observed Mrs. Brown interact with students. Mrs. Brown does expect a lot out of her students, however, out of what appears to be frustration she often treats her students without respect in the things she says to them and the voice she uses.

3. When Mrs. Brown's classroom was next to mine, on many occasions I could hear her yelling at students in a harsh and demeaning manner. This occurred frequently last year, but I have also heard her yelling at students this year as well. Last year when I asked her what was going on since I could hear her yelling at student clear in my room, she became very defensive towards me.

4. I have heard Mrs. Brown tell students things such as "you're a liar", "you are lying" and "you are cheating." I have also heard other words from Mrs. Brown towards the students that I feel are damaging to the children. These words are harmful to children's self-esteem. Other methods of classroom management need to be used to correct and guide children. Her conduct at times is harmful to children and demeaning. I think her overall performance as a teacher is not good for children. When Mrs. Brown has been in my classroom teaching Title I this year, I have been concerned about Mrs. Brown's self-control, and her treatment of children. I have paid close attention and seek to protect my children from Mrs. Brown by checking on them when Mrs. Brown is with them.

---

be advised of the names and the nature of the testimony of witnesses against him or her, (3) at a reasonable time after such advice, the teacher must be accorded a meaningful opportunity to be heard in his or her own defense, and (4) that hearing should be before a tribunal that both possesses some academic expertise and has an apparent impartiality toward the charges" (emphasis added).

5. The children react to Mrs. Brown's negative demeanor toward them with negative responses. I have observed children become belligerent, noisy or hostile toward Mrs. Brown when she condemns them.

6. Typically, if the children are not understanding a lesson Mrs. Brown's response is to repeat herself in a louder voice accusing the children of not listening when, in fact, they don't understand.

7. When Mrs. Brown is in my classroom and treats a child in a manner which I do not feel is appropriate, or begins to appear frustrated with a student, I try to intervene and help the child. For example, I may give an explanation in a calm voice or help the child work through a problem.

8. From my observations of her teaching, Mrs. Brown has tried very hard since January of this year to change her teaching delivery and class management methods. Initially Mrs. Brown demonstrated a kinder and gentler approach to the children. However, during that time I have observed her exhibit the previous agitated, frustrated and impatient attitude toward students. It would be my observation that Mrs. Brown does not recognize these behaviors in herself and therefore cannot necessarily sustain the control and make the lasting changes in her method of delivering instruction and managing students.

9. Earlier this school year, Mrs. Brown and myself were both working with students in my 4th grade class with electricity. Mrs. Brown was working with a student that struggles with school. While the student was sitting right next to Mrs. Brown, Mrs. Brown turned to me and asked sarcastically, "Do we have any batteries for brains in here." I did not respond to the derogatory comment, which I felt was offensive and highly inappropriate to say to any student. Mrs. Brown then repeated the statements, asking, "Do we have any batteries for brains in here." Because I did not respond in like manner, I answered firmly, "No Mrs. Brown!", and turned my back to continue working with a student.

10. A few days later when I was working with the student that Mrs. Brown had been working with before, the student told me that she knew she was stupid because she needed batteries for her brain. Obviously, such comments tear students down. I care deeply about my students and their welfare. As much as I care about

Mrs. Brown, the demeaning innuendos and put downs of children must not be allowed to continue.

11. On another occasion early in the 2017–2018 school year I was present on the playground while waiting for a bus with several teachers, including Mrs. Brown, parents, and the children. Mrs. Brown in front of all of the children, the other teachers, and the parents said to one of the parents present in a loud voice that all could hear that, "Your daughter is lying to me again." Megan was among the children. The mother responded, "Megan is Lying?" Mrs. Brown announced more loudly, "Megan is lying about her math assignments." I went over and put my arms around Megan and said quietly to her, "Megan is not a liar", in an attempt to repair the damage. Calling any child a liar at any time is unprofessional and contrary to our duties as teachers and to make such a statement to the child's parent in such a manner is also unprofessional.

12. Mrs. Brown has kept students after school and yelled at them irregardless of who could or could not hear. Last year, I observed or overheard Mrs. Brown talking to parents about their children, accusing them of lying or being mouthy after treating the children disrespectfully herself.

13. Late last fall children in my class mentioned that Mrs. Brown told them they needed to be on their best behavior as she was going to be evaluated by the Principal the next day and she threatened them to be good.

14. In my opinion as a professional elementary educator, Mrs. Brown's conduct in repeatedly yelling at students, speaking to them in a demeaning manner, making students feel inferior, failing to respect students, and using her position of authority over students is inappropriate. Our role as teachers is to nurture students to do their best and build them up.

This testimony, along with the testimony of Mrs. Brown herself as the first witness called at her hearing before the board of education with regard to the standard of performance expected, resulted in the termination of Mrs. Brown's contract by a unanimous vote of the board of education with one abstention. It was the right result and would not have happened but for the integrity and courage of her peers.

Your teachers overall want children to learn and be in a safe environment. But often they feel powerless to do anything about it because (1) they do not want to be a tattletale, (2) they fear the administration will do nothing about it, and (3) if they do so, they might be next. If, however, the teachers see that the administration is indeed going to do something, and they trust the administration to follow through, they will step up most of the time and be your most powerful witnesses. Such was the case above, and the veteran teacher was terminated to the benefit of the students and the school overall. That said, the administration must take care to confirm the information provided by the teacher, just as you would with a complaint or concern of a parent or student. You will always be faced with evaluating the veracity of a witness, and you will not be perfect, but you will be right most of the time.

Your assignment:

1. Write a paragraph about your thoughts after reading "The Judgment of Peers." In doing so, answer these questions:
   o Who bears ultimate responsibility for the quality of teaching? The teacher? The principal? Both?
   o Then after reflecting on whose job it is, what parts of it fall to which people?
2. Reread the "Ask and Analyze" section of *Teach Like a PIRATE* on pages 33–53.
3. Review your formative observation tool/form.
4. Review your summative evaluation tool/form.
5. Review your performance summary form (if you have one).
6. Answer the following questions:
   o Upon what educational model is your instrument based?
      ▪ Hunter's ITIP?
      ▪ Danielson's domains?
      ▪ Marzano's framework?
      ▪ Other?
      ▪ A hybrid of the foregoing?
   o Has your school district adopted an instructional framework and education model, and if so, which one?
   o Is your instructional framework and education model embedded in your evaluation instrument?
   o Have you been trained on your school district's instructional framework and education model?
   o If so, does that training occur every year?
   o Is your training on your instructional framework and education model documented? If so, how?

7. Write a memorandum answering the following questions:
   o Do the forms provide a structure for you to accurately apply each criteria/ domain/element reflecting the standard of performance expected of teachers in your school district?
   o How would you use the forms to accurately apply each criteria/domain/element fairly, accurately, and honestly?
   o How would you improve these forms to accomplish the above referenced goal of assisting teachers to improve and meet the standard of performance expected?

CHAPTER 8

The Key Component or the Kiss of Death (or the Lifeline)

Now here is the kiss of death. After each lesson sit down by yourself & think, "If my son or daughter were correctly rostered in this class, would I be comfortable with the lesson & the effort I put forth today?" If your answer is yes, you can sleep tonight. Whatever the answer, ask yourself what went well, what didn't, how I do it better, etc. The best teacher never rests on their laurels.[88]

—Tony Danza quoting Harry Gilbert, a pseudonym

You are only as good as your last case.

—Edwin C. Perry, Esq.,[89] to Rex Schultze, 1983.

One of the glaring deficiencies we find in most teacher competency cases is a lack of emphasis on effective and complete lesson planning by the administration, by the teachers generally, and by the teacher in question. Generally,

- there is no template (see below) for the form and content of lesson plans;
- there is no emphasis on the need for complete and effective lesson plans (what about the poor substitute teacher—a lost day of instruction for students?); and
- there is no standard of performance among the entire staff for effective and complete lesson planning—the district standard of performance!

Good lesson planning is the *key* to success in the process of teaching and learning. A teacher who is prepared is well on his/her way to a successful instructional experience. Good lesson planning opens up everything.

First and foremost, it is fun! Fun for the teacher, and fun for the students. Maybe not fun like an amusement park, but the fun of the experience it allows for the teacher to create, present information, and then run with it to allow students to apply their new knowledge and develop a higher level of thinking skills (see discussion of Bloom's Taxonomy below) and thereby the learning that follows.

---

[88] Danza, *I'd Like to Apologize to Every Teacher I Ever Had*, 36.
[89] Ewin C. Perry was a distinguished attorney, mentor, friend, and senior partner in Perry, Guthery, Haase & Gessford, PC, LLO.

Second, it is freeing. It allows for reasoned experimentation by the teacher, and possibly out-of-the-box thinking by the students. Sometimes you will hit it out of the park, sometimes you will miss and strike out, but you take the risk, and all learn—teacher and student. Hopefully you will bat above .500.

Third, it provides the opportunity to be creative, answering the question, "How can I make this a real learning experience?" Warning, however, sometimes there is an unintended consequence.

Bull's-Eye

In 1957, we moved to Valparaiso, Nebraska, where my dad was superintendent of schools and my mother taught home economics and science.

Being the child of the superintendent and science teacher carried additional responsibilities. After concluding my half-day kindergarten class, I went to my mother's science room. She told her six-year-old son to walk downtown to the grocery store operated by a gentleman named Harry Jones and pick up a brown paper bag. So, dutifully, I walked the three blocks down the gravel roads of Valparaiso to the Jones Market—the local grocery store and meat market.

When I walked into the store, I told Mr. Jones, "My mom asked me to pick up a brown paper bag." Mr. Jones said, "Well, Rex, it's not quite ready, but come with me." He led me to the back of the store and into a room that had a concrete floor with a drain and some hanging apparatus in the ceiling. He said, "Rex, stand right here and don't move." He then walked out into the alley, and I heard a loud noise, a bang, which I eventually realized was a gunshot. He then led a cow, still walking, into the room. The cow paused and then collapsed.

Mr. Jones leaned over the now dead (as opposed to "mostly dead"[90] when the cow walked into the room) with a knife and removed the cow's eye, put it in a paper bag, handed it to me, and said, "There you go, Rex." Stunned, speechless, and not quite understanding, I took the paper bag with the cow's eye inside back to my mother's science room, where I assume it was eventually dissected by her students. It's amazing what a child can learn simply by hanging around teachers as parents. By that assignment, Mr. Jones made me understand the concept of death and renewal all at once.

My mom unintentionally gave me a lesson I would never forget, and her class got to experience the dissection of that bull's-eye!

---

[90] A line by Miracle Max (the Billy Crystal character) from the movie *The Princess Bride* when Inigo (the drunken swordsman) says Wesley, the hero, is dead:

Finally, it was my experience as a teacher that a significant by-product of good lesson planning was that there were (and are) fewer discipline problems.

The development of interesting lessons takes a great deal of time and effort and, as noted above, the willingness to experiment. Yet, it is where the craftsmanship of teaching begins (or the opportunity for same).

All teachers should understand that they are not an island unto themselves in the development of lesson plans. A principal should be one of the first sources for teachers to guide and develop the skills involved in creating effective weekly and daily lesson planning. Outside resources, mentor teachers, department members, and templates, all are sources for structure and content. As with anything, it is a learned skill, one that continually develops throughout a teacher's career.

Again, the key is for principals to make lesson planning a priority to help teachers in doing their job—a difficult one in the Information Age. That said, while a principal should review a teacher's lesson plans as needed, making the production of lesson plans on a weekly basis as a punitive measure should be avoided except in the most egregious circumstances involving insubordination, e.g., the refusal of a teacher to do lesson plans (a matter that involves other just cause elements).

Danielson and McGreal describe the importance and skill of effective lesson planning:

> Planning is an important skill in its own right, distinct from a teacher's ability to conduct a successful instructional experience for students. Planning requires thoughtful consideration of what students should learn; the nature of the subject; the background, interests and skills of learners; and how to engage students in a meaningful way with the content. Skilled planning requires a thorough knowledge of the subject, but such knowledge is insufficient. Teachers also need knowledge of content specific pedagogy—how to engage students meaningfully and in increasingly complete ways with the content.[91]

For me, the first step in any task, such as writing this book, is to have an organizational structure. Where do I start? Where do I finish to get the desired result? While Danielson and McGreal provide in their rubric the characteristics that a teacher should demonstrate in their professional performance, their approach to the structure (skeleton) upon which those teach-

---

Miracle Max: "Hoo hoo, look who knows so much, heh? Well, it just so happens that your friend here is only *mostly dead*. There's a big difference between mostly dead and all dead. Please, open his mouth. Now, mostly dead is slightly alive. Now, all dead...well, with all dead, there's usually only one thing that you can do."

Inigo: "What's that?"

Miracle Max: "Go through his clothes and look for loose change."

[91] Charlotte Danielson and Thomas L. McGreal, *Teacher Evaluation: To Enhance Professional Practice*, 48.

ing skills are to be shown follows the tried-and-true Madeline Hunter ITIP[92] model with a few changes in nomenclature. See Appendix B.

As stated in Chapter 4, we are focusing our consideration of teacher preparation of instruction using the Instructional Theory in Practice (ITIP) framework for instruction and a hybrid version of Charlotte Danielson's *Enhancing Professional Practice* as incorporated in part into our model lesson plan template (Appendix B). The ITIP model provides a time-tested structure for planning and delivering effective lessons, and the hybrid Danielson model is, as noted, the predominant measuring tool for establishing the domains of teaching

---

[92] While the term the "skeleton" may seem a bit macabre (and I would note that this is not an anatomy lesson), the point I am trying to make is that every lesson must be based upon a framework, with the elements of good teaching proving the muscles and the organs that animate the skeleton. The ITIP model provides that basic framework through seven elements for lesson planning and delivery. Again, as noted, this framework has been incorporated into the lesson planning structure for both the Danielson and Marzano educational models.

Here are the different steps:

A. Getting students set to learn: The first two elements are interchangeable. As stated earlier, a distinctive review is optional. However, typically at the beginning of the lesson, the teacher may briefly review previous material if it is related to the current lesson.

1. Stated objectives: Letting students know where they are going. Giving them a sense of where they are headed belays the feeling of being a hostage in a learning experience. This step gives students direction and lets students know what they are supposed to accomplish by the end of the lesson.

2. Anticipatory set: Getting students ready and/or excited to accept instruction, also known as the hook. (Please note that giving directions may be part of the procedural dialogue of a lesson, but in and of themselves directions are *not* an anticipatory set! The key word here is "anticipatory," and that means doing something that creates a sense of anticipation and expectancy in the students—an activity, a game, a focused discussion, viewing a film or video clip, a field trip, or reflective exercise, etc.) This step prepares the learner to receive instruction much like operant conditioning.

B. Direct instruction and checking for understanding: This part involves quickly assessing whether students understand what has just been demonstrated or presented.

3. Input modeling / modeled practice: Making sure students get it right the first time depends on the knowledge or processes to be shown or demonstrated by an expert, or by someone who has mastered what is to be demonstrated or shown. In addition to the instructor, prepared students can certainly model the focused skill, process, or concept for peers. Instructors could also use a video for this portion.

4. Checking understanding: Teachers watch students' body language, ask questions, observe responses and interactions in order to determine whether or not students are making sense of the material as it is being presented. This portion takes place as instruction is being given. This is a whole class exercise, one in which the instructor carefully monitors the actions of the learners to make sure they are duplicating the skill, process, procedure, or exercise correctly.

5. Guided practice: Takes place after instruction has been modeled and then is checked for understanding to make sure students have it right! The question here is can they replicate what you want them to do correctly? Students are given the opportunity to apply or practice what they have just learned and receive immediate feedback at individual levels.

C. Independent practice: These last two components can be interchanged.

6. Independent practice: After students appear to understand the new material, they are given the opportunity to further apply or practice using the new information. This may occur in class or as homework, but there should be a short period of time between instruction and practice and between practice and feedback. Essentially, they are doing a learning task by themselves.

D. Closure: Bringing it all to a close, one more time.

7. What did they accomplish? What did they learn? Go over it again. As you can see, this model is highly repetitive. It is really a drill model and, as I indicated earlier, not conducive to support a number of high-level thinking or feeling functions without some serious alteration or modifications.

responsibility. As discussed, lesson planning and preparation is the hard work of teaching, work that can be made much easier if the teacher follows a structural approach.

That does not mean that they can't "depart from the text."[93] In fact, they should take the license to find or use the teachable moment, but they have the foundation (there is that word again) to return to after the diversion—a place where both the teacher and the students can rely upon. As Dr. Pace notes, "Principals have a responsibility to define what we mean when we adopt curricula. Is it to be delivered exactly as written without deviation? (I HOPE NOT) Or is it to be used as a guide, according to their professional judgment, formative assessment, goals of the district, and engagement with the professional learning community?"

Let's explore the model lesson plan template, Appendix B, and the knowledge that you as the expert educator must have to guide your staff.

- *ITIP*: Regarding ITIP as applied by the model lesson plan template, you must be able to (or learn how to) answer these questions effectively to lead your staff.
  - o *Lesson structure*: How does that lesson structure assist the teacher, and thereby the student learners, to organize and assimilate the concept or standard being taught that day or as part of particular unit of study? Do you know and understand the lesson plan template you hopefully have in your school district and upon which you have trained your teachers?
    - *Lesson objective / instructional outcomes*: Why must teachers develop and establish effective learning objectives? Where do these objectives come from? Are they driven by the curriculum or by state standards, or both? And if both, how do you integrate them into effective lesson planning?
    - *Relationship to unit structure*: How do your teachers develop a sequential approach to build on previous learning?
    - *Instructional material / resources*: Who can assist your teachers in the incorporation of the myriad of instructional materials, technologies, applications, equipment that can engage learners—media director, technology director?
  - o *Methods and instructional strategies*
    - *Anticipated student misconceptions*: How do you convey to your staff the ability and skill to have a wholistic "10,000 foot" view of where students are at in learning concepts that build upon each other to a result, e.g., leaving the bread crumbs for students to follow and avoid getting lost in the trees?
    - *Concept prerequisites*: Again, how do you convey the need to organize instruction that builds on prior learning?

---

93 From a story I read to my kids, "A Wish for Wings that Work" by Berkeley Breathed, published by Little, Brown and Company in 1991.

- *Anticipatory set*: What should an anticipatory set look like? Have you personally developed examples that you can share with your staff?
- *Instructional activities (input)*: Why must the teacher-lead input provide a variety of learning opportunities to reach all types of learners? Do you know and understand how to develop and incorporate higher level of thinking activities and the development of such skills?
- *Wrapping up / synthesis / closure*: Closure is the step where you wrap up a lesson plan and help students organize the information in a meaningful context in their minds. This helps students better understand what they have learned and provides a way in which they can apply it to the world around them.[94]
- *Differentiation according to student needs*: How do you inculcate in your staff a focus on the need to check for understanding for all students regardless of special learning needs, and a commitment to reteaching when necessary? What should guided practice look like? What are engaging guided practice options that can be utilized by your staff regardless of the subject or discipline being taught?
- *Assessment (formative and summative)*: What ideas can you provide to your teachers on the variety of the means of assessing student learning? How do you relate to your staff the importance of effective assessment of student learning to guide adjustments in teaching methods and student progress?

An element that is consistently present in lesson plans in those teachers who are struggling (and whose evaluations I get to read as a result) is a plan that only spoon-feeds information; i.e. "Read Chapter 10 and do this worksheet"; and, takes a "teach thyself" approach to

---

[94] https://www.thoughtco.com/lesson-plan-step-5-closure-2081851.

"A strong closure can help students better retain information beyond the immediate learning environment. A brief summary or overview is often appropriate; it doesn't have to be an extensive review. A helpful activity when closing a lesson is to engage students in a quick discussion about what they learned and what it means to them.

"It is not enough to simply say, 'Are there any questions?' in the closure section. Similar to the conclusion in a five-paragraph essay, look for a way to add some insight and/or context to the lesson. It should be a meaningful end to the lesson. Examples of real-world usage can be a great way to illustrate a point, and one example from you can inspire dozens from the class.

"Look for areas of confusion that students might experience and find ways in which you can quickly clarify them. Reinforce the most important points so that the learning is solidified for future lessons.

"The closure step is also a chance to do an assessment. You can determine whether students need additional practice or whether you need to go over the lesson again. It allows you to know that the time is right to move on to the next lesson.

"You can use a closure activity to see what conclusions the students drew from the lesson to ensure they are making the appropriate connections to the materials. They could describe how they can use what they learned in the lesson in another setting. For example, ask students to demonstrate how they would use the information in solving a problem. Ensure that you have a selection of problems ready to use as prompts.

"Closure can also preview what the students will learn in the next lesson, providing a smooth transition. This helps students make connections between what they learn from day to day."

their jobs with little or no student involvement or engagement. In other words, the teacher has made no investment in doing the hard work.

As Tony Danza's mentor at Northeast High in Philadelphia told him, "You can't learn for them... It's about getting them involved in their own education."[95]

The well-known Bloom's Taxonomy is a classification of the different objectives and higher level of thinking skills that educators set for their students (learning objectives). The taxonomy was proposed in 1956 by Benjamin Bloom, an educational psychologist at the University of Chicago. The taxonomy has had many iterations over the past sixty-three plus years, but it remains a vital structure to incorporate into great lesson plans. The terminology has been recently updated to include the following six levels of learning. These six levels can be used to structure the learning objectives, lessons, and assessments of your course:

- *Remembering*: Retrieving, recognizing, and recalling relevant knowledge from long-term memory.
- *Understanding*: Constructing meaning from oral, written, and graphic messages through interpreting, exemplifying, classifying, summarizing, inferring, comparing, and explaining.
- *Applying*: Carrying out or using a procedure for executing or implementing.
- *Analyzing*: Breaking material into constituent parts, determining how the parts relate to one another and to an overall structure or purpose through differentiating, organizing, and attributing.
- *Evaluating*: Making judgments based on criteria and standards through checking and critiquing.
- *Creating*: Putting elements together to form a coherent or functional whole and reorganizing elements into a new pattern or structure through generating, planning, or producing.[96]

Planning requires thoughtful consideration of what students should learn, the nature of the subject, the background, interests and skills of the learners, and ways to engage students is a meaningful way with the lesson content. And, it is very hard work. Tony Danza discussed the advice he was given about lesson planning:

David reminds me that teachers prepare lesson plans to help them stay on track. Which is why he had me slave for three solid days over my plan for today. As David explained to me more than once, lesson plans have to encompass not just what I teach but also how I teach and how I plan to assess my students' retention of the material. Each lesson must have a goal

---

[95] Danza, *I'd Like to Apologize to Every Teacher I Ever Had*, 45.

[96] See also "Bloom's Taxonomy 'Revised' Key Words, Model Questions, & Instructional Strategies," https://coe.uni.edu/sites/default/files/wysiwyg/BloomRevisedTaxonomy.pdf.

and each class three parts: the "do-now" or warm-up exercise, the main activity, and the wrap-up.[97]

A Standardized Lesson Plan Structure

Again, the district should have a standardized expectation of lesson plan content, whether it is the ITIP model, or the modified version thereof developed by Danielson or Marzano. It should provide a uniform approach to lesson planning by your entire staff; it must be based upon your educational model. Significantly for you as a principal, it establishes a structure to provide your expert assistance in each domain, criterion, element, or other aspects of your instructional framework and education model.

Finally, in this regulated environment around education, state learning standards and requirements can be overemphasized and drive instruction in an unhealthy manner. A planning template can help you help your staff to put those standards in their proper place in the science of teaching. The lesson plan templates for both Danielson and Marzano have a place for state standards that is tied to the objective of the lesson. State standards, however, should not dominate lesson planning. Rather, they should be integrated into the lesson as a teacher plans his/her framework; it is part of this particular skill that must be taught and/or supported with your staff.

Once you adopt a lesson plan template, you must teach your staff what a good lesson plan includes, and provide examples, models, demonstrations just as you would teach a subject to a classroom of K–12 students, and thereby set the goal for them to work toward developing lesson plans using the template. Additionally, you should challenge your staff to (1) make sure that their lesson plans would allow a substitute to provide meaningful instruction on days when the teacher is gone, and to (2) ask themselves the question that Harry Gilbert asked Tony Danza, "If my son or daughter were correctly rostered in this class, would I be comfortable with the lesson & the effort I put forth today?"[98]

You may (will) get some pushback from veteran teachers who feel that they know better. A master teacher, Gary Largo, a social studies teacher in Scottsbluff High School for the past forty-two years,[99] described lesson planning from a veteran teacher's point of view as follows:

> There is no doubt that lesson planning is crucial. That said, what sort of planning works for one teacher may not work for all teachers. For some, a detailed plan, like those promoted by Hunter and Danielson, work well

---

[97] Danza, *I'd Like to Apologize to Every Teacher I Ever Had*, 18.

[98] Danza, 36.

[99] Gary Largo. One need only to walk into Gary Largo's room, and learning starts. Historical pictures, sayings, books galore—it is a place of constant learning. It may be cluttered a bit, but it is a placed where visual and manipulative learners can literally see and touch history. Encouraging teachers to use their classroom as a real place of learning is a good thing that should be encouraged by principals.

while for others, a list of topics scratched on a post-it note will suffice for a great lesson.[100]

Seat-of-the-Pants Teaching

Mr. Largo's statement above that "a list of topics scratched on a post-it note will suffice for a great lesson" does not hold water (see *My Cousin Vinny* infra). While there may be a teachable moment that you can scratch out quickly and present, a great one-time lesson on a Post-it does not provide an ongoing consistent planned approach to a curriculum. That does not mean that a spur-of-the-moment idea should not be pursued, but seat-of-the-pants teaching does *not* meet your district's standards. While those of us who have taught have all done it (myself particularly after a late girls' basketball game more than once, not something I am proud of, by the way), there must always be an overall lesson plan for the day, unit, and subject matter. Every teacher must follow the adopted lesson plan template to a major extent, even if a teacher has demonstrated through their performance that they are a master teacher, such as Mr. Largo.

Time to Plan

Mr. Largo's major point is that teachers need time to lesson plan. It is one thing to have a lesson plan template, but it will not be effective to improve student learning if there is not sufficient time to prepare such lessons.

> Time is the key ingredient in lesson planning. Teachers must be given time to work and trusted to do so. Staff development should consist of giving teachers time to work on what is important to their job, not to jump through the latest hoop discovered by an administrator at the latest meeting they attended. Teachers should be given time to collaborate and to experiment. With this experimentation must come the realization on the part of the teacher and the administrator alike that sometimes experiments fail, but that there is value in such failures.[101]

As the educational leader in your school, you must strategize with your staff how to provide time for them to plan individually and collectively. You should also be involved in and lead the collective efforts to coordinate instruction in departments, emphasize the importance of planning, to encourage collaboration and sharing of ideas and approaches to instruction, focus on the planning and delivery of higher levels of thinking exercises for

---

[100] Gary Largo.
[101] Gary Largo.

students (Bloom's Taxonomy), and support the tremendous effort it takes to plan lessons for 176 or so teaching days.

Stated simply, you need to find the time within the workdays of the school year. Expecting teachers to use their summer months to plan for the school year, while a great individual practice, is technically outside the contract year (usually 185 to 190 days). It is important! *Find the time!* Early dismissal. A dedicated plan day. A retreat for departments on an early dismissal afternoon—away from the school. Starbucks? It does not have to be fun (though it can be), but it should be on the one hand relaxed and interactive, and focused and accepted as a priority on the other.

Experimentation

Mr. Largo also encourages patience, allowing teachers time to grow over time.

> Finally, there has to be a realization that becoming a master teacher will not happen overnight; excellent lesson plans will not magically appear like mana from heaven. A willingness to coach and a willingness to allow for failure and redemption are keys to being a master administrator working to help teachers master their craft. Questions like, "Have you thought about doing such and such?" as opposed to "Do it this way!" will help move teachers along the path we all desire—a path that leads to quality instruction for all students. If the judge in your concluding movie had not given Vinnie some leeway, he would never have risen to the occasion and proven his clients innocent even though their Pontiac pointed to their guilt."[102]

We were all babes in the woods in the beginning. As noted before, our evaluation instruments rate all teachers, probies and tenured, young and old, on the same standards. Yes, you should objectively apply those standards of performance equally to all teachers, but those standards and the ratings produced by the application thereof must be seen by the teacher and by you as the evaluator as building blocks—elements of the teaching profession that need to be worked on or maintained or (God forbid) are found as exemplary and should be shared with others.

The coaching aspect that Mr. Largo notes cannot be overemphasized. Remember, coaching is not always telling. Coaching can be "let's look into this together; let's both learn." You do not have to be a know-it-all; you need to be an encourager, guide, resource, and colleague. A joint conspirator to try something different. Sometimes it will work, sometimes not, but if

---

[102] Gary Largo.

it is adequately planned, 99 percent of the time, students will get something out of the effort made, and that is the goal after all.

"Suckiness"

Good planning calls for diversification of the delivery of lessons to reach all types of learners and encourage rather than hinder creativity by lockstep/structured—one-size fits all—approach to lesson planning and delivery of instruction. "For many students, school is filled with monotony, drudgery, and a soul-killing suckiness" (Dave Burgess, *Teach Like a PIRATE*, 55).

Please stop here and reread the "Transformation" section of *Teach Like a PIRATE* on pages 55–63.

So, how do you alleviate the suckiness? As the building leader, you probably know the names of every child in your school—at least you should know each of them. In fact, you should not only know their names, but you also know each child's background, certainly behaviorally if they appear often in your office, but you also should know in a general way their individual educational fingerprint. You must be the hub of information on students so you can guide teachers on the type of learner each student presents. If you do not know the student personally, then you should encourage communication between the staff members as the student moves through the grade levels teacher to teacher. By knowing your students and working with your teachers to plan remarkable lessons that provide a stimulating and engaging experiences for students—some of the suckiness will go away.

The following is an example of a principal and teacher working together to recognize a student's special talents, and plan and present learning opportunities to allow him to grow outside the norm and eliminate suckiness for him.

Aiden

So…let me tell you about Aiden. Aiden was a genius before his time. His classmates did not understand his humor; both his intelligence and genuine love of word manipulation were well beyond the comprehension of anybody in his developmental age group. Aiden and I hit it off immediately. His sense of humor matched mine exactly. When he came to my classroom, I think it was the first time in his life where his sense of humor was actually publicly noticed and appreciated.

In the past, he had been punished, yelled at, and even ostracized for the brilliant things that he came up with on the spot in class and in everyday conversation. He had very low self-esteem because of the way he had been treated by his peers and sadly, by his teachers, for his insistence on bringing to light coincidental or unintended hilarities of everyday discussion.

The phenomenon that happened in my classroom was that instead of receiving shushes and eye rolls, he received my genuine mirth and praise. He quickly learned that my favorite type of humor was the type that was witty and circumstantial. When he thought of a funny remark that pertained to what had just been said, he created a habit of looking at me through a "side eye" to see if I had noticed and understood his comment. Inevitably, I always did notice and understand his remarks. In fact, I loved them. Instead of students dismissing his blurted jokes, puns, facts and ideas, they began to try to imitate them. They saw that it was the way into my heart, and they wanted desperately to be a part of the joke that they didn't understand. They had always been a part of the crowd who survived by discluding those who were different, but I gave him a voice where non-understanding meant being left out of the joke.

One day, my principal came to my classroom to do an informal observation. He told me with a look of gratification that Aiden seemed confident, happy, and understood in the environment I had created. At first I didn't understand how this was a compliment until I later learned about Aiden's experiences in previous years. He had been routinely punished, ignored, and even told to stop blurting in his past classrooms. *My principal, who had known Aiden since he was in Kindergarten, told me that Aiden was thriving. This kid was able to think of things in ways unlike anything I've ever seen.*

The sad thing was, he was not equipped for a public education system that values students who follow arbitrary rules without causing disturbances, can answer multiple choice questions without asking questions the teacher has never thought of, or pushing the depth of knowledge past what was expected in curriculum standards. He was kicked out of the differentiated program because "his thinking was too out of the box". For instance, in his differentiated class, while talking about Pascal's triangle, he interjected

WHO ARE YOU WHO ARE SO WISE IN THE SCIENCE OF TEACHING?

with a valid question about whether or not deep sea animals that could live in extreme pressure, low oxygen and low-light atmospheric conditions would also be able to survive or create adaptations to survive in deep space.

How is this not a child that needs to be challenged beyond what state education legislators have deemed worthy for children of his age to know?

How can we not validate a valid question that has never been asked?

This is why our industrial and scientific programs fall short to other countries. I wish with all my heart that that differentiated teacher would have taken that conversation thread and presented it to the rest of the "gifted" group to see what their responses could have blossom into. In some ways, differentiated programs reward students who have mastered the system of remember, retrieve, respond and apply in a way that does not award students who think in ways others don't understand. *The world has never been changed by people who were understood by the majority and could regurgitate inapplicable information.*

That gifted teacher probably rejected Aiden's valid inquiry because it was not what followed her pre-scripted lesson plan and therefore made the conversation out of her control. No wonder Aiden felt ostracized; if he could not present his intriguing question to the group that was meant to push boundaries, who could he really ask?

One day, whilst on the playground, Aiden summoned me to where he was sitting on top of the monkey bars with a little half-grin on his face. I immediately knew he was setting me up but couldn't tell how, so I played a long and he asked me while sitting there swinging his feet, "Ms. Shemek, do you look up to me?"

The great mystery to me is whether or not popular opinion had been correct that he belonged on the autism spectrum, or if maybe he just never had been given the opportunity to be understood and scaffolded at his unique creative level. He did not understand how to socialize because developmentally, in many ways, he was beyond the level of his peers. This created an environment for him where none of his teachers understood how to support a student of his intellect and audacity at his given age that they were used to.

When Aiden went to 5th grade, he waltzed into my classroom on the first day of school and grabbed my teacher microphone from me with confidence. He resolutely addressed the entire class of new fourth grade students that he did not know and confidently used body language in front of a crowd. He jabbed his thumb toward me in the front of the classroom and told this new group of kids that "You guys are lucky. You've really got a good one here." He went on and told the new group of kids that he would be the local fifth grade celebrity and he would come in every single day to make sure all of the kids in my new fourth grade class were appreciating me (and also to tell a joke). And he did.

The truth is, I know how hard it was for him to put himself out there and face a crowd. I know how hard it was for him to do something that was possibly socially unacceptable. I know how much he just wanted to be heard and validated for the amazingly brilliant out of the box ideas that he had. But what he really did, standing in front of that class with confidence and defending my honor, was show me that I could make a difference for kids who deserve to be recognized for the way they were created to be intelligent and appreciated. Albert Einstein said, "If you always judge a fish by its ability to climb a tree, it will live its whole life believing that it's stupid."

The challenge is to reward principals who appreciate teachers with this mentality, reward teachers who have the permission from administration to uplift students with different types of intelligence, and embrace a system that recognizes that there are many types of geniuses that may not fit into traditional standardized test success—but that may someday change the world. If as a society we agree that the majority of future jobs for our young student population will include roles yet unimagined nor expected, how can we afford to not support an education system that recognizes instead of represses this trait in our students? [103] (Emphasis added)

The lesson of "Aiden" is that one of the difficult challenges for teachers, and the principals who lead them, is to find the time and make the effort to plan or adjust instruction to recognize special talents, allow a child to express themselves, yet maintain a classroom where all students can learn. The writer of Aiden clearly has strong feelings about not leaving children behind or ignoring their talents. I elected not to edit them out, as I think they reveal the challenges some teachers face and their feelings that principals must respect and address—providing guidance, support, and (if necessary) redirection. From personal experience, a classroom environment that restricts or demeans, even scars a student, will have lasting effects on the student, often for a lifetime. It is a difficult balancing act, and principals need to observe teachers informally, watch the students, and provide advice, guidance to help teacher plan lessons that maximize the school day for each child. This may sound unrealistic, you may miss some, but if one does not try, the why are we here?

Summary of the Kiss of Death

In sum, rather than the kiss of death, good lesson planning can (and should) be the first piece of a lifeline for struggling staff, a boon to your proficient and distinguished staff, and a treasure trove for your students. It is the foundation (there is that word again) for all that that comes after the classroom! As stated by Dave Burgess in *Teach Like a PIRATE*:

---

[103] Cassie Geier, fourth-grade teacher, Lakeview Elementary, Lincoln Public Schools.

The power of a lesson cannot be maximized without incorporating a masterful presentation. It's like riding a bike with flat tires. You may be doing everything right, but you're working harder than necessary and getting sub-par results. *When you have crafted an engaging lesson for your material it is like coasting downhill on a perfectly tuned bicycle with two fully inflated tires.* Everything seems easier because the students are drawn into your material as if by some magical or magnetic force.[104] (Emphasis added)

Dr. Riley comment: To not have a lesson planning philosophy and practice in a school district makes it complicit to the unsuccessful teaching occurring in classrooms. Many districts have moved away from requiring lesson plans due to the time commitment for teachers and principals. We've gotten lazy. It is well established that effective questioning is tied directly to the levels of thinking in Bloom's Taxonomy. I have met few teachers who have the ability to question at the various levels off the cuff. Effective questioning has to be well planned prior to and well-timed within a lesson. Lesson plans don't have to be long, arduous documents. However, they need to help us prepare for each and every class and make us think so that we can challenge our students to think.

Your assignment:
1. Read Chapters 6 and 7 of *I'd Like to Apologize to Every Teacher I Ever Had*.
2. Identify the instructional framework and educational model adopted in your school district. (If you do not have one, select one of the above and discuss adopting a model with your superintendent and BOE.)
3. Identify those domains, criteria, elements that you found difficult. If difficult to you, they are probably difficult for your teachers.
4. Find your lesson planning template for your instructional framework and education model. If your school district does not have one, you can certainly use the template in Appendix B attached hereto.
5. Reread part 2, "Creating Engaging Lessons," from *Teach Like a PIRATE*.
6. Prepare a week's worth of lesson plans in your subject area of endorsement—selecting a unit of your curriculum in that area. Include in your lesson plan the concepts found in part 2, "Creating Engaging Lessons," from *Teach Like a PIRATE*.
7. Prepare a plan for finding time for teacher to prepare lesson plans, individually and collectively, i.e., how would you fit it into your school year? (Be creative! Your superintendent can only say no so many times!)

---

[104] Burgess, *Teach like a PIRATE*, 75.

8. Determine if your lesson plans meet your goals for student engagement and partic- ipation, e.g., are there higher levels of thinking opportunities for students to take responsibility for their own learning?
9. Remember, the lesson plan should reflect what you would expect of your teachers!

PART 3
The Teaching

CHAPTER 9

The Communication—A Two-Way Street

[T]he most frequent concern I hear…is teacher's doubt
about whether they're making a difference.[105]

—Tony Danza

Teachers make a difference! Let's get that out there right away. All of us can remember a teacher who made a difference to us—probably several teachers over our academic lives. They taught us little things and big things. Things that we built on and allowed us to move to the next level in life.

Coach Jacobson

His name was Larry Jacobson. He was a football star at Kearney State College—a running back; solid; about 5 feet, 8 inches; a lantern jaw;[106] square; a no-nonsense demeanor; yet had a kind approach to kids. He was my fourth-grade PE teacher. To this day, I do not remember why, but he taught us little 9-year-olds how to direct snap (center) a football (you put the laces of the ball on your fingertips, and as you center the ball through your legs to the quarterback, you roll the ball with your wrist so that the QB receives it with the laces in his fingers ready to throw the ball). So, fast-forward 5 years. I am a skinny (112-pound) 14-year-old wanting in the most desperate way to make the Morton Junior High Panther ninth-grade football team. Obviously, I want to be an offensive juggernaut, and I get in the line with the ends, as I am going to use my unusual speed (about 6 seconds in the 40) to make catches and score touchdowns. (Frankly, I am not going to make the team as an end). Just then, the coach walks up, sees all the kids in the ends line with one quarterback and one center, a bigger kid named Tom, and asks if anyone can center the ball so he can start another QB to throw to the multitude of aspiring ends. So, I raised my hand and say, "I know how to center the ball." The coach waved me over. I centered the ball with all the skill that Coach Jacobson taught me. At the end of the day, I was one of the first ones called to get a helmet and to make the team. I was joyous! Not that I ever

---

[105] Danza, *I'd Like to Apologize to Every Teacher I Ever Had*, 217.
[106] A long, thin jaw and prominent chin.

centered the ball all season. Tom did that. But in the old one-platoon football of the day, you played both ways. The center was always a linebacker. Well, Tom was too big to be a linebacker, so he came out and I went in as the linebacker, all 112 pounds of me. Our team was not very good, and I got run over a lot, but I played, and had a great life experience, all because Coach Jacobson taught me a particular skill.

PS. Coach Jacobson went on to become the head football coach at my high school (Burke High School in Omaha) and had a very successful career. Sadly, he passed away recently, and is missed and treasured by his students and players, a truly great teacher.

PSS. I never played padded football again. I became a runner of cross-country and track, realizing my limitations. When I was a senior, I had Coach Jacobson for PE again. To get an A in the track unit of the PE class, you had to run a mile under 6 minutes. As we lined up to run, he whispered in my ear, "If *you* want an A, you had better run it in under 5 minutes." Jeez, I thought, not fair. I just ate lunch. I did it and got my A. He was always coaching us to do our best.

Be the Coach

You are the coach of your teaching staff. You are the person who can teach them to center the ball, give them the skills to build their teaching career, and grow as teachers. This is true of both beginning and veteran teachers. The first thing to do with your staff is to remind them that we should all be lifelong learners.

As the coach or teacher of your staff, you will use all the skills you learned when you were a classroom teacher. As in the classroom, you are the leader of learning. In Dave Burgess's *Teach Like a PIRATE*, he used the acronym PIRATE that he says is "in part inspirational manifesto and part a practical road map." He describes his purpose is to create "a system that can, like a treasure map, guide your [teachers] to the reward of a total transformation of your [the teacher's] classroom and your [the teacher's] life as an educator."[107] The acronym involves passion, immersion, rapport, ask and analyze, transformation, and enthusiasm—PIRATE.[108] Kind of cool, don't you think?

Mr. Burgess's work is exciting, and I hope you have taken the opportunity to read his book. After all, it was your assignment at the very beginning. We are not, however, going to recite his work here except to refer to a couple of other of his ideas a bit later.

---

[107] Burgess, *Teach Like a PIRATE*, xi.
[108] Burgess, xiii–xiv.

General to Specific

Often in the practice of law when writing a brief or organizing an opening or closing statement, we work from general to specific. In other words, first provide an overall view of the issue or issues at hand and the principles undergirding those issues, and then drill down to the ways those issues and principles relate to the specific facts of the case.

Similarly, as a principal, an approach to coaching your staff is to provide all staff with teaching theory and practice to improve teaching and student learning. Such an effort sets an underlying standard that supports the standard of performance expected of your staff and sets forth the domains, components, and elements of the education model.

In presenting these best-practices materials and ideas, as with students, you need to impress upon your staff that you expect them to reflect those ideas in their teaching, from their preparation of lessons to instruction, to assessment of student learning, and to their professional decisions regarding adjustment of instruction to reach all learners. Your teaching of your staff should add an extra dimension to the expectation of what constitutes good teaching in your school, e.g., the proficient level.

A Two-Way Street

Coaching/teaching requires the same type of lesson planning, preparation, and instructional skills as in the classroom. Teachers will expect you to demonstrate the same level of performance that you expect of them. "What is good for the goose is good for the gander."[109] It is your opportunity to show your stuff, and it will add to your credibility as an evaluator of your staff. In fact, you may find it a bit intimidating. Don't let it be. Your teachers know the challenge, so let them see you work hard and be willing to let them tell you where you can improve. It should be a two-way street.

Listen

Teachers are just like students. They do not like to be talked to or lectured too much. They prefer interactive learning and learning from one another. One of the most important skills you need as a principal is that of listening. Listening involves first providing the opportunity for others to interact with you so you have something to listen to; and second, actively encouraging your teachers to share with you and others their experiences, successes, failures, and struggles, and collectively discussing approaches to resolving those issues. That

---

[109] The phrase is used to say that one person or situation should be treated the same way that another person or situation is treated. If he can go out with his friends at night, then she should be able to, too. What's good for the goose is good for the gander. https://www.merriamwebster.com/dictionary/what%27s%20good%20for%20the%20goose%20is%20good%20for%20the%20gander#:~:text=Definition%20of%20what's%20good%20for%20the%20goose%20is%20good%20for%20the%20gander,US&text=%E2%80%94used%20to%20say%20that%20one,is%20good%20for%20the%20gander

is also coaching. And sometimes teachers just need someone to talk to, listen, understand, and commiserate a bit. Finally, as you coach your staff, as with students, you need to check for understanding, which involves questioning and listening.

Communication

As you work from general to specific with a teacher, the best or the poor ones, you need to communicate your expectations and have them communicate back their response to those expectations. In assisting principals on personnel matters, the questions that are always asked are

- How did you communicate with this teacher?
- How often?
- What help did you provide?
- Did you listen to him or her about concerns and issues, and understand their struggle?
- How did the teacher respond?
- What did you do to constructively assist them?

As your lawyer getting you ready for a hearing in a competency case, if the answers to these questions establish that you were actively involved in helping (coaching) the teacher, your testimony takes on a level of credibility that a fact finder (board) will appreciate and thus be more willing to accept the resulting recommendation regarding the teacher's contract.

Integrity

It is essential in your coaching of teachers that you are perceived by the teacher (and others, including your board) as truly working to make them better at their profession. Integrity requires truthfulness.[110] Your integrity is measured every day by every teacher on your staff. As Gary Largo noted:

> Administrators need to know that they are being evaluated by the teachers all the time and that their conduct impacts the working environment. A teacher's working environment is a student's learning environment and that working environment is impacted by the actions of administrators.[111]

---

[110] *Merriam Webster Dictionary*'s definition of integrity:
noun
the quality of being honest and having strong moral principles; moral uprightness
[111] Gary Largo.

As educators, we find it difficult to say the hard things. We are trained to be nurturing and empathetic. While we would not want you to lose that trait, at the same time, you as a principal have a job to do. Your charge is to provide a quality education to every student, and your assets are to assure that outcome. As such, you need to coach your teachers that part of growing is to accept that no one is perfect, and that you do not expect perfection. You are not like Yoda of *Star Wars* who famously said, "Don't try. Do!" There has to be some try and trial and error. This approach requires your teachers to accept that they will not always get proficient ratings on the domains, components, and elements of the evaluation instrument. Some may get a basic or (God forbid) an unsatisfactory. You have to have the courage to call the ball.[112] As Dave Burges states in *Teach Like a PIRATE* in an essay entitled "Don't Let Critics Steal Your Soul":

> You will be criticized! In fact, the more you step outside the box and reject the culture of conformity, the more of a target you will become. When criticism comes, take a moment to evaluate it. Is criticism an opportunity for growth? If so, learn from that instruction. But realize too that your critic may have no idea what they are talking about! In that case ignore it.[113]

The key to understanding the foregoing quote is to make sure that you, as the principal, clearly know what you are talking about, and that ignoring it will be at the teacher's peril. You do not always have to be right, but if you offer criticism, you must have a basis for it.

Be clear and concise when working with your teachers. Have first-person interactive conversations with input from the teacher. A teacher who understands the reason for your criticism, they will better accept it. In other words, coach them up to make a difference.

Pride in Your Profession

Finally, you must exude pride in the teaching profession. You must convey to your teachers that attitude and encourage them to do the same. You and your teachers know (or should know) that teachers change lives—forever. As noted, they are the difference makers. The following is one such story.

---

[112] When landing US aircraft carriers, call the ball is a request to sight the lights from the multicolored optical landing system that shows a pilot to be on the correct approach path or how to correct his/her approach path.

[113] Burgess, *Teach Like a PIRATE*, 165.

Chiara

My wife, Sharla, and I have had the privilege of hosting five foreign exchange students, essentially parenting five seventeen-year-olds for a year. It was a wonderful, enriching experience for us and our children, and I think for the students themselves. Our last student was from Italy, a young woman named Chiara. She came to us with a bit of a chip on her shoulder, informing us that she was rebelling against her mother, that American schools were way too easy, that she was studying the arts in Milan, and finally, that she was a vegetarian. (A year without meat was tough for me. "Is this real meat?" Yes, my wife is a saint!)

Well, we worked on all the above issues, except how she felt about American schools and her arts focus in secondary school both here and in Milan. From this point on in the story, Sharla and I can take no credit whatsoever.

Now foreign exchange students in the Lincoln Public Schools are required to take a complete curriculum, including math and science. Chiara enrolled in physics. Soon, she started talking about how she liked school. She was amazed by the East High football games. In Italy, school is over at 2:30 p.m. and you go home. She couldn't get over the fact that out of a school of approximately 1,500 students, over half were involved in some manner in the games, on the team, the pep squad, the drill team, the band, or the students in the stands. Suddenly, American schools were unique and different, all in a good way. Chiara also found school more challenging than she anticipated, particularly physics. She loved physics and her teacher. Having finished the nine-month school year, she cried when going home. She told us she had learned so much and was going to transfer to a science-oriented high school when she got home.

Chiara did just that. She graduated from the science high school and went to university, graduating with a degree in physics. She then earned her master's degree in particle physics, which I understand is very complex. (Duh!) She began working on her doctorate in the same discipline. Four years later, she received an internship at the Fermi Institute at the University of Chicago, the institute named after Enrico Fermi, the theoretical physicist who deciphered the means to create the atomic bomb.

Chiara now has her doctorate and is working at the Large Hadron Collider (LHC)[114] particle accelerator[115] located on the border of Switzerland and France.

---

[114] The Large Hadron Collider (LHC) is the world's largest and highest energy particle collider and the largest machine in the world. It was built by the European Organization for Nuclear Research (CERN) between 1998 and 2008 in collaboration with over 10,000 scientists and hundreds of universities and laboratories, as well as more than 100 countries. It lies in a tunnel 27 kilometers (17 miles) in circumference and as deep as 175 meters (574 feet) beneath the France-Switzerland border near Geneva.

[115] An apparatus for accelerating subatomic particles to high velocities by means of electric or electromagnetic fields. The accelerated particles are generally made to collide with other particles, either as a research technique or for the generation of high-energy X-rays and gamma rays. See https://www.energy.gov/articles/how-particle-accelerators-work.

Chiara recently got married to another scientist!

One teacher, her American physics teacher in a public school, changed her whole life! Something we should all be proud of. I know Sharla and I are proud of the accomplishments of "our kids" and the education they received here.

PS. Our other four kids are in order, a CPA in Germany, a financier and now rancher in Brazil, a doctor in Germany, and a computer programmer from Korea now working in California. All had part of their education in America.

Dr. Riley's comment: Over the years, I have found the best coaches to be people who have an intense interest in improving others. The best high school coaches spend a great deal of time planning so as to put their players in a position to succeed. They build their offenses and defenses on the skills of the players they have, not on fitting their players into their system. When things are going well, they credit their players. When things aren't going well, they blame themselves and ask, "What can I do better." These are tenets of leadership, and leadership is at the very base of an effective teacher evaluation process.

Your assignment:
1. Reread part 3, "Building a Better Pirate," of *Teach Like a PIRATE*.
2. Write a one-page (12-point font) memorandum applying to your experience as an educator on the essay on page 155 of *Teach Like a PIRATE* entitled "Life Isn't 100% or Fail."

CHAPTER 10

The Documentation—Being There and MBWA

Have the courage to be calm.[116]

—Tony Danza

Document, document, document! We have all heard that from other administrators and from lawyers. Lawyers (and judges) in particular like paper (at least something they can print) that provides written evidence that you as the building principal told the teacher what was observed, and that documents the direction and/or assistance provided. In fact, from the beginning, this book has been about documentation. Documentation as the foundation for your training and for giving your teachers notice of the expectations for their job, their professional duties. See Chapters 5 and 6.

Documentation as a Fact of Life in Public Schools:

Teachers know and understand documentation. They have to do it every day! As our society demands more and more accountability for what is taught and what is learned, the paperwork becomes at times oppressive and overwhelming, and can diminish teacher preparation and effectiveness in the classroom.

The first thing we are going to address under this heading of documentation is to encourage you, as building principal, to review the breadth and depth of the documentation required of your staff and to provide templates and other time-saving means to efficiently handle the demands placed upon them. Efforts on your part (or by the district itself) to use templates and technology to allow teachers to meet the documentation demands will benefit everyone and allow teachers to teach. Such assistance will also help you with the response to the recalcitrant teacher who says I cannot get it all done; you can respond that the documentation requirements have been streamlined to help the teacher get the work done.

Artifacts:
- *Historic artifacts*: The documentation efforts of teachers in their daily work described above create artifacts[117] of their work. In addition to the general artifacts provided

---

[116] Danza, *I'd Like to Apologize to Every Teacher I Ever Had*, 110.
[117] *Merriam Webster Dictionary*'s definition of artifact:
noun
    1a: a usually simple object (such as a tool or ornament) showing human workmanship or modification as distinguished from a natural object

through the introductory tools we have discussed, there are teacher—or depart-ment—specific artifacts that document a teacher's performance. These are to be reviewed, analyzed, synthesized, and evaluated to reach a conclusion regarding areas where a teacher is distinguished, proficient, basic, or unsatisfactory. Your task is akin to putting together a puzzle with the picture coming into focus the more pieces you see that fit. We have already discussed some of the baseline artifacts, some produced by the teacher and some by you or other principals who came before you. These artifacts include some historic documents:

- o Prior evaluations
- o Current evaluations
- o Exemplary performance commendations and awards from the board, admin-istration, other staff members and students
- o Improvement plans, current and former
- o Teaching certificates
- o Transcripts showing course training
- o Continuing education classes or experiences

At times, administrators new to a building will say to themselves or to their teachers that everyone starts with a clean slate and that prior evaluations will not be consid-ered unless there is a major issue (a mistake). As a principal, it is your duty to know as much about your staff as possible so you can monitor learning in the classroom, where it is needed most, and determine the strong and the weak as far as the abili-ties of your staff. It may be that the prior principal did a good job of evaluating and supporting her staff. But the opposite is also often true. The prior principal did not evaluate, did so only occasionally, or adopted the approach that all teachers are above average (the easy, lazy approach) and rated everyone the same. (The evaluations are done, and no one is unhappy. Of course, the losers are the students and your school district.)

In short, the historic artifacts are part of the documentation that either estab-lishes the foundation for your work with a teacher or, in the absence thereof, results in you having to start from scratch with your staff.

---

b: something characteristic of or resulting from a particular human institution, period, trend, or individual

c: something or someone arising from or associated with an earlier time especially when regarded as no longer appropriate, relevant, or important

2a: a product of artificial character (as in a scientific test) due usually to extraneous (such as human) agency

b: an electrocardiographic and electroencephalographic wave that arises from sources other than the heart or brain

c: a defect in an image (such as a digital photograph) that appears as a result of the technology and methods used to create and process the image

James B. Gessford: Prior favorable evaluations. A review of numerous cases, commentaries, and a good deal of practical experience reveal at least one common theme which permeates evaluation law and many teacher discipline situations. The "prior favorable evaluation" theme is a claim which seems to occur again and again. The following provides at least some authority and ideas for a response to such a claim. In *Newcomb v. Humansville R-IV School District*,[118] a tenured or permanent teacher dismissal was upheld on the basis of incompetency and inefficiency. The teacher claimed the board's decision was contrary to law, in that for fourteen years the district annual evaluations rated her skill and competence as satisfactory. The teacher maintained the board's decision was erroneous because it contradicted its own records from previous years. In rejecting the argument as "illogical," the court stated: "[The] Board was not required to make its decision about Newcomb's competency and efficiency in 1993–'94 based solely on her performance evaluations in prior years. Achieving tenure does not insure that a teacher will be eternally competent and efficient in the teacher profession. The legislature implicitly recognized that fact when it included incompetency [or] inefficiency in the line of duty as one of the six causes for which a board can terminate a permanent teacher's contract."[119]

It should also be noted that the Newcomb court emphasized the less-than-favorable written "comments" in the prior evaluations, even though the teacher was graded as having "met performance expectations." Thus, even in the face of prior satisfactory evaluations, negative written comments have some evidentiary value.

- *Preparation artifacts*: We have focused on great lesson preparation as the sound foundation for a successful teaching experience for the teacher and learning experience for the student. It is in the lesson planning that students can be given the opportunity to do the engaging. In most schools today, a teacher's lesson plans are online in the school network. They are easily accessible by you, the principal, and therefore reviewable on call. Obviously, they should be preserved, not only week to week, but also year to year for comparison and reference by you and the teacher. Stated simply, lesson plans and the materials compiled to support those lesson plans are literally the framework to begin your analysis of teacher performance and upon which you will base your assistance to the teacher.
- *Classroom artifacts*: In addition to lesson plans, the work product of the teacher and the students can provide a window into what is being taught, how it is taught, and what is being learned. We all have experienced the worksheet teacher. Read the book and do the worksheet. There is very little instruction and certainly no higher level

---

[118] 908 S.W.2d 821 (Mo. Ct. App. 1995).
[119] Id., 825.

of thinking and questioning skills required of the teacher or the student. Obviously, a review of lesson plans should tell you the means of delivery instruction and the guided practice following same. But you can really see what is happening by obtaining and reviewing the work being done in the classroom. These artifacts will tell you what and how a concept is being taught, and the means of assessing student learning and understanding. These artifacts include worksheets or other teacher-produced assignment sheets and materials used to provide visual and manipulative instruction, such as PowerPoints, videos, lab instruction and experiments, writing assignments, and the instructions for same. Students experience their teachers in their direct interactions and in their assignments. The assignments provide a window into classroom life that observations cannot see. These artifacts enable the evaluator to witness the teacher's plan coming to life for the students.

Your access to and review of these artifacts are an opportunity for you to learn, obtain ideas that you can share with other teachers, and determine the level of student engagement for and by students in that classroom. As you work with your teachers, you gather these artifacts and reach a conclusion with regard to their use. You may find them effective, not effective, an indication of a lack of preparation, or a myriad of other determinations based upon your education and training as to what is good teaching under your educational model.

- *Computer usage artifacts*: Your school district should and probably does have a computer usage policy and procedure. That policy will provide that there is no expectation of privacy of the teacher's usage of that school-supplied computer. In this information age with these machines at our fingertips at all times, we all (teachers, administrators, and lawyers) get lax in our use of computers that are not our own and that allow others to see what we are doing. Most all school professionals use their computer for appropriate uses. But there are always those who do not follow this dictum. You must inform your staff of the rules involving the use of the school-owned computer and systems for personal e-mails and such which is prohibited and enforce those rules for your own good and that of the teacher. The history of computer use can provide the artifacts to establish whether a teacher is on task and performing his/her duties competently.

The Home Shopping Network:

A principal, doing her normal walk around the school, noticed that every time she walked past the high school German language class of Frau Blücher (neigheeeee!),[120] she was sitting at her desk, no matter what time in the class period the principal walked by. The principal asked a student about what was going on in the classroom and was told that the teacher was always on her phone or at her computer and that little if anything was being taught.

The next day the principal walked into the teacher's classroom. The students were disengaged, and the teacher immediately stood up and began "instructing" the class. It was clear that the students did not know what the teacher was talking about. There were no materials on the students' desks, and it was obvious that no real teaching was occurring.

When the principal got back to her desk, she called the superintendent who in turn called the school attorney. After hearing the details of what had occurred, the school attorney suggested that the principal take immediate possession of the teacher's school computer and have the technology coordinator investigate the teacher's computer usage.

This is what the principal wrote in the reasons section of the cancellation hearing disclosure letter:

> Students have reported to the Administration that you have been on your personal cell phone and using the computer during class time. Such reports were confirmed during an examination of your computer usage since November 19, 2014 and continuing through January 30, 2015. The search of your computer established conclusively that you were on your computer accessing websites, including the Home Shopping Network and other websites while on duty and when you should have been engaged in teaching students. The information accessed was unrelated to any instructional purpose and clearly involved personal inquiry and business. (See attached computer usage log based upon an examination of your classroom computer.) Significantly, on most days such computer usage occurred at the beginning of each class period when you were to be providing instruction to students. You should have been initiating class through the statement of the lesson, the objective thereof,

---

[120] Frau Blücher is a character in *Young Frankenstein*, a 1974 American comedy horror film directed by Mel Brooks and starring Gene Wilder as the title character, a descendant of the infamous Dr. Victor Frankenstein, and Peter Boyle as the monster. The supporting cast includes Teri Garr, Cloris Leachman, Marty Feldman, Madeline Kahn, Kenneth Mars, Richard Haydn, and Gene Hackman. Why does Frau Blücher's name scare horses in *Young Frankenstein*? Some speculate that the horses in the film react violently to Frau Blücher's name because it means glue in German.

providing an anticipatory set, providing instruction and modeling as a set up for checking for student understanding and learning, and providing guided practice and closure. In other words, engaged in performing your teaching duties. You were asked by the Administration to provide a copy of your phone usage records for school time, and you refused to provide the same. On that basis, the Administration must rely upon the reports of students that you are frequently on your personal cell phone during class time.

The teacher's contract was canceled without a hearing. The teacher resigned. She was doomed by her own actions and left a trail of evidence on her computer, an artifact she could not erase.

- *Professional development artifacts*: Throughout the school year, schools generally provide staff development learning opportunities for their staff. The materials and the content of presentations should be maintained and remain available to staff. Attendance sheets for these events should be made available for each and maintained to confirm a teacher's attendance and hopefully participation in some manner. You could also provide for teachers to develop and maintain a log of professional development activities for their use and your review.
- *Parent-student-colleague communications artifacts*: Parent and community communications are a skill in itself. Under NDE Rule 10, two of the four required areas of evaluations are professional and personal conduct. It is interesting that in the Danielson domains professional and personal conduct are not a real emphasis, but often it is this aspect of the teaching profession that presents the most day-to-day problems for you as the principal and the teacher. Samples of a teacher's communications with parents should be well written, education focused, and accurate in reporting student achievement or classroom issues. They should include a plan for addressing the problem(s) and strategies for parents to use to assist the learning (at least try to engage them in their child's learning). The same goes for a teacher's communications and interactions with colleagues. A teacher can be a very good teacher (or at least be knowledgeable in his/her endorsed area), but if he/she is not a team player or does not treat others with respect, they can challenge the culture of the school quickly.
- *Collection of artifacts*: All the above described types of artifacts should be gathered by your teacher as directed by you as principal and is maintained in a kind of portfolio that you review regularly with both probationary and permanent staff. If teachers know what you will be looking for, they are more likely to make sure they have the

artifact materials, which in turn means that the artifacts will be incorporated into their teaching, and therefore, student learning is enhanced.

Documenting Management by Walking Around (MBWA):

One of the most often asked questions from principals is "If I observe something about a teacher's performance that is significant, and I write something down, do I need to give it to the teacher right away?" The answer is an unequivocal *no*. As a principal, you are the eyes and the ears of your school as a whole; you need to see and know everything, if possible (though as we have noted before, "life isn't 100% or fail"). An effective administrator is one who is (1) visible (rather than in his/her office all the time), (2) accessible, and (3) observant. Your teachers should expect you to be around, looking in on their classrooms, stepping in, and standing in the back, and be prepared for you to stop in for an entire instructional period, announced or unannounced.

James B. Gessford: Unannounced observations.[121] A new argument being made in the courts by some teachers is that excessive or unannounced observations may violate the Americans with Disabilities Act (ADA). For example, in *Borkowski v. Valley Central School District*,[122] a library teacher who had sustained neurological damage in a car accident fifteen years earlier claimed that the school district should have accommodated her mental disability by providing her a teacher's aide to help her control her class. The Second Circuit held that she should be allowed to take her case to trial. The court concluded its opinion by discussing, but not deciding, the issue raised by the library teacher involving unannounced observations, stating:

> Ms. Borkowski also claims that the School District's use of unannounced observations unfairly disadvantaged her in view of her difficulty in dealing with multiple stimuli. Under Section 504, an employer must take care that its evaluative techniques measure the job-related skills of an individual with disabilities and not the disabilities themselves. See 34 C.F.R. § 104.13 (b); 45 C.F.R. § 84.13(b); cf. 42 U.S.C. § 12112(b)(7) (Americans With Disabilities Act). * * * We need not reach the separate question of whether the School District's use of unannounced observations was itself discriminatory under Section 504. We very much doubt, however, that, as Ms. Borkowski suggests, the School District could

---

[121] Gessford, "Termination of School Employees: Legal Techniques," Evaluation, 1995, 2-8 to 2-9.
[122] 63 F.3d 131 (2nd Cir. 1995).

adequately perform its legitimate and important function of evaluating its probationary teachers by foregoing unannounced observations and relying on announced observations alone.[123]

My father, Dr. Robert Schultze, some forty years ago, told me that as a junior high principal in a school of 1,200 students, he visited every class in his school every day, just a look-see, but sometimes, he stood in the back and took in the lesson delivery and classroom environment. His staff loved him. Not that he was easy. He was fair and honest. He also told me that when he saw something that would help a teacher, or something in the teacher's performance that might need correcting, he would write it down and revisit it the next time he was in the classroom. Once he had what he felt was enough information to reach a conclusion about his observation, he would gather and coalesce the information, write up the collected observations with the dates and classes where the issue or matter was observed, and his conclusion based thereon. He would then sit down with the teacher and go over what he had observed. Sometimes it was exemplary performance; sometimes, deficient performance. Once written and reviewed, he would give the teacher a copy of the memorandum and put a copy in the teacher's file to be referred to when working with the teacher. Eventually it was used as a measure of performance in that teacher's evaluation.

What was good practice forty years ago is good practice today. Write down what you see. Write a note or an e-mail to yourself. It is okay to create your own memory file about your teachers, collectively or individually. It is your information until you decide to act on it. When that time comes, you document your observations and conclusion, provide it to the teacher, and discuss the issue with him or her.[124]

Documenting Social Media

The level of social media sophistication varies among principals and their teaching staff. Twitter, Instagram, etc., (that is the extent of a baby boomer's knowledge of such things) are fine for personal communication, but not professional communication.

From a legal standpoint, any communication by school employees, administration, teachers, or support staff on the school district's equipment is subject to a public records request.[125] As such, you should be very careful before you hit "send," because what you write

---

[123] Id., 143.

[124] Dr. Pace's comment: Several years ago, a principal I had worked with in his master's sent me a photo of the office of another of our grads he had recently hired as assistant principal. It was a shot of the AP's empty office. The caption showed the AP's name, followed by "Instructional Leader," because he was out where the action is. Teachers don't improve with the instructional leader sitting in an office pushing paper.

[125] See your state's public records act.

may soon be public. That not only refers to e-mail but also any other electronic device, whether your own or the school's system upon which you are conducting school business.

That does not mean that you should not use e-mail to communicate with your staff. E-mail is a very effective way to inform and guide your staff, collectively or individually. E-mails from you and from a teacher or teachers provide a nearly perfect documentation of the date, time, and place of an interaction on a performance issue. In short, e-mails are documentation that should be preserved and organized to be accessible to you in your overall review of a teacher's performance.

Another issue with social media is conduct by teachers and administrators on social media in what they consider their private lives. If such conduct is violent, lewd, harassing, unlawful, or another form of conduct (drunkenness) that could influence the teacher's students or the students of the school as a whole, untoward conduct may have a nexus (a connection) to the teacher role that results in some form of discipline or cancellation or termination of the teacher's contract.[126]

The Birthday Party

It was a warm summer Friday night. It was his twenty-third birthday. He and his friends were in a downtown trendy bar area. They were in the restaurant's outside seating, laughing, having fun, and drinking—to an excess. Phones were out. Videos being taken and exchanged. A very popular rap song was blasting from the bar's loudspeakers. The rap song's lyrics are edgy and included *the* racial epithet and the f-bomb (as we called it in the old days) repeatedly. Everyone, including the birthday boy, was singing the lyrics—including the aforementioned words—loudly, and their performance was being videoed by someone. He posted the video of this birthday celebration on Facebook and Twitter. Acquaintances saw the video and responded via e-mail that the post was offensive due to the lyrics of the rap song and encouraged him to take it down. He did not remove it.

Subsequently, e-mails were sent to the school district that employed him as a ninth-grade teacher and coach, the local newspaper, and others, describing the conduct of the partygoers with the video attached. In the meantime, he responded to one of the e-mails sent by an African American friend, BOYS (evidently meaning Being Obnoxious Youthful Souls).

---

[126] "In order to dismiss a school board employee for acts performed at a time and place separate from employment, the Board must demonstrate a 'rational nexus' between the conduct performed outside of the job and the duties the employee is to perform" (Syllabus Point 2, *Golden v. Bd. of Educ.*, 169 W. Va. 63, 285 S.E.2d 665 [1981]).
Woo v. Putnam Cty. Bd. of Educ., 202 W. Va. 409, 410, 504 S.E.2d 644, 645 (1998).

So the administration had the ninth-grade teacher / coach's birthday conduct to address. The first question was whether there was sufficient nexus between his conduct that summer night and his job teaching and coaching students aged fourteen to sixteen years old. In other words, was there *a 'rational nexus' between the conduct performed outside of the job and the duties the employee is to perform.*" Whether such a connection exists depends on the facts and circumstances of the conduct and also the facts and circumstances of the school and community.

Alcohol abuse by students is a major issue in every community, and specifically the school community. Further, the concurrent racial issues in the country were another exacerbating factor—singing the N-word and disrespecting the person of color who called him out on his conduct as offensive (BOYS). Does such conduct establish that he (our young teacher) does not have the character necessary to mold young minds? When interviewed by the administration, he apologized, was truly remorseful, and in a mature manner, he expressed an understanding of the depth of his error and impact on his position as a teacher.

The question to you as the school principal is "What would you do in this circumstance?" Does it matter he is a high school teacher rather than a first-grade teacher? Does it matter that he is also a coach?

So, do you recommend to the board cancelation of his contract? If so, do you think you have enough to convince the board of education or possibly a judge that there was a rational nexus? Or, is there any other option?

Answer this question for yourself, and then look at the footnote below to find out what the school district decided in this case.[127] Then decide whether you agree with the disposition reached by the administration.

The lesson here is that part of every teacher evaluation process is the evaluation of a teacher's personal and professional conduct. It therefore behooves the building principal to regularly remind staff members, particularly the newer/younger staff members, that they are called upon to be exemplars for their students and a colleague to their fellow teachers; and in this day and age of cell phone cameras and social media, they must guard and protect their reputation and integrity. As they say, once one's reputation is lost, it is very difficult to get it

---

[127] The administration offered the teacher a reprimand if he would agree to all its terms and waive any right to a hearing thereon, and if he did not accept the reprimand on those terms, the administration would process with cancellation. The reprimand required him to (1) allow the administration to inform others (board, parents, etc.) of the facts and the disposition of the matter; (2) accept the placement of all the investigatory information and the reprimand in his permanent personnel file; (3) speak to his colleagues at the school where he was assigned, all the school district's new teachers about his conduct, and the student he coaches about the abuse of alcohol and the need to be socially aware, and the fact that it nearly cost his job and professional standing; and (4) inform himself of the social mores and standards across cultural lines, including the use of and participation in pop culture. Here, the administration felt secure in their choice and could hopefully say in time that they "saved that one!"

back, and past sins follow us for a long time—sometimes forever. So, professional educators need to think before acting. Their career may depend upon it.

Documentation during Observations (Formal and Informal)

Documentation during classroom observations should follow the educational model set forth in your evaluation instrument. Appendix D is the teacher classroom observation (TCO) form that has been created based upon the summative evaluation form, Appendix C. While the TCO uses the nomenclature of the summative evaluation form, there are opportunities for you to insert your observations within each component and element thereof, and reach conclusions applying the model to the teacher's instruction and classroom management, the two major domains for a classroom observation.

Note that the TCO form first has you review the teacher's lesson planning, again, the key to a successful lesson and student learning. Second, the TCO form has you listen and script the lesson observed; the idea is to avoid looking at your TCO form and missing what is going on in the classroom between the students and the teacher. The third step is to review and consider what you saw, and then go through the elements of the ten (10) components and identify those elements you observed and those that you did not.

Your "Summary and Notation of Exemplary Performance and/or Suggestions for Improvement" comments at the end of the TCO form should include complete sentence narratives of what you saw or did not see. You should use the magic words of the model and explain them clearly so the teacher knows the "good, the bad and, the ugly"[128] and can understand where he/she sits in each component and the elements thereof.

This may seem daunting, but the form leads you and the teacher through the process, from preconference and lesson plan review, to observation, to post-conference. It is your opportunity to teach, and the teacher's opportunity to improve. It is the type of effective documentation that provides credibility and integrity to the entire evaluative process. The intent of the TCO form format in Appendix D is to make it easier to say the hard things, as it is in black-and-white right in front of you and the teacher. *The key is sticking with the standard of performance, and jointly engaging in learning and applying the science of teaching to in turn give students the tools to be engaged in their own learning.*

---

[128] *The Good, the Bad and the Ugly* is a 1967 movie. In the Southwest during the Civil War, a mysterious stranger, Joe (Clint Eastwood), and a Mexican outlaw, Tuco (Eli Wallach), form an uneasy partnership. Joe turns in the bandit for the reward money, then rescues him just as he is being hanged. When Joe's shot at the noose goes awry during one escapade, a furious Tuco tries to have him murdered. The men reteam abruptly, however, to beat out a sadistic criminal and the Union Army and find twenty thousand dollars that a soldier has buried in the desert.

Dr. Riley's comment: Documentation is a pain, until you need it and don't have it. When this happens, it's all on you. Documentation is essential. Solid documentation is evidence that you truly care about the teaching and learning that goes on in your classrooms.

Your assignment:
1. Read Chapters 7 and 8 of *I'd Like to Apologize to Every Teacher I Ever Had*.
2. Read the "Enthusiasm" section of *Teach Like a PIRATE*.
3. Make a list of all the artifact documents that you have at your disposal in your school district.
4. Create an MBWA file and organize it in a fashion that allows you to make entries daily of your observation of school operations, teacher performance, and student issues.
5. Using the teacher classroom observation form in Appendix D, conduct an observation of two teachers, one probationary and one permanent, and compare your product with the current template you are using for classroom observations (if it is other than the TCO form).

CHAPTER 11

The Assistance—"Teach, Don't Tell"[129]

Made a difference to that one![130]

—*I'd Like to Apologize to Every Teacher I Ever Had*

Most states have a probationary period for teachers new to the school district. In Nebraska, we have a three-year probationary period. Generally, the three-year probationary period is set aside to allow schools to observe, develop, and train new teachers. As discussed in "The Assets," you and your school district have made an investment in each of these new staff members, and you must nurture that investment like any other.

The Dilemma and Approach

A dilemma for building principals when working with a staff with new and experienced teachers is described succinctly by Charlotte Danielson:

> Teaching, alone among professions, makes the same demands on novices as on experienced practitioners. The moment first-year teachers enter their first classrooms, they are held to the same standard, and subjected to the same procedures, as their more experienced colleagues... *When the principal arrives to conduct an observation of a novice teacher, she holds the very same check list as that used for experienced teachers...* Although the school district must ensure that all teachers (including beginning teachers) have at least a certain level of skill, the procedures used might be somewhat different for novices than for their more experienced colleagues.[131] (Emphasis added)

---

[129] Dr. Todd Whitaker.

[130] Danza, *I'd Like to Apologize to Every Teacher I Ever Had*, 251–252. As Tony Danza is leaving Northeast High School, he finds a gift from his assistant principal, Ms. Dixon. He writes, "I find a polished wood rectangle embellished with a metal scroll. The inscription on the metal scroll tells a story of a huge storm that roils the sea and washes thousands of starfish up onto the beach. The clouds break, and the sun comes out and begins to bake the starfish. A man wanders by and sees the thousands of stranded stars. He doesn't know what to do at first, but then he starts to throw them back in the water one by one. Another man comes by and says to him, 'What are you doing? There are so many, you are not making much of a difference.' The first man bends and picks up another starfish, throws it in the water, and says, '*Made a difference to that one!*'" (emphasis added).

[131] Danielson and McGreal, *Teacher Evaluation: To Enhance Professional Practice*, 5–6.

Dr. Riley's comment: When hiring a first-year teacher, I never expect a seasoned professional. The colleges and universities have done their job, and now it's time to do ours. A thorough orientation process, complete with an experienced teacher serving as a mentor, provides a good start for a young educator. This orientation period can last more than a year. Introducing the young teacher to district philosophy, curriculum/standards, instructional priorities, and the evaluation system requires the investment of time and resources.

The statutes and regulations of most states set forth the type of assistance required for teachers, probationary and permanent teachers alike. Most require in some form that probationary teachers be provided "a list of deficiencies and a list of suggestions for improvement and assistance in overcoming the deficiencies" and "follow-up evaluations and *assistance when deficiencies remain*"[132] (emphasis added).

What Is Assistance

You may think you know what assistance means, but let's look at it anyway. It is a noun. It involves action and active participation by both the assistor and the assistee (both new words according to my word checker, but you get the gist). Stated simply, it involves the action of helping someone with a job or task. But in looking at the synonyms of assistance, it is clear that it is much more.

Assistance involves
- help,
- aid,
- abetment,
- support,
- backing,
- succor,
- encouragement,
- reinforcement,
- relief,
- intervention,
- cooperation,
- collaboration,
- a helping hand,
- a hand,

---

[132] Neb. Rev. Stat. §79-828(2).

- a good turn,
- a favor,
- a kindness,
- ministrations, and
- services.

All of these synonyms apply to assistance to your teachers! And within each of these synonymous terms, such assistance can also require the provision of resources and/or information to help someone.

What does assistance to a probationary teacher to address identified deficiencies or enhance performance look like? Or stated another way, what assistance does an administrator need to provide when a teacher calls for *help*?

Help!

The following is a summary of the efforts of a real principal and a real first-year teacher to address classroom management issues as written by the principal in a summary for the end of year evaluation of that teacher. We have, of course, "changed the names to protect the innocent."[133] We have named the protagonists Mickey Jagger as the teacher and Ringo Starr, as the principal (yes, I am using those names! 😊).

Memorandum

To: Mickey Jagger
From: Ringo Starr, Principal
Re: Summary of Assistance during the 20__–20__.

The purpose of this summary is to provide an overview of your performance this year. The issues and deficiencies in performance, the assistance provided, and outcomes of such assistance in your teaching to date.

August–September:
You and I met regularly with another first year science teacher on a weekly basis to discuss their experiences in the classroom, any issues or questions, and provide guidance and assistance to both of the teachers.

---

[133] Quote from introduction to the fifties TV show *Dragnet* by Jack Webb. One of *Dragnet*'s trademarks is the show's opening narration: "Ladies and gentlemen, the story you are about to hear is true. Only the names have been changed to protect the

The topics discussed were open, with most conversations relating to student conduct and classroom management. From these meetings it became apparent that you were having some issues with classroom management and issues with specific students.

In September, we spoke with regard to one specific student whom you indicated was disrupting your classroom daily and that you had no control over him. We talked about some strategies to use with the student. After some consideration it was determined that it was in the best interest of the class that the student be removed from the classroom. We also decided that I would come into your classroom and observe to give you feedback on instructional and classroom management approaches.

The classes observed went fairly well, but you said that I should come all of the time, as the students were well behaved when I was present.

In late September, I suggested that we videotape a class while you taught when I wasn't present to allow me to evaluate your teaching and approach to classroom management issues. Video tapes were made nearly every day, most of the time during the 6th and/or 8th period biology. All of the video tapes were of an entire instructional period. You and I reviewed the tapes for general classroom observation and comment, and other times we reviewed a particular situation or classroom incident.

I sometimes reviewed the tape separately, and then we would meet to discuss what I saw. I noted any deficiencies that I had observed in your instruction or classroom management, and I provided you with suggestions to address the issues observed. Suggestions pertained to improving your overall teaching with specific recommendations regarding managing student conduct, and adjustments you should make in your teaching. Specifically, I suggested that you incorporate more structure to your classroom; requiring students less freedom of movement to assist you in maintaining student focus.

October:
The video tape review process continued through December, when the camera was removed, as it was that the video tape process had served its purpose of providing you feedback and suggestions for improvement.

---

innocent." This underwent minor revisions over time. The "only" and "ladies and gentlemen" were dropped at some point, and for the television version, "hear" was changed to "see." Variations on this narration have been featured in subsequent crime dramas, and in parodies of the dramas (e.g., "Only the facts have been changed to protect the guilty").

During the month of October, you and I dealt with sending students to the principal's office due to discipline issues, including excessive talking or paper throwing (minimal behaviors that appear to escalate to the point of disrupting the entire class). I met with you and noted that there were clearly continuing difficulties with classroom management issues. We discussed strategies to assist you in keeping the focus of the class on the learning objective for each day through well planned lessons and avoiding the "power play" classroom management technique. I advised you to use the "proximity" technique (stand close to the student with a quiet admonishment one-on-one, while continuing to teach). You stated that you would try to use those techniques.

November:
During November, you continued sending students to the office for disciplinary reasons. At this point, I started to see multiple offenders from the class. I met with you and discussed further ideas to assist in handling the classroom and addressing student conduct. We determined that I would start giving additional assignments from the office to help detour behavior. We also discussed the need to implement the strategies we had discussed to maintain control (classroom structure, proximity, lesson planning), and that you were losing the respect of the students when you could not control behavior. We focused on the classroom environment Domain headed, "Respect and Rapport". I expressed to you my concern with the number or referrals that I was seeing. You stated that you would take a look at your classroom management as well as your discipline procedure. We discussed the idea to give the students clear cut expectations and let them make a conscious choice to misbehave.

December:
You began referring a student named Jack on a regular basis to the office. You stated that Jack is purposely disrupting the class, jumping from his chair, flashing things on his phone in the middle of class. [Yes, "Jumping Jack Flash!" Sorry, I just could not pass that one up!] We had a meeting with the student and admonished the student to correct his behavior. After the meeting we talked about how to best deal with Jack. During our conversation you stated that you didn't want to dedicate that much of your time to someone that wasn't putting out any effort in the class. At this time, you and I began to review email communications from the

student's parents. We then met with the student's father and developed a discipline plan for the student in your classroom.

January:

On January 12, 20__, you and I met to address 1st semester issues and set goals for 2nd semester. I provided you with a document entitled 2nd Semester Science Goals, addressing classroom management issues. We focused on what you had learned from the experience of the first semester and that you could use this new semester as a fresh start. We reviewed the Science Goals in detail and discussed the implementation of the strategies outlined in the documents and their practical application in the classroom. You expressed thanks for the help and said that you would work to implement the strategies and ideas in your classroom.

On January 20th, I conducted walk though observations of your classroom to see how you were progressing with the implementation of the Science Goals. On that day you expressed frustration with specific students, and problems with students not complying with your directives. It was disturbing that you had very little that was positive about students, nor did you indicate any pleasure or satisfaction from your teaching.

I was pleased however that you initiated a discipline strategy involving a "Think-Time Form" that students came to the office to fill out. If a student failed to modify their behavior after filling out the form, they were sent to the principal. But, for one reason or another, students continued to be sent to the office. The pattern of problems with classroom management you experienced in the First Semester was continuing into Second Semester.

February.

In early February, a 7th grade student left class to come to my office for refusing to do push-ups. You were directing kids to do push-ups for forgetting their book. Requiring "push-ups" is a form of corporal punishment and is contrary to school district policy and state law. You were told to discontinue such a practice.

In mid-February, I was informed by the Technology Director that you had broken the "white board" in your classroom out of anger. You stated you were upset with the class and yanked on a cord that the tech director told you to leave alone.

Subsequently, an incident occurred where a student was making comments to you regarding your teaching. In response, you sent the student to the office, shortly after that you sent two other students to the office. The students related that you had become angry over the student's comments and sent them to the office. When contacted, you admitted that you had lost your "cool". We again discussed your classroom management skills and the means of avoiding such incidents—avoid power play situations and use other less confrontational and disruptive approaches.

Informal classroom observations were ongoing throughout the months of January and February via walk-through observations. A formal observation was done on February 23, 20__.

March:
On March 3, 20__, you sent an e-mail that was unprofessional to the parent of a student that resulted in a combative "back and forth" between you and the parent. The triggering incident was an inappropriate drawing made by the student when a sub was watching the class. I met with you and we covered 3 points:

1. Handle your class. Must manage all student behavior.
2. Professionalism. Give Parents facts… Don't preach.
3. Don't try 3 or 4 management strategies and then give up. Keep trying.

On March 9, 20__, you sent an email to the parents of two students. The facts of the e-mail were true but the last sentence "questioned their [the students'] character." The parents of the student were very upset. Again, I told you to give parents the facts, and don't tell parents how to parent or question their integrity or that of their students.

Also, on March 9, 20__, you became involved in a verbal confrontation with a parent in the hallway. The parent was upset about not being notified of a detention. The parent became argumentative, and you allowed yourself to become involved in a confrontation. When I spoke with you about it, you felt you were in the right and "didn't want to back down from her." We talked about it not being appropriate to argue in the hallway and that you needed to end the argument and be the professional. I told you that (1) you should never argue with a parent. If an argument appears to be developing it is better to disengage the conversation and find a later time to talk, and (2) the hallway or classroom with students present was not an appropriate place to carry on such a discussion, that you should have found a place where this discussion could be held in private.

On March 10, 20__, I was notified by a 7th grade parent that you called your class "a-holes." When I asked you about this, you said, "I'm not going lie, yes I did." I told you to apologize and address the matter immediately.

I told you we would talk soon, and that is when I set up the March 12th meeting. I met with you on March 12th. We reviewed your Summative Evaluation that I had prepared based upon your formal evaluation and the informal evaluations, formative work, and other contact throughout the semester and incorporated your 1st semester summative findings to cover the entire school year, including the issues with student and parents. We focused on the domains and elements for "Professional Conduct" and "Classroom Management" and discussed your performance under each of the elements of those domains. Your rating on those elements was basic in some, and unsatisfactory in others. Notwithstanding the assistance provided, your classroom management and professional conduct declined as the school year progressed despite our joint efforts to fix them. And, I told you that I would be reviewing your overall performance and would let you know my recommendation on the renewal of your contract for next year.

On March 18, 20__, I met with you and delivered to you an Appraisal Report of Teaching Performance, a Notice of Deficiency and an Assistance Plan of Action. You know your science subject matter. We just need to continue to work on your classroom management and communication skills. As we move forward for the balance of the school year, let's focus on your lesson planning, and student engagement, which will go a long way in addressing the classroom management issues you have experienced.

Note here that:
1. The principal used the first person to discuss what occurred during the year rather than a cold third-person approach;
2. The principal tied his work with the teacher to the standards of performance in the evaluation instrument;
3. The principal provided very specific recommendations and resources to address the classroom management issues that the teacher was struggling with;

4. The principal gave the teacher time to work through issues, and provided creative means of observing and assisting the teacher through the videotaping of her class;

5. The principal noted the positive (her knowledge and teaching ability), but provided something to focus on as the school year progressed; and

6. The principal took the risk of continuing to work with a teacher who had some real issues her first year, seeing potential in a person who might otherwise leave the profession. The measure in Danielson's rating method is whether students will be harmed if the teacher continues. Here, the conclusion was that at this point they would not.

Was the principal's handling of the teacher perfect? No, but it is an illustration of the hard work needed to assist young teachers to hang in there, learn and, hopefully, eventually succeed. *Like the starfish in Tony Danza's story, the principal worked to save this one.*

Will the principal succeed in his effort? The principal can only provide the guidance, resources, and the opportunity. As Tony Danza learned, "You can't learn for them. They [the assistee] have to do the work."[134]

The Fundamentals of Assistance

Our touchstone for assistance is again the essential elements of Section 79-828(2) and 007.06 of Rule 10 here in Nebraska. The touchstones are

1. a list of deficiencies,
2. a list of suggestions for improvement,
3. assistance in overcoming the deficiencies, and
4. follow-up evaluations and assistance when deficiencies remain.

The Plan of Assistance

At the end of the narrative of assistance provided to Mickey Jagger above, the principal presented her with an appraisal report of teaching performance (the summative evaluation of her overall performance to date), a notice of deficiency, and an assistance plan of action.

What should that plan of assistance look like? The fundamental elements of assistance noted above literally provide the template for every plan of assistance. Let's break them down element by element as they should be used in a plan of assistance.

---

[134] Danza, *I'd Like to Apologize to Every Teacher I Ever Had*, 45.

A List of Deficiencies

Any listing of deficiencies in performance that are the basis for a plan of assistance should be organized in a general-to-specific manner. First, list the standard of performance that the deficiency relates to. For example, in the case of Ms. Jagger, using the Danielson domains, one of her areas of deficiency is in Domain 2: The Classroom Environment, Component 2a: Creating an Environment of Respect and Rapport; and 2d: Managing Student Behavior. In listing the deficiency in these components, your plan of assistance could look like this:

Deficiency: Domain 2—Creating an Environment of Respect and Rapport: The Classroom Environment, Component 2a

Level of Performance:

Element	Standard of Performance	Teacher Performance
Expectations	Proficient = Teacher-student interactions are friendly and demonstrate general warmth, caring, and respect. Such interactions are appropriate to developmental and cultural norms. Students exhibit respect for the teacher.	Basic = Teacher-student interactions are generally appropriate but may reflect occasional inconsistencies, favoritism, or disregard for student cultures. Students exhibit only minimal respect for the teacher.
Monitoring of Student Behavior	Proficient = Student interactions are generally polite and respectful.	Basic = Students do not demonstrate negative behavior toward one another.

Deficiency: Domain 2—The Classroom Environment, Component 2d: Managing Student Behavior.

Level of Performance:

Element	Standard of Performance	Teacher Performance
Expectations	Proficient = Standards of conduct are clear to all students.	Unsatisfactory = No standards of conduct appear to have been established, or students are confused as to what the standards are.
Monitoring of Student Behavior	Proficient = Teacher is alert to student behavior at all times.	Basic = Teacher is generally aware of student behavior but may miss the activities of some students.
Response to Student Behavior	Proficient = Teacher response to student behavior is appropriate and successful and Teacher respects the student's dignity. Student behavior is generally appropriate.	Unsatisfactory = Teacher does not respond to misbehavior. The response is inconsistent and overly repressive. Teacher does not respect the student's dignity.

While you need not use the foregoing format, the concept is to inform teachers of the standard expected and compare that to their level of performance in each element. They can visualize the skills they need to develop to meet the standard of performance expected that is right in front of them—being proficient.

The next portion of the list of deficiencies is to describe the actual conduct and incidents (see Ms. Jagger above) that you have observed, and your conclusions based upon those observations that are the basis for your ratings on each element of the domain and component at issue. Be specific. Do not make generalized statements without a basis. It undermines your credibility. Use dates, class period, or times. Use your MBWA notes and e-mails to yourself and/or the teacher as a basis for your narrative of the performance that is not meeting the standard. Remember, recounting the problems allows the teacher to reflect on that issue or incident, and think through other approaches and options to address, in this case, her class-room management. This approach helps the teacher use her problem-solving skills—Bloom's higher level of thinking. Ms. Jagger looks at the above components, sees the standard, and hopefully evaluates, analyzes, applies the component/element, and on that basis, she begins to aspire to meet that standard.

A List of Suggestions for Improvement

The operative word here is "hope." It is here that you say, "You can do this, and here are some suggestions to get to the standard expected." But, as is said repeatedly in Tony Danza's book, "You can't do it for them." Here, Mickey Jagger needs to (1) accept that her classroom management is indeed deficient; (2) want to be an effective teacher to all students and wants to improve; (3) feel that there is a workable solution to the issues with her classroom management and is willing to work to incorporate them; and (4) make the necessary changes in her approach, a process that may take time, even a new school year, with a new class, where she can start anew.

As you formulate your suggestions for improvement, consider the admonition of Maddie Fennel in Chapter 2. Focus only on two to three necessary changes at a time. *(Please stop here and go back to Chapter 2. Reread the section on what a teacher wants. It will provide you further guidance as you work on your improvement plan and particularly your suggestions for improvement.)*

Another major point to convey to your teacher, as you begin working on ideas and approaches to improve performance, is that no one is perfect. *Stop here again and read "Life Isn't 100% or Fail" from* Teach Like a PIRATE *by Dave Burgess.* Burgess says, in part:

> During a recent new teacher training, a second-year teacher asked me a fantastic question. After watching me demonstrate lots of student engagement strategies and techniques, she asked, "When you use these strategies, do you have full engagement from one hundred percent of your students?" I said, "Ok. I am going to tell you the real deal. What I have is more engagement than I would have had if I didn't use these techniques.[135]

What should suggestions for improvement look like? Whatever you as the expert educator determine will best serve the teacher and her students to improve learning. In some ways, it is the creative part of your job. And Dave Burgess' notes above to the young teacher applies equally to you. Your suggestions will *not* be effective 100 percent of the time. Some

---

[135] Burgess, *Teach Like a PIRATE*, 155.

ideas will fit, others will not, and some will provide more effective teaching techniques, but not resolve all issues.

Assistance in Overcoming the Deficiencies

The key to any effort to provide assistance to Mickey Jagger is the sincere effort by you *and* the teacher (Mickey), effort that involves trial and error, successes and failures, and—most of all—an investment of time on your part. Letting a teacher know you have given suggestions to sink or swim without support in giving effect to your suggestions is unfair and, frankly, negligent on your part. That does not mean you have to be in the classroom every day. It means that you need to be paying attention and being a resource, doing the follow-up discussed below.

There are a myriad of ways of providing assistance. Those typically suggested are
- recommending coursework of some kind (in person or online),
- conducting regular observations and follow-up discussion,
- videotaping of classes (Mickey and the principal tried that with some success),
- providing a mentor and/or observing the mentor's classroom, and
- going over again the tools discussed in Chapters 5 and 6.

Really, probably all the above, and more. Again, imagination is your friend as long as you are in it with the teacher together. In short, you are a resource and can offer resources.[136]

However, there are the Rex rules for resources.

The Rex Rules for Resources (The 3 Rs)

Rule number 1: Read, review, and know the content of any resource you recommend. *Do not violate this rule!*

Rule number 2: Resources must be tied directly to addressing an identified deficiency and the desired enhancement.

Rule number 3: Real assistance—*no busy work*! The teacher is busy enough and has no time for unhelpful tasks that may simply be perceived as punishment or, worse, a setup for failure as a means to an end. If this is the perception, your efforts are a waste of time.

---

[136] *Merriam-Webster Dictionary's* definition of resource:
noun
a stock or supply of money, materials, staff, and other assets that can be drawn on by a person or organization in order to function effectively.

Effective improvement plans require investigation into best practices, consideration of the results desired for student learning and how best to get there, and investment in critical thinking and well-planned action. As you write improvement plans for your teachers, remember that teachers are your assets and your responsibility, and you are striving for his/her success; such an effort requires a realistic step-by-step approach which may take more than one school year.

Follow-up Evaluations and Assistance when Deficiencies Remain

We alluded to follow-up evaluations and assistance in the foregoing, but a couple of comments about this required task in the statute are appropriate at this point. From a legal standpoint, it means that you cannot simply observe, evaluate, and deliver the evaluations at the same time you deliver the nonrenewal letter. Such action is not only contrary to the statute and court interpretations of same, it is also a failure to do the job of a principal/evaluator.

Obviously you should arrange for follow-up observations, announced and unannounced, and summative evaluations. *Yes, a summative evaluation in the middle of a quarter or semester.* A summative (discussed in detail in Chapter 13) provides a wholistic view of the teacher's entire performance—*the big picture.* Teachers need that picture to know where they are; they truly want to know. Be candid. Say the hard things. It also provides the evidence of what is working and what is not. It allows adjustment of the improvement plan to implement new strategies, to get rid of what is not working, and try another idea or method. All done in the spirit of helping and with the light of hope and support for success.

Every improvement plan should have a time line for improvement. Most plans say that improvement must be immediate and continuing, and there is nothing wrong with such a directive. It works well with objective requirements, like the teacher getting her lesson plans in on time. But, such time lines should outline specific work, tasks, or changes that make sense, and provide adequate time for implementation. Ms. Jagger should be given time to try different approaches to her classroom management, even with a new class next year. Sometimes success takes time and trial and error.

As should be clear at this point, an effective improvement plan involves a process. It should be continuous, not a means to an end. Often you will get asked by a teacher when they will come off an improvement plan. My answer would be never. Teachers should always strive to improve, and the improvement plans should have identified weaknesses in the teacher's performance. Ms. Jagger will likely always be challenged by classroom management issues and will need to continue to learn to strategize as she has different students in her classes that present different challenges behaviorally or in learning styles. So, you and your teachers need to understand that we all continue to learn and hopefully get better every day, every school year, through our professional lives.

Final Note

A final note to you as the evaluator in writing improvement plans and the effective use thereof:

- Do *not* write them and then ignore them. If you do, you have not done your job, and eventually that will catch up to you.
- Again, do not place time lines on yourself. You are busy. Failing to meet a time line will come back to haunt you in a hearing.
- Get back in the classroom and see how your investment is doing.
- Evaluation and observations do not end on April 15 (or whatever date is set by the statutes in your state for notice of nonrenewal or termination at the end of the contract year). Your work with the teacher should go to the end of the school year and beyond to the next.
- There should be a year-end summative and review of the summative evaluation and improvement plan.
- There can and probably should be check-ins during the summer, cheerleading for preparation for the next school year.
- There should be a meeting before the next school year starts to set the stage for better and hopefully improved performance. Such a meeting should include a review of the improvement plan again, prior evaluations, the work the teacher has done over the summer break to improve his/her skills and lesson preparation for the upcoming school year, and—based on the foregoing—a clear discussion of expectations and performance requirements.

Teachers like Ms. Jagger, who struggle through some or most days, should not be alone or feel alone. Having been there on some days, it is often a helpless and defeating experience. They need to know that someone has their back. That someone is you. Your assistance and counsel are invaluable, even if it is to listen, and then help the teacher critically think through the issues with their job. All this so you can say with some pride and satisfaction, "Made a difference to that one!"

All this takes time, but it is worth it! The parents and students may not know of your effort, but your teacher will, and the students will benefit.

Dr. Riley's comment: Placing a staff member on a growth plan is serious business. Your primary goal is to improve the instruction and learning experiences for the students in that teacher's classroom. There is another issue to consider. When you have a teacher that is working at a level below what is expected, every other teacher in the building knows it. If you don't address the problem, you have just accepted a lower standard of teaching for your school.

Your assignment:

1. Read Chapters 9 and 10 of *I'd Like to Apologize to Every Teacher I Ever Had*.
2. Using the evaluation instrument used in your school district, write an improvement plan for Mickey Jagger. Be sure to incorporate elements required by Section 79-828. As part of your preparation of Mickey's improvement plan, reread pages 19 to 32 of *Teach Like a PIRATE*. Include a narrative for your improvement plan that you would use to relate the discussion of "Rapport" to Mickey.

PART 4
The Skills

CHAPTER 12

The Composition—The Art of Painting, Drawing a Picture of Observations, Guidance, Support, Directives, Expectations, and Results

Ms. Dixon also has tricks of teaching. "Ever heard of a six-word memoir?" she asks me. I have no idea what she's talking about. "Hemingway wrote the first one: 'For sale: Baby shoes, never been worn.' A whole life story in six words. Try it on your students Tony. It will make the children think. And that's what we want them to be doing, critical thinking, not just rote learning. But they will also like this assignment because it is short, and they do like short. Best try it yourself first though"[137] (emphasis added).

—Tony Danza.

We all took composition during our educational journey, most times twice, once in high school and once in college. The ability to compose, to put down on paper (or these days on a computer, laptop, or cell phone, using Twitter, Instagram, e-mail) your thoughts, concepts, or ideas for the purpose of communicating to others (or yourself) is a skill. An essential skill for a school teacher and a very essential skill for a building principal. In fact, I thought about titling this chapter "The Communication" but, in retrospect, decided that focusing on the ability (or skill) of being able to express one's self to others individually or collectively was the way to go. So here we go.

The definition of the noun "composition" from our Merriam-Webster Dictionary includes elements like "work of art, work, creation, literary/musical/artistic work, opus, oeuvre, piece, arrangement, poem, novel, play, drama, symphony, concerto, opera, painting, drawing, picture."[138] As this quote emphasizes, most of us think of the term "composition" as a form of art. However, as you read the entire definition in the footnote below, you can

---

[137] Danza, *I'd Like to Apologize to Every Teacher I Ever Had*, 50–51.
[138] Definition:
   noun
      1. the nature of something's ingredients or constituents; the way in which a whole or mixture is made up
      1a. the action of putting things together; formation or construction
      1b. a thing composed of various elements
      2. *archaic*: mental constitution; character
      3. *archaic*: a compound artificial substance, especially one serving the purpose of a natural one
      4. *linguistics:* the formation of words into a compound word

see that "composition" has applications across all disciplines of learning, not only linguistics, but also math, science, including physics. Have you ever seen the movie *Good Will Hunting* with Matt Damon?[139] Damon's character solves a complex theorem written on a classroom blackboard which had been assigned as a challenge to a linear algebra class when his job was a janitor. *That was composition.* We will talk a bit more later about the application of the concept of composition with your staff.

The Basics of Composition

We have all been taught that good compositions nearly always have three main parts (the big three):

- Introduction: The first paragraph is often an introduction, a paragraph that introduces the topic, says something interesting about it, and states the thesis.
- Body: Following the introduction are several paragraphs called the body. These paragraphs give readers specific information about the topic, supporting and developing the thesis. The body of all good compositions are organized carefully with a beginning, middle, and end. The body is well developed with facts, examples, incidents, or reasons to make a clear point.
- Conclusion: The conclusion, which is often one paragraph, gives readers a final interesting point to think about.[140]

The big three form the foundation of any composition. As we move forward in this chapter, keep the big three in mind as the foundation of all your communications with your teachers (and other staff) in e-mails, memos, to the entire staff or individuals. The foundation will help you provide complete expression of your thoughts and the concept(s), infor-

---

5. *mathematics:* the successive application of functions to a variable, the value of the first function being the argument of the second, and so on

6. *physics:* the process of finding the resultant of a number of forces

7. a work of music, literature, or art

7a. concerto, opera; painting, drawing, picture

7b. the action or art of producing a work of music, literature, or art

8. an essay, especially one written by a school or college student

9. the artistic arrangement of the parts of a picture

10. the preparing of text for printing by setting up the characters in order

11. a legal agreement to pay an amount of money in lieu of a larger debt or other obligation; an amount of money paid under a legal agreement

[139] *Good Will Hunting* is a 1997 American drama film directed by Gus Van Sant and starring Robin Williams, Matt Damon, Ben Affleck, Minnie Driver, and Stellan Skarsgård. Written by Affleck and Damon, the film follows twenty-year-old South Boston janitor Will Hunting, an unrecognized genius who, as part of a deferred prosecution agreement after assaulting a police officer, becomes a client of a therapist and studies advanced mathematics with a renowned professor. Through his therapy sessions, Will reevaluates his relationships with his best friend, his girlfriend, and himself, facing the significant task of confronting his past and thinking about his future.

[140] https://www.custom-essay.net/parts-of-a-composition.

mation, or directive(s). What follows are suggestions for refinement and adaptation of the big three to provide substance to your communications with your teaching staff as you teach, guide, and evaluate their performance to improve student learning.

The Skill of Writing to Teach Teachers

We are going to focus initially on the skill of composing written communication to teachers both in form (the words to use) and substance (the ideas to be conveyed). The composition concepts apply to all forms of communication with your teachers, collectively or individually. Generally, this skill involves several elements found in our *Merriam-Webster Dictionary*'s definition. Concepts like:

- "The nature of something's elements; the way in which a whole or mixture is made up."
    - As we have discussed, teaching is a science, and as with any science, there are ingredients that must be incorporated into the mix of planning and presenting lessons and in managing one's classroom.
- "The action of putting things together; formation or construction."
    - The action of the coalescing of the myriad of concepts and requirements within the science of teaching set forth in the rubrics/domains or criteria of the instructional model adopted by your school district and set forth in your evaluation instrument.
- "A thing composed of various elements."
    - Tying together the individual elements of the skills, duties, and responsibilities of a professional educator's (teachers, counselors, speech pathologists, school psychologists) to provide an overall picture of their professional performance. Again, capturing *the big picture*!
- "The successive application of functions to a variable, the value of the first function being the argument of the second, and so on."
    - While a math concept in the definition, the successive application of functions to help a teacher build from one rubric, domain, or criteria to another or move from unsatisfactory to basic to proficient to distinguished fits into effective composition to teach the teachers.
- "The process of finding the resultant of a number of forces."
    - Here again, a physics-focused concept, but equally applicable to teaching (not telling) your teachers how to use effective lesson planning to provide varied instruction to meet the needs of all different types of learners (auditory, manipulative, etc.) to provide varied input to learners and application of the concept being taught through the input portion during guided practice and independent practice and assessment that follows to guide needed further

instruction to the group or individual, e.g., teaching to understanding. These forces put into play by the teacher directly affect classroom environments, individual student engagement, and ergo, they lessen student discipline issues. Mastering these forces (a cause-and-effect analysis) also supports an essential component of teaching teachers and is difficult on one hand but can be freeing on the other.

As noted before, you should use Bloom's higher level of thinking skills (we need them as much as students)—the *old* versions are application, analysis, synthesis, and evaluation, while the *new* versions are applying, analyzing, evaluating and creating—to address all the parts of an issue, whether lesson planning, instruction, or classroom management, and factor in each variable to arrive at a thoughtful solution to an issue for an individual student, an entire class, or the teacher his/her self.

Old Bloom's Taxonomy	New Bloom's Taxonomy
Evaluation	Creating
Synthesis	Evaluating
Analysis	Analyzing
Application	Applying
Comprehension	Understanding
Knowledge	Remembering

The original Bloom's Taxonomy has always seemed to me (a social studies teacher) to be more of a scientific experiment approach to a problem or subject. The revised Bloom's Taxonomy (Bloom's revised) is more applicable to the skill of composition that a building principal needs to teach, guide, and nurture the school's assets—the teachers. Applying Bloom's revised, we could articulate its application to composing a narrative on a domain/rubric/criteria of your instructional model based upon observations, formal and informal or MBWA, reviews of artifacts produced by, and assessments of student progress by that teacher as follows:

The principal

1. remembers the skill (standard of performance) set forth in the instructional model as a master teacher;
2. understands through thorough expertise as a master teacher the behaviors or actions of the teacher with regard to that skill;
3. applies the skill (again, the standard of performance is proficient) set forth in the instructional model to the teacher's demonstrated performance;
4. analyzes the information gleaned from the observation in conjunction with the tools given to the teacher(s)—again, job description, contract, evaluation instrument and instructional model, teacher handbook, etc.;
5. evaluates the information and arrives at a conclusion with regard to the teacher's performance and reaches a conclusion based upon sound teaching science-based facts; and
6. creates an articulate, clear, and concise communication with the teacher from the results of the first five elements of Bloom's revised, the skill of putting it all together to teach and guide.

Some Basic Rules

There are some basic rules to effective composition of communications with your teachers.

First and foremost, *teachers are not third persons*! They are your colleagues and your students in some ways. You should communicate with them *at all times* on a first-person basis. *Do not refer to them as Mr. Jones or Mrs. Robinson.* Your communication needs to be one-on-one communication. "You" and "me." You do not have to be friends, and there is certainly a need to keep your relationship at arm's length to maintain the professional relationship that you are there for all teachers equally, but you should be professional colleagues who can communicate respectfully and directly.

Second, be consistent in the way you refer to the teacher in your documentation given directly to the teacher. Do not start out the communications (memo, e-mail, or an observation or evaluation) in first person and switch in the middle of the documents to third person. It sounds oxymoronic, but I assure you it happens (see discussion of grammar below).

Third, be sure (and this is essential) to spell-check and grammar check your writing. There is nothing worse than going into a hearing and presenting a communication from a principal to a teacher to the board of education and having it be full of grammatical and spelling errors. You are being presented as an expert educator. Remember, the fundamentals of education are reading, writing, and arithmetic. You are already a leg down in the hearing if that happens. The lawyer for the teacher you are seeking to dismiss will not pass that up. It is what we lawyers call low-hanging fruit, and we cannot resist. Writing well takes time, but good, accurate, and well-written product shows investment, interest, and a desire to help the teacher. So be careful, as once you send the document, you cannot retrieve it. You can correct it, but still it is there.

Fourth, use the magic words, the language of the individual rubrics/domains/criteria for the standard of performance expected in the case of the Danielson rubrics—proficient. Your teachers should have been taught what each standard means, and how to apply each one through your setup efforts at the beginning of the year and through teacher in-service. They should be familiar with the descriptors of what constitutes good teaching. Remember, we no longer use the "I know it when I see it" approach.

Fifth, be honest. Say what needs to be said. Teachers want the truth. They want to be evaluated and need to be confirmed when they are doing well, and told when they do not meet district standards, individually and collectively, and in writing. If you are honest with your staff, they will respect you, seek you out for assistance, and bounce ideas off you. In our office, we always say, "Mark the box!" which means be willing to mark "unsatisfactory" if the teacher's performance is deficient. However, we also say that you must then explain why you rated the teacher as not meeting district standards. Soften the blow, while allowing you to recommend nonrenewal or termination if your effort to improve performance does not bear fruit.

Sixth, work with the teacher incrementally. As Maddie Fennel noted in Chapter 2, do not expect perfection immediately. It takes time. While you should note all deficiencies, note the most critical and seek improvement on those, which in turn will provide a basis for improving the other areas of deficiency. Remember our statutory guide in Nebraska, Section §79-828(2), which states:

> The probationary certificated employee shall be observed, and evaluation shall be based upon actual classroom observations for an entire instructional period. If deficiencies are noted in the work performance of any probationary certificated employee, the evaluator shall provide the probationary certificated employee at the time of the observation with a list of deficiencies and a list of suggestions for improvement and assistance in overcoming the deficiencies. The evaluator shall also provide the probationary certificated employee with follow-up evaluations and assistance when deficiencies remain.

In other words, use the statutory guide (and Rule 10). Here it is again: To help the teacher build a foundation upon which to move to the next step, think general to specific. Let's climb this little hill so we are in shape to climb the mesa, and then move to the mountain. No one is perfect, even the best. As a principal, it is your duty to encourage and support each teacher to get better every day. A daunting task but the most important one in your school.

Seventh, and this is key, you must draw on and incorporate all the foundational elements that you have developed personally and have taught your staff as discussed in the preceding eleven chapters.

Composition of Informal Communication with Teachers:
Less Can Be More—The Six-Word Memoir

Finally, while narrative compositions can (and will) sometimes be several sentences, sometimes less can be more. At the beginning of the chapter, we quoted Tony Danza's book on pages 50 to 51 and his conversation with Mrs. Dixon, the tough assistant principal. While the quote related to having the students write a six-word memoir, it can equally be applied to teaching and guiding teachers, a teaching memoir. Stating Mrs. Dixon's idea another way, it will make the teacher you are working with think. And that's what you want him or her to be doing. Critical thinking of how to plan lessons, how to vary instruction, how to deal with classroom management issues. While it may be a short assignment, it will engender self-reflection and rededication to the teaching task. It is something that should be done periodically. Additionally, your making this assignment sincerely to promote improvement in performance is clear evidence of your commitment to improvement to the teacher and, if necessary, in any personnel issue down the road.

Dr. Riley's comment: Pay particular attention to Rex's third point in his basic rules. Many people write like they talk. It doesn't work. You become a better writer by reading good literature written by good authors. Model their sentence structure, grammar, use of tense, etc. This is something you can do every day. You become a better writer by writing. When you write letters or send e-mails to staff, parents, or community members, have a trusted colleague read your work before you send it. Insist they be brutally honest.

Your assignment:
1. Read Chapters 11 and 12 of *I'd Like to Apologize to Every Teacher I Ever Had.*
2. Select one teacher on your staff and identify (1) a deficiency in meeting *or* (2) a successful meeting of a district standard set forth in the rubric/domain/criteria in your evaluation instrument, and incorporate all seven (7) of the composition elements set forth in this chapter to craft a narrative that is clear, concise, and meaningful to the teacher. Then give it to the teacher and ask what they get out of the discussion set forth in your written narrative *without* your explaining any portion thereof until you have heard their complete response. So take a shot at it and see how it comes out!

CHAPTER 13

The Summative—The Delivery of the Results of Your Joint Efforts

You can't learn for them Tony.[141]

—David, Tony's mentor

Composition of Formal/Summative Communications with Teachers

Formal or summative evaluation documents must by their nature be more detailed, providing the overall big picture, rather than the more day-to-day informal communications on situational observations and interventions by you as the principal discussed previously. As noted briefly above, it is in the formal/summative arena that you bring to the table *all* the foundational work and artifacts you have provided to and instructed the staff on in prior years, at the beginning of the year, and during the current school year.

Included in these foundational documents are the job descriptions applicable to the teacher's position, contract terms, lesson planning template, the teacher handbook, the student handbook, board of education policy, and the teacher evaluations process and instrument, in-services on your educational model, district and school or department goals, student discipline and classroom management training, and the like, collectively referred to hereafter as the "foundational documents."

The summative is a document where through your narrative, you can engage the teacher and be creative in guiding him/her toward improvement of their skills by giving the *big picture* of where they are at and where they need to go.

Most importantly, it is the resting place of the informal observations made throughout the semester or school year, those notes to self or to the teacher that have coalesced into a conclusion regarding the teacher's performance.

---

[141] Danza, *I'd Like to Apologize to Every Teacher I Ever Had*, 45–46.
Tony went on to relate a conversation with his mentor David:
David: "You can't learn for them Tony."
Tony: "But I get the feeling some just don't want to work."
David: "There's a difference between not wanting to work and not wanting to learn. The student has to, at the very least, be interested in learning. It might make it more interesting for them if they like you, but teaching is not a popularity contest. It's about getting them involved in their own education… Get out of the way, let the kid's do it."

The foundational documents should be referenced as a source establishing the standard of performance expected of teachers in your district, and the terms therein should be incorporated into your compositions of your formal communication regarding a teacher's performance in his/her summative evaluations.

A. *The structure of the summative*: What you are composing in the teacher formal/summative evaluation process is a teaching as a science-based conversation about the teacher's performance, supporting a rating of distinguished, proficient, basic, or unsatisfactory (again, Danielson's rubric ratings), regarding each rubric/domain/criteria set forth in your evaluation instrument. You must compose a reason for the rating you give a teacher for each element of a rubric/domain/criteria. This appears on its face to be an impossible task, but as we will see, it can be done by development of a well-crafted summative evaluation document that guides you as the principal and the teacher through each rubric/domain/criteria in a linear and focused manner.

B. *A framework for a formal/summative composition*: We discussed above the basic elements of a composition and used the revised Bloom's Taxonomy to outline the critical-thinking process that should go into the composition of a teacher evaluation narrative which you could use as a structure for your composition. You certainly should use those critical thinking elements.

    1. *IRAC*: In law school, I was taught a very simple organization for writing a legal brief on an issue that works well with any problem-solving process. It is called IRAC (as opposed to Iraq the country). The acronym means

      • *Issue*: What is the issue, problem, or achievement that is up for discussion, decision, or guidance?

      • *Rule*: What is the standard of performance that the teacher has or needs to achieve?

      • *Analysis*: What ideas do you and the teacher have to address the issue as it applies to the rule (standard of performance)?

      • *Conclusion*: What are your suggestions for improvement where deficiencies exist or accolades for meeting or exceeding the standard of performance to support and supplement the teacher's efforts? (Remember, this is a growth process, not a punitive process. Hopefully, a struggling teacher also does good things, so say so).

    2. *The Eight-Step Approach*: Another approach structure used by a larger school district in Nebraska uses a formula for structuring the composition of a narrative of performance for its struggling teachers. The school district graciously provided this time-tested pathway for providing staff with great communication. For our purposes, we will call it The Eight-Step Approach.

- *Component 1*: Establish the problem (the deficiency).
  - o Identify the domain/rubric/criteria not being met.
    - ▪ Quote it.
    - ▪ Explain it.
- *Component 2*: Give specific examples of when you have noticed the issue (the evidence).
  - o What is the basis of the evidence?
    - ▪ Classroom observation
    - ▪ MBWA
    - ▪ Observations of others
- *Component 3*: Describe the effect on the learning environment and/or working environment (the application).
  - o Apply the evidence to the deficiency in the performance of the domain/rubric/criteria/element.
  - o Focus on the effect on student learning or safety.
- *Component 4*: Your directive (the guidance, assistance, and resources).
  - o What exactly do you want them to do?
    - ▪ Be clear and concise.
    - ▪ Be selective. Work on one or two things and keep other issues as to-dos, if not critical, but note them. *No busy work!*
    - ▪ Use your foundational material provided at the beginning of the school year and throughout the year and direct assistance provided to the teacher.
    - ▪ Use your expertise or that of others.
- *Component 5*: A measurable time frame for when you expect change to happen (the opportunity).
  - o When do you want things done?
  - o Again, be clear and concise, but also practical.
  - o On their schedule, not yours!
  - o Allow time for the teacher to learn the concept and apply it, just like teaching a student.
- *Component 6*: Specific strategies for implementation. You may need to teach the employee what to do (the suggestions).
  - o Where does the teacher go from here?
  - o Refer the teacher to:
    - ▪ Educational model–based document
    - ▪ Outside materials, classes, or other self-improvement measures (that you have read)
    - ▪ Mentoring from you or other professionals

- *Component 7*: Your rationale for the recommendation (the conclusion).
  - Where is the teacher at, and where are they going?
  - Do not sugarcoat the issue that needs fixing, but also use encouragement.
  - Offer yourself as a continuing resource:
    - Your expertise
    - Your care and support

The following is a short example of the application of the foregoing approach to composing a narrative.

There have been times when I have walked through your classroom that there is no definite start of class. For example, when I was doing a walk-through last Tuesday, I noticed that the bell rang and 4 of the 24 students were out of their seats talking to each other. This off-task behavior has a negative impact on the structure of your classroom environment, and you are not using the full instructional period. I am recommending that you research and reflect on effective anticipatory set/sponge/bell ringers. Effective anticipatory set/sponge/bell ringers are methods to hook students into learning and utilize the full instructional period.

The first seven components are met in the foregoing composition of a narrative to a specific rubric, domain, or criteria.

Using the above narrative design in an evaluation and improvement plan will provide you the *structure* to clearly and consistently provide accurate and meaningful guidance to your staff and will measurably improve *student learning*.

- *Component 8*: Your support for improvement and hope (the encouragement).

  I would suggest an eighth component to the narrative design, encouragement. You have said the hard things, those that will be perceived as critical and, by some, defeating. It is in the overview or summary at the end of a rubric that you provide guidance and directives but, critically, also encouragement. You are *not* trying to get rid of the teacher. You want him or her to succeed. To do so, they must see a way out of the noted deficiencies in performance.

It is a delicate balance to critically evaluate and yet provide hope. Teachers are particularly sensitive to criticism. (Well, I guess we all are, to some extent). We do not financially reward teachers for excellence. Teachers are paid for years of experience (to the limit of the vertical columns on the salary schedule) and for graduate education (again, to a limit for the education columns on the salary schedule). As such, teachers perceive themselves as equal in all respects to their peers. To be singled out as not meeting district standards even in one area can be difficult to accept for most. So, you as a building principal are in this conundrum as a teacher/coach of your teaching team.

On the one hand, you can be the tough taskmaster like Coach Dale in the seminal sports movie *Hoosiers* played by Gene Hackman, who announced his approach to coaching to a skeptical town passionate about high school basketball (to heck with teaching history). "I'm gonna break them down and then I'm gonna build them back up."[142] On the other hand, as teachers who are trained to nurture students, we know that "it takes a million compliments to build you up. And one insult to send it all crashing down."[143] In evaluating teachers and composing narratives in formal/summative evaluations, you need a little of both.

3. *Applying the Eight-Step Approach*: The Eight-Step Approach can be incorporated into a summative evaluation document stating the area of the teacher's job duties, the component of the evaluation document, and the rubric setting forth the standard of performance expected. The approach allows for a breakdown of the rubric by element that we discussed earlier. Now we are going to fill in the blanks in a manner necessary to focus the teacher on each of the critical portions of the rubric. This structure allows you as the principal to focus on those elements that need improvement and those that are satisfactory or even exemplary with an area for comments following each element, e.g., a narrative design that tries to find the proper balance between tearing down and building up and maintaining the dignity and spirit of your staff.

---

[142] Coach Dale, *Hoosiers*, Metro Goldwyn Mayer, released November 14, 1986.
[143] Drake. https://www.azquotes.com/quote/1196484.

To Teach or Not to Teach, That Is the Question: The Case of the Dilemma of the State Standards

I am not very good at accepting change. Being a baby boomer, getting a grasp on how to use all the new technology has been at times challenging. Sometime in your professional life as a principal, you are going to run into a teacher like me, where change is required and the teacher either resists or overreacts or, worse, gives up.

One such case involved a veteran teacher and a new principal. The teacher (we will call her Mrs. Robinson[144]) had been with the school district for fourteen years and had taught fifth grade, fourth grade, and (at the time of the principal arriving at the school) second grade. As the principal began her efforts to get to know her staff with walk-throughs (MBWA in action), she noted that Mrs. Robinson's second graders were always at their desks doing worksheets or that Mrs. Robinson was reading to the students. There were no activities or action in the classroom. The principal also noted that Fridays seemed to be testing days. Yet, notwithstanding the paperwork being done by the students, Mrs. Robinson had few, if any, grades recorded on the school district's smart school recording program.

A look around the classroom showed no evidence of manipulatives or displays to engage student interest. Simply, it was Dullsville.[145] The principal also consulted with the third-grade teacher to see how students in Mrs. Robinson's second grade were prepared for the next step in their education. The third-grade teachers said that their incoming students were generally behind and had difficulties with participatory classroom activities.

The principal spoke to Mrs. Robinson about these informal observations and inquired about the lack of activities and recording of grades. Mrs. Robinson responded that she was focused on teaching to the state standards as she had been told that it was essential that her students meet those standards. The principal asked to see Mrs. Robinson's lesson plans, and Mrs. Robinson stated she did not have her lesson plans for the week at school, that they were at home. The principal informed Mrs. Robinson that her lesson plans should be at school to be available for a substitute and, more importantly, as a guide for Mrs. Robinson in her planned lesson. The principal reminded Mrs. Robinson that her lesson plans were to be formatted following the Danielson lesson plan framework (see Chapter 8 and Appendix B), a framework that included an area to note the state standard(s) to be taught and incorporated into the lesson objective. Mrs. Robinson again noted the need to teach to the state standards.

At that point, the principal realized that Mrs. Robinson needed help to accept the need to plan effectively and help to make a commitment to make use of the lesson

---

[144] A homage to the infamous Mrs. Robinson in *The Graduate*—Anne Baxter.
[145] Something or someplace that is dull or boring.

planning training the school district had provided in prior years. The principal met with Mrs. Robinson to develop a plan to address these deficiencies in her performance that included (1) a review of the Danielson rubrics for lesson planning and the Danielson lesson planning template and (2) suggestions of learning activities that could be designed to incorporate the concepts that students are to learn as specified by the state standards while teaching the curriculum.

Mrs. Robinson was not excited about the principal's efforts to improve her performance. Lesson plans continued to provide few, if any, activities, continued to be based on rote learning, and remained focused on the standards.

It came time for the principal to prepare the summative evaluation for Mrs. Robinson in February. The principal, guided by the Eight Step approach, prepared the following summative scoring and narrative to support a finding of unsatisfactory performance for the planning rubric of the school district evaluation instrument.

Warning: This is a somewhat harsh evaluation designed to provide you with a pointed illustration of a narrative composition. This is not a template for all narratives.

Anywhere Public Schools—Summative Evaluation Form

The following Anywhere Public Schools—Summative Report is based upon classroom observations, formal and informal evaluations, and review of instructional artifacts, including lesson plans, student assessments instruments, and other areas of the duties assigned to certificated teacher of the Anywhere Public schools, as set forth in Board of Education policy, administrative regulations, contract and job descriptions. The Summative report is cumulative and incorporates performance by the certificated teacher on a continuous basis during the employee's tenure with the School District.

Performance Rating Key:

Level of Performance	Numerical Rating
Unsatisfactory	1
Basic	2
Proficient	3
Distinguished	4

PLANNING:

Component 1: Lesson Planning, Alignment with State Standards & RC Curriculum, and Instructional Materials Prepared.

Standard of Performance = Danielson Rubric—"Proficient Level":

There is evidence of consistent planning of daily instructional goals, strategies, and methods of assessment. The teacher can provide a clear rationale for the design and sequence of units. Evidence indicates that instructional content is consistently aligned with the local or state standards. Plans indicate that the instructional goals of the curriculum are met. There is evidence that the lesson plan provides opportunities to accommodate individual student needs. The teacher is prepared for class with all necessary materials and equipment readily accessible.

Level of Performance	Numerical Rating
Unsatisfactory	1

Standard of Performance and Comment:
- There is evidence of consistent planning of daily instructional goals, strategies, and methods of assessment.
  - Comment: *[Component 1: Establish the problem (the deficiency)]* There is little evidence that you have consistently prepared lesson plans that contain daily instructional goals, strategies, and methods of assessment. In fact, you frequently have not had your lesson plans for the week available in your classroom; they should be at school to be available for a substitute, and more importantly, as a guide for your instruction. Further, upon review of the lesson plans you have provided, there is virtually no evidence of consistent daily, weekly or unit planning with daily instructional goals, strategies, and methods of assessment of student learning. Rather your lesson plans simply list the state standard code numbers to purportedly be met for that particular day. It follows that your lesson plans to date do not follow the Danielson lesson plan template upon which you were trained

    [Component 2: Give specific examples of when you have noticed the issue (the evidence)] As we have discussed, your lesson plans contain only references to the state standards for the 2nd grade curriculum or copied from

the Core Reading Program Wonders. Some Math lessons are copied from the Math Resource EnVision. Your plans do NOT contain any of the essential elements of the lesson structure outlined in the Danielson template provided to you and again attached hereto, a bell ringer (anticipatory set), a stated objective, and creative input of information to students through a variety of means, visual, auditory, manipulative, etc.

[*Component 3: Describe the effect on learning environment and/or working environment (the application)*] The result is instruction that is based upon rote learning from the text and students completing worksheets. This approach to your teaching does not reflect the creativity our students deserve to engage them in their own learning. Lessons should provide students with an "input" of knowledge, and then an opportunity to move toward higher levels of thinking to invest them in the learning process. Lesson plans that are based upon stated (and posted in some manner for students) daily instructional goals, and then a variety of strategies and applied activities to engage students in learning the instructional goal allow for an exciting and fulfilling learning environment of our students, that is fun for all. You then follow-up with a creative means of measuring student learning so you, as the teacher, can assess the level of student understanding and reteach as necessary. While our students must be provided instruction to meet the state standards, that should be the "result" of a well-planned lesson (e.g., the goal).

[*Component 4: Your directive (the guidance, assistance, and resources)*] As noted, you have been provided the Danielson lesson plan template and training on the use of that format for lesson planning. Attached is a copy of the PowerPoint we reviewed at the beginning of the school year both this year and the previous year. We reviewed the template and PowerPoint in our recent meeting. The expectation is that you will prepare (create) lesson plans that follow the Danielson template, a framework that includes an area to note the state standard(s) to be taught and incorporate same into the lesson goal.

[*Component 5: A measurable time frame of when you expect change to happen (the opportunity)*] You shall prepare lesson plans that follow the lesson plan template effective IMMEDIATELY and shall continue same into the future.

[*Component 6: Specific strategies for implementation (you may need to teach the employee what to do—the suggestions)*] There are several resources available in our professional library that provide instructional ideas for a variety of learning activities. One such resource is the book "*Teach Like a PIRATE*" by Dave Burgess; which is a fun and engaging book that emphasizes out-of-the-box approaches to lesson planning and lesson delivery and assessment.

[Component 7: Your rationale for the recommendation (the conclusion)] Lesson planning is the hard work of teaching, but as Tom Hanks character says in the movie A League of Their Own, "It is the hard that makes it great!" It will take some time for you to develop those skills, but the reward will be immeasurable for you and the students. It will require of you a rededication and excitement for the task at hand. That rededication and excitement must begin NOW.

- The teacher can provide a clear rationale for the design and sequence of units.
    o Comment: It follows that where there is a lack of effective lesson planning, there will be a total absence of any rationale for the design and sequence of units other than the table of contents of a textbook or curriculum. This discussion incorporates all the elements covered in the foregoing sub-rubric.
- Lesson design consistently followed.
    Comment: The lesson plan format has not been followed at any time during the school year. This discussion incorporates all the elements covered in the foregoing sub-rubrics.
- Evidence indicated that instructional content is consistently aligned with the local or state standards.
    Comment: While, as noted above, lesson plans contain information copied from the Core Reading Program Wonders and some Math lessons are copied from the Math Resource EnVision, there is no cohesive structure that sets out the instructional content to present the learning objective as set forth in our school district and state standards. This discussion incorporates all the elements covered in the foregoing sub-rubrics.
- Plans indicate that the instructional goal of the curriculum are met.
    Comment: Your plans do not contain any stated instructional goal, objective, or learning outcome. This discussion incorporates all the elements covered in the foregoing sub-rubrics.
- There is evidence that the lesson plan provides opportunities to accommodate individual student needs.
    Comment: Totally absent from your lesson plans are any noted plans or opportunities to check for understanding, re-teach a concept to be learned or otherwise accommodate individual student needs. This discussion incorporates all the elements covered in the foregoing sub-rubrics.

- The teacher is prepared for class with all necessary materials and equipment readily accessible.

    Comment: Again, any mention of necessary materials and equipment is totally absent from your lesson planning, let alone any reference to where they are located so that they can be "readily accessible" to the student or any substitute teacher. This discussion incorporates all the elements covered in the foregoing sub-rubrics.

Overall Comment:

[Component 8: Your support for improvement and hope (the encouragement)] While the foregoing notes unsatisfactory performance, the weakness in your lesson planning skills is something that can be rectified. As noted, it will involve hard work, and trial and error, but I am confident that you can make this change. Your prior evaluations reveal that you have the subject matter knowledge. You clearly care about your students. You have the professional skills and tools; you now simply must make the effort. I am here to assist you in this process, to be a resource, to listen, to review and to suggest approaches to improve your planning of daily instructional goals, strategies, and methods of assessment.

The foregoing is an example, not a template. In the end, there is no right or wrong approach to composing an evaluation narrative. You have to develop your own style and means of teaching and coaching your staff, just like Gene Hackman in *Hoosiers*. The key is to do this hard work with integrity and apply your expertise to help your teachers help children learn how to learn.

Encourage Teacher's Thoughtful Response

In most states, there is either a statutory or regulatory requirement that the teacher has a right to respond to any evaluation or improvement plan.[146] As a principal and evaluator, you should encourage the teacher to respond. That response can be in agreement with the observations and suggestions for improvement and requirements of the summative evaluation, or pointing out areas of concern or opposition to the suggestion in the improvement

---

[146] 79-8,109. Teacher, administrator, or full-time employee; personnel file; access; written response; attach.

"Any teacher, administrator, or full-time employee of any public school district shall, upon his or her request, have access to his or her personnel file maintained by the district and shall have the right to attach a written response to any item in such file. Such teacher, administrator, or employee may in writing authorize any other person to have access to such file, which authorization shall be honored by the district. Such access and right to attach a written response shall not be granted with respect to any letters of recommendation solicited by the employer which appear in the personnel file. No other person except school officials while engaged in their professional duties shall be granted access to such file, and the contents thereof shall not be divulged in any manner to any unauthorized person."

plan. In asking the teacher to respond, you should encourage the use of the teacher's higher level of teaching skills. See discussion of Bloom's Taxonomy, e.g., the teacher should show that they have used the skills of application, analysis, synthesis, and evaluation in responding to the conclusion reached and directives made in the evaluation. This approach provides the professional dialogue between educational colleagues to achieve improved student learning.

You should keep the encouragement of a response approach in mind, as a summative evaluation that is developed and written will avoid pitfalls of unintentional punitive measures or placing the teacher on the defensive. Both of which are difficult to overcome once out there. In the end, you may not adjust or modify the summative as written, but the fact that you have incorporated the opportunity to the teacher to respond, considered the response, and moved forward from that point is an essential part of your job and supports your position as an expert that has considered all aspects of the circumstance surrounding the teacher's performance.

Your assignment:
1. Read the epilogue of *I'd Like to Apologize to Every Teacher I Ever Had.*
2. Using the foregoing components to write a narrative, select two teachers that you supervise and have observed for the immediate past school year, and for each teacher, write a narrative for a domain/rubric/criteria or element in your instructional framework and education model as shown in your evaluation instrument. Draw a picture of observations, guidance, support, directives, expectations, and results.
    o Teacher number 1: Select a teacher that is having difficulties, one that does not meet district standards in a specific domain/rubric/criteria/element and help them!
    o Teacher number 2: Select a teacher that is *not* having difficulties, one that does meet district standards in a specific domain/rubric/criteria/element. "No one is perfect." How can they improve?

CHAPTER 14

The Closure—Where the Rubber Meets the Road

Kids learn better when classes are fun, and how can teachers make education fun when they feel humiliated and have the district constantly breathing down their necks?[147]

—Tony Danza

You have composed your summative evaluation for a teacher. What now? You present it to him or her. If it's a probationary teacher, you will make this presentation twice a year, once in December and once in March (or if you are piled up, April, but not too late in April!). If it's a permanent teacher, it likely will be in March or April, or anytime during the year if that teacher is on an improvement plan. While you may feel some trepidation that presenting what you perceive (and likely the teacher will perceive) as a negative appraisal, the result should not come as a surprise to the teacher. You have put in the work with the teacher. Hopefully the teacher has reciprocated and put in the work to meet the standards of performance and your assistance in working toward that goal.

While the teacher may feel like those at Northeast High School in Philadelphia that you are "constantly breathing down their necks" and make them feel humiliated, hopefully those that can view the process as professional improvement and not as a means of unfairly getting rid of someone will accept the findings and suggestions for improvement in the summative. There will always be the teacher who is the victim. But, if you have done the preparation and laid the foundation (that word again) that we have discussed throughout this book, your staff as a whole and individually will begin to accept the overall evaluation process as legitimate and valuable.

At this juncture, it is important to remind ourselves that summative evaluations must provide an objective overview of a teacher's performance. While it may point out areas of deficiency, it *must* also emphasize the exemplary performance and the obvious efforts taken by a teacher to benefit the children the school serves. Stated bluntly, no teacher's performance is all bad. If it is, they should have been encouraged to find another profession long before now.

Once the summative is presented to the teacher, and it's reviewed in detail, you will provide the teacher with a copy. On occasion, a teacher may refuse to sign the summative documents in the place provided for affirming that they have received same. In that event,

---

[147] Danza, *I'd Like to Apologize to Every Teacher I Ever Had*, 197.

do not make a big deal of it. Simply write in the place of the signature that the document was presented to the teacher and the teacher refused to sign the summative. Include the date and time of this occurrence.

Per your evaluation procedure and instrument, the teacher has a right to provide a written response. The timing of such response should be set forth in your school district's policy. The response should be placed in the personnel file of the teacher attached to the summative evaluation. Further, you should read the teacher's response carefully. Do not just stick it in the file. The response will tell you a lot.

- First, it will let you know whether the teacher thinks you have any idea what you are talking about.
- Second, it will allow you to determine whether any of your suggestions or directives for improvement were heard.
- Third, it will tell you whether *there is still a chance* and whether the teacher is willing and/or able to continue to work toward meeting district standards.
- And fourth, it will tell you if *the time has come* to end the employment relationship and move toward a recommendation of nonrenewal or termination.

"So you're telling me there's a chance?"[148] Hopefully the teacher's response is positive, and "improvement is likely with experience, and little or no actual harm is done to students." (See basic rating level under Danielson in Chapter 7.) While noting some disagreement, the teacher's response shows a willingness to work at correcting deficiencies while appreciating your notations of good or exemplary performance, again, a needed inclusion in any summative. The summative and the teacher's response should be the springboard for preparation for the remainder of the school year in which the summative is issued and of the ensuing school year. It should be revisited before the end of the school year and again at the beginning of the school year and provide a basis for a plan of improvement if deemed appropriate by you, the decider.

In sum, while this chapter is called "The Closure," for the teacher you are still working with, it is simply the closure of one evaluation cycle and the beginning of another. It is literally the foundation (there it is again) for going forward.

The time has come; actual harm will be done to students if the teacher continues! If, on the other hand, (1) the teacher responds in a negative manner to your attempts at assistance in a manner that establishes a lack of desire, effort, or ability to improve his/her performance to even the basic level of performance; or (2) if the teacher responds positively, but his/her

---

[148] A line from the 1994 movie *Dumb and Dumber*.
Lloyd Christmas: What are the chances of a guy like you and a girl like me…ending up together?
Mary Swanson: Not good.
Lloyd Christmas: Not good like one in a hundred?
Mary Swanson: I'd say more like one in a million.
Lloyd Christmas: So you're telling me there's a chance?

performance taken in sum leads you to the objective determination that he/she does not have the skills to "enable the teacher to grow and develop" in the areas of identified deficiencies; and (3) improvement is unlikely with experience, and actual harm will be done to students, *then*, you will be faced with a decision whether to recommend to your superintendent that the teacher's contract be non-renewed or terminated at the end of the contract year (or, if extreme, be canceled immediately [see above discussion]).

The "Whole Enchilada"!

If, after you meet with the teacher to review his/her summative evaluation, you make the decision to recommend the ending the teacher's employment, the next step is to put together all your documentation that supports your recommendation of nonrenewal, termination, or cancellation—the whole enchilada. Once you, with the assistance of your school attorney, put the enchilada together, your school attorney will draft for you the Notice of Recommendation letter advising the teacher of the administration's decision to non-renew, terminate, or cancel the teacher's contract. These documents will be delivered to the teacher in person by you and the superintendent. At that meeting, you will provide the teacher with the Notice of Recommendation *and* the collected documentation supporting the reasons for the recommendation, all exhibits to be offered, and a list of witnesses. In other words, your entire case that is the basis for your recommendation.

Dr. Riley's comment: Most people want to please their boss. When working with a staff member who isn't meeting instructional/professional expectations, you will find some that can accept the recommendations and make the recommended improvements. You will also find some that can't improve and some that will refuse to improve. Fortunately, the can'ts and the won'ts are in the vast minority. The can'ts usually resign (through your empathetic counseling) and move on. The won'ts are the ones you usually end up facing in a hearing.

The Association

A few words about the role of the Nebraska State Education Association (NSEA) and local affiliates and its involvement in the nonrenewal/termination/cancellation process. The NSEA is a professional association of educators, not a union in the general sense of that described by Tony Danza in the quote at the beginning of this chapter. Its purpose generally is really threefold: (1) to provide legislative lobbying to support public school teachers and their interests; (2) to provide a stable health and dental insurance program; and (3) to provide legal services and representation in the event of a continuing contract issue with a member, e.g., nonrenewal, termination, or cancellation. With regard to the latter issue of representation, the NSEA has a duty to its members to provide an adequate and competent defense.

One of the first questions your legal counsel will ask is whether the teacher at issue in a continuing contract matter is a member of the NSEA, as that status will affect the approach to be taken going forward with the process. The legal counsel used by the NSEA is very good. They are also knowledgeable about the legal process and the practical considerations presented in every case. The NSEA, through its attorneys and UniServ representatives, can be a resource to counsel a teacher out and get a resignation. But be aware, they can spot errors by the administration in following the statutory process we have been discussing and will vigorously pursue a defense on that basis. So, let's make sure we cross our "t's" and dot our "i's."

The Juice

When you reach the determination that your efforts over time for and with the teacher have failed to sufficiently improve performance and student learning is being inhibited thereby, you will need to (1) compile all the foundational materials that you have at your disposal, those things we have discussed in Chapters 1 to 13; (2) begin work with your school district legal counsel (you should be working with legal counsel experienced in education law and culture, the legal process, and the personnel hearing process) to put together the case and assure that the statutory processes are followed to a tee; and (3) discuss your work with the teacher and your findings and recommendations with your superintendent to see if you have the juice (support) of him or her and (most importantly) with the board of education. By the juice, we mean, "Do you have the political support of the superintendent and/or the board based upon the position in the community of the teacher in question?"

The Juice

Unfortunately, life has little bumps in the road, and even when you have done your job as a school administrator, outside circumstances may affect the result of your efforts at evaluating staff. This can be particularly true in a smaller community, where everyone knows everyone and everyone's business, and where a teacher might have a special relationship with the board of education or community.

One of the first questions a school attorney asks the superintendent and/or principal is whether they have the "juice", meaning, do they have the purchase in the community to non-renew, terminate, or cancel the employment contract of the teacher in question. It is an unfortunate fact that whether you perceive you have the juice raises significant

---

WHO ARE YOU WHO ARE SO WISE IN THE SCIENCE OF TEACHING?

questions and choices as to how to handle a personnel matter. Choices that may impact your standing in the community, your job, and even your career. As the saying goes, "Know when to hold 'em and when to fold 'em," and when your integrity and professionalism require you to go forward, notwithstanding the risk professionally or personally.

Several of these circumstances come to mind, but we will focus on two of the more interesting cases.

The football coach. In one instance, a very successful football coach was also the school's biology teacher. The coach/biology teacher had a very physical approach to his relationship with students, once kicking one of his players in the behind with enough force to knock the student over and bruise him in that sensitive area. One day in biology class, students were assigned a lab project. They were to work in teams on the experiment and record their results. Two girls were working together, one of whom was the daughter of another teacher in the school and the eventual valedictorian of her senior class. We will call her Julie. The teacher walked past Julie, who was sitting on a stool, and her partner and mentioned that Julie should be more actively involved in the experiment rather than being the data collector. A few minutes later, the teacher again approached Julie and her partner with Julie still sitting on her stool. This time, the coach/biology teacher grabbed Julie's long ponytail and forcefully jerked her up off the stool, startling Julie, causing her to cry out in pain and with hurt emotions. The coach/biology teacher stated, "I told you to get up and work on the experiment."

Obviously, everyone in the small school heard of what was in legal terms a criminal assault and battery, witnessed by several students. Julie's mother, the teacher, went to the administration with her concern about the coach/biology teacher's actions.

The administration immediately suspended the coach/biology teacher with pay pending a hearing before the board of education on the administration's recommendation that the coach/biology teacher's contract be canceled.

A public hearing was held before the board of education (see process below). The feeling in the community was supportive of the coach, notwithstanding his conduct, so much so that the student and her teacher mother would not testify at the hearing. The attorneys for the administration, the teacher, and the board of education determined that in lieu of live testimony, the student could submit an affidavit setting out what had happened to her. Unusual, as there was no opportunity for the teacher to cross examine the student, but here, the facts were not in dispute. The teacher's attorney did not want the board of education to have to face the student or her parent to avoid sympathy. The focus needed to be on keeping the coach.

After this legal maneuvering, the hearing commenced with the school gym jammed to capacity to see the spectacle and support the coach. The administration knew they were doomed. The teacher admitted his conduct. The hearing was rather short. The board

187

deliberation continued for more than two hours, when the attorney for the board came to the attorneys of the administration and teacher and said the board was deadlocked between cancellation and retention of the teacher and wanted a way out. A settlement was reached to roll the teacher back four steps on the salary schedule and allow him to continue. Obviously, the administration did not have the juice.

PS. Ten years later, the coach again abused a student. His football teams were not as good. He was fired.

Was the administration wrong in going forward? Not necessarily. Sometimes you must stand by your principles.

These are very tough situations. A key approach to help avoid them is the preparation of your board, getting them focused on the "students first, adults second" approach. You or your legal counsel should also educate your board on the current focus of the law on physical and emotional abuse of students and the increase in lawsuits under Title IX, Section 1983, the Nebraska Tort Claims Act, and new federal anti-abuse legislation that creates significant liability for school districts.

In short, you must have your case made and put together and *know the lay of the land before you pull the trigger on recommending the nonrenewal, termination, or cancellation of the continuing contract of a teacher or administrator.* Once your case is fully developed, then, and only then, do you initiate the statutory process.

Settlement

As noted above, 99 percent of the cases where you as the principal have done your job as described herein, those cases will settle. Under current NSEA practices, most probationary teachers will resign without any specific resignation agreement or monetary settlement. On the other hand, for permanent (tenured) teachers, those cases will usually involve a resignation agreement that will include a resignation by the teacher, some form of monetary payment—cash and/or continued health and dental insurance for a period of time in exchange for a complete release of any and all claims against the school district, board member, or administrators. A clean separation.

The following story is instructive on the political considerations as well as the educational approach when all the work with the teacher has not resulted in performance that meet district standards and the principal has compiled this thick notebook of evidence, and has recommended to the superintendent that the teacher's contract be terminated.

Teacher of the Year!

Ring, ring. Marcia answers the phone.

"Anywhere Public Schools, Marcia here."

"Hi, Marcia, this is Greg at the law firm."

"Do you want to talk with Dr. Peterson?"

"Yes, is she available?"

"I will put you right through."

"Thanks."

"Dr. Peterson, may I help you?"

"Hi, this is Greg. I received a call this morning from legal counsel for Mr. Crosby, about the termination hearing in three weeks, and inquiring about possible terms of a settlement of the matter that would include a resignation with some form of payment to him."

"Well, Greg, I am not sure we as the administration are very interested in a settlement other than a simple resignation. Our team has put a lot of time into trying to help Mr. Crosby, and the board of education will support our recommendation of termination."

"First, Dr. Peterson, I am required to convey any offer to you. The attorney suggested a payment of $8,000 in exchange for Mr. Crosby's resignation and a complete release of the school district for any possible discrimination or contractual claims during his employment, plus a letter of recommendation."

"Again, we have done all of this work. Why should Mr. Crosby be financially rewarded for not meeting our district standards as a classroom teacher."

"I understand, but my job is to advise you based upon the facts, including the costs—both monetary and community costs. Certainly, the choice is yours."

"Well, what are your thoughts, Greg?"

"From a monetary cost point of view, we have our case ready, so preparation is basically done. But, as we approach the hearing, we will need to spend 15 hours to prepare you and Principal Stills and Assistant Principal Nash. Another 10 hours of prehearing prep by our office. Then there is the hearing, which will last about 20 hours over three days—Thursday night, Friday night, and all day Saturday. Our attorney's fees for preparation and the hearing will be around $13,500. The attorney for the board of education will be around $6,000. The cost for the court reporter will be around $2,000. So just for the hearing, we are at $21,500, and that may be low.

"I would note that during the 20 hours of the hearing, neither you nor more importantly will the board members be paid anything.

"Then there is the community issue. The hearing will be held in the gymnasium. Mr. Crosby, as you will recall, was chosen as Teacher of the Year just two years ago. While his popularity was the result of being a buddy to the kids, and he was not an effective classroom teacher, the community does not know that and there will be droves of folks—students and parents at the hearing. So, the board will be looking over our shoulders to a bunch of unhappy people. And, even if these people listen to and understand the evidence, they will not like that you belittled Mr. Crosby in public.

"I can't put a dollar value on the community disruptions, but it is a cost.

"Obviously, it's up to you? What do you think? How should I respond to the teacher's counsel?"

"Take the deal!"

Your assignment:

1. Write a step-by-step outline leading up to the delivery of the summative evaluation based upon the evaluation procedure adopted by your school district. Do not miss a step, as failure to follow the procedure to the letter may cause problems during the hearing process.

PART 5
The End Game

CHAPTER 15

The Testimony—A Time to Shine

"This profession requires a highly specialized and valuable mix of personality, perspective, and skills for success"[149] (emphasis added).

—Tony Danza

Well, here we are at the culmination of all your work with the teacher that is the subject of the due process hearing in which you are about to testify. You are ready. You have laid the foundation. You have the education, training, and experience to establish yourself as an expert in elementary and/or secondary instruction in the public schools. You have invested the time and effort to teach, assist, and guide the teacher to improve his/her performance to meet the school district's standard(s) of performance expected of all teachers performing the same or similar duties. You have observed the teacher and compiled the data and documentation that constitutes the record of his/her performance. Based upon all this data, documentation, and observations, you have reached a scientifically based opinion which is the basis for your recommendation to the board of education that the teacher's contract be non-renewed, terminated, or canceled. You have done all of this with integrity, not based upon personal bias but based upon the best educational interests of the students in your school building, and the district as a whole.

You are, therefore, qualified by your knowledge, skill, experience, training, or education as an expert under Section 702 of the *Rules of Evidence*. You are an expert that can provide the board of education with the scientific, technical, and other specialized knowledge of teaching with the content and in a manner that will assist the board to understand the evidence and to determine if there is a just cause basis for the termination or cancellation of a teacher's continuing contract. In so doing, you can and will testify in the form of an opinion regarding whether the teacher met the standard of performance expected of other teachers performing the same or similar duties.

A Mindset

To be an expert, you must think you are an expert and prepare yourself accordingly. You are on the stage and have the opportunity to inform the board of education of how the

---

[149] Danza, *I'd Like to Apologize to Every Teacher I Ever Had*, 253.

teacher evaluation process that they adopted is applied to their teaching staff to support student learning. It is a time to show off your knowledge. They hired you and expect you to be an expert, so be an expert. Make them want to know what you know. Like the judge in *My Cousin Vinny* when Mona Lisa says, "Would you like to hear more?" Vinny says, "I would love to hear this!" and the Judge says, "So would I."[150]

Special Treatment

As an expert, you get special treatment. Unlike other witnesses, fact witnesses, e.g., what did you see, hear, feel, etc., you can rely on what others saw, felt, or heard, things we lawyers call hearsay. Thus, in forming your opinion, you can rely upon observations or statements of others, and determine their relative credibility. (Caution is made here, as our courts have put little credence to the opinions of students with regard to each performance.)[151]

The Building Process

So, what does effective expert testimony look like? It is organized, very much like the organization of this book. Not an accident!

It is a building process, just like an actual building.
- You start your testimony by laying the foundation of your education and training.
  - Education:
    - College:
      - BA
      - MA
      - Doctorate or specialist

(Expound on your educational training, not just college but elsewhere, e.g., this symposium.)
  - Continuing education:
    - Seminars attended and classes taken to enhance teaching an administrative skill
    - Treatises and articles read
    - Publications that you subscribe to and routinely read
  - Teaching experience
    - Show that you have done the work to be a master teacher.
    - Show that you are continuing to work to enhance your knowledge to continue to be a master teacher.

---

[150] *My Cousin Vinny*, 20th Century Fox, 1992.
[151] *Hollingsworth v. Board of Education of the School District of Alliance*, 208 Neb. 350; 303 N.W.2d 506 (1981).

- o Training in educational models
  - ▪ Introduce the educational model and evaluation process based thereon will make them better teachers and in the end make their job easier on a daily and annual basis.
  - ▪ Trained on evaluation instrument.
  - o Lay a foundation upon which to build credibility to the evaluation instrument and supporting documentation that the board of education has adopted, and you are implementing.
- Then the notice of job duties and expectations given to all staff
  - o Job description
  - o Teacher handbook
  - o Contract
  - o Etc. (See Chapter 6, "The Tools and set Up.)
- Then the teaching and training you gave to your staff *and* to the teacher that is the subject of the hearing
  - o Introduce how you have in-serviced your teachers on instructional techniques and best practices.
  - o Copy of material provided: outline and/or PowerPoint?
- Then your application of the job duties and expectations and teaching and training for working with and improving the teacher's performance and thereby student learning
  - o Introduce the teacher at issue:
    - ▪ Positions
    - ▪ Years in the school district
    - ▪ Your experience in working with the teacher
  - o Opportunities to observe the teacher:
    - ▪ Informally
    - ▪ Formally
- Then your review of the evaluation history and earlier evaluations (yours and others)
  - o When the issues with the teacher's performance arose.
  - o How the issues with the teacher's performance arose.
  - o What you observed and documented.
  - o Take the board through the documentation.
  - o All documentation: evaluations, e-mails, notes, memorandums to the file, etc.
- Then your effort in advising the teacher of noted areas of deficiencies, provided with suggestions and resources for improvements, follow-up evaluations, and areas of proficient or exemplary performance (it can't be all bad!).
  - o List of deficiencies noted, with an explanation of each
  - o List of proficient and/or distinguished in performance, with an explanation of each

- o Resources provided
- o Mentoring opportunities
- o Regular meetings
- o What your assistance provided to the teacher to improve his/her performance
  - ▪ Improvement plans
  - ▪ Directives
  - ▪ Resources
  - ▪ Assistance
  - ▪ Follow-up evaluations
- Then your use of higher levels of thinking, skills of application, analysis, synthesis, and evaluation, to arrive at conclusions that are used in assisting the teacher
  - o Explanation of significant factors, incidents, observations that are indicia of the teacher's performance, and your analysis of same
  - o Discussion of general conclusions reached
- Then you take the conclusions reached in the application of the measuring devices adopted by the board of education, the evaluation instrument, and educational model, and connect them to the teacher performance.
  - o Summative evaluation of performance or conduct by the teacher.
    - ▪ Discuss ratings of the teacher on the educational model criteria or domains.
  - o Discuss the narrative explanation of the rating to the teacher on the educational model criteria or domains.
  - o Meets the standard of performance or does not meet the standard of performance on the educational model criteria or domains.
  - o What the result of your efforts at assistance provided to the teacher to improve his/her performance.
  - o Artifacts of teacher's response to improvement plans and assistance.
  - o Follow-up assistance and your response thereto.
- Then arriving at your final recommendation
  - o What your findings are based upon, observations, and/or documentation
- Then your opinion
  - o Opinion testimony

Question: Based upon your "knowledge, skill, experience, training, and education" and your efforts to improve the teacher's performance, do you have an opinion as to whether the teacher, through his/her performance of his/her duties, meets the standard of performance expected of other teachers performing the same or similar duties?

Answer: Yes!

(Stop there, follow-up questions to follow).

Question: And what is that opinion?
Answer: It is my expert opinion that the teacher, through his/her performance of his/her duties, *does not* meet the standard of performance expected of other teachers performing the same of similar duties.

Question: Would you explain to the board of education the basis for your opinion?

(Now is the time to tie all the evidence together.)
- Review all the evidence in summary.
- Review your efforts to improve the teacher's performance.
- Review the final summative evaluation.
- The significant issues it discusses.
- Your conclusions based thereon.
- Your finding that the teacher does not meet district standards.
- Based upon the foregoing testimony, do you find that the teacher's performance as a teacher in this school district is just cause standard:
    - o [ ] Incompetent
    - o [ ] Neglect of duty
    - o [ ] Unprofessional
    - o [ ] Insubordinate
    - o [ ] Immoral
    - o [ ] Other conduct which interferes substantially in the continued performance of the teacher's duty

Final question: What is your recommendation to the board of education with regard to the continued employment of the teacher by the school district?
Answer: I recommend that the teacher's employment be terminated/canceled immediately, as the case may be.

"You've been a lovely, lovely witness!"

Your testimony should be logical and linear, following the bread crumbs of your documentation all the way home to the end opinion.

Subject to Challenge

Although rare, the teacher's lawyer may attempt to challenge your ability to give an opinion on the basis of a lack of foundation or attack your credibility in teaching an opinion. If it is a foundational challenge, the lawyer may ask to voir dire you as the witness. It might look something like this:

"Mona Lisa Vito and the 327 with a 4-Barrel Carb"[152]
"Your Honor, I object to this witness. Improper foundation."
"I am not aware of this person's qualifications."
"I'd like to voir dire this witness as to the extent of her expertise."

If that should happen, let the lawyer have it like Mona Lisa Vito! You have the ammo!

Your assignment:

1. See the Web addresses below for the video of the expert testimony of Ms. Mona Lisa Vito from the movie *My Cousin Vinny*, truly a classic.
   Mona Lisa Vito Foundation Vour Dire Questions: https://www.youtube.com/watch?v=GTPUzRXozF0
   Mona Lisa Vito Expert Testimony—"The Defense Is Wrong": https://www.youtube.com/watch?v=CFdJza0AbeA
   My Cousin Vinny Trial Defense Case Dialogue: https://www.law.indiana.edu/instruction/tanford/web/movies/MyCousinVinny.htm
   My Cousin Vinny—Mona Lisa Vito Foundation and Expert Testimony Dialogue: https://illinoiscaselaw.com/expert-witness-defined-by-marisa-tomei-from-my-cousin-vinny/

2. Write a paragraph discussing how you see Mona Lisa's testimony applicable to the testimony of a principal at a hearing for the nonrenewal, termination of cancellation of a certificated teacher or administrator.

3. Now, write your own script of your testimony at a teacher termination hearing based on a fact basis from a teacher you have observed and evaluated who did not or does not meet district standards (please keep all names fictional).
   (a) Remember, you will be testifying before your board of education, so show off!
   (b) Your script should provide the following:
      i. Foundational testimony to qualify yourself as an expert under *Rules of Evidence* Section 27-702.

---

[152] *My Cousin Vinny*, 20th Century Fox, 1992.

ii. Factual testimony of the evidence supporting your determination to recommend to the board of education the nonrenewal, termination, and cancellation of the teacher.

iii. Opinion testimony stating your opinion as to whether the teacher should have his/her contract non-renewed, terminated, or canceled.

CHAPTER 16

The Hearing—A Long Day's Journey into Night[153]

This profession [is] emotionally grueling.
—Tony Danza, *I'd Like to Apologize to Every Teacher I Ever Had*, 253 (emphasis added)

Getting Ready for the Hearing: Preparation of the Principal for His/Her Testimony

Even though you are totally prepared, you will be very nervous about the hearing. It is only natural. I can tell you that as the attorney, the lawyer is always nervous too. There is always some uncertainty about due process hearings even when you are totally prepared. Personnel hearings are about the human condition, and you are dealing with a lot of humans at the hearing, the teacher, his/her lawyer, six to nine board members, counsel for the board, your superintendent, and nearly everyone in the community sitting in the audience. It is a show to them. They do not want to miss anything, and you are the star witness.

Now that you are scared to death, it is your lawyer's responsibility to prepare you for the hearing. In Chapter 15, "A Time to Shine," we discussed in detail your powerful position as an expert in the science of teaching. So now let's get down and dirty on how you will prepare for a formal due process hearing. Here are the steps to that preparation:

- You, the principal, prepare with your legal counsel with whom you should have been working once the teacher was identified as having difficulty meeting school district standards. It is thorough and intense and requires you to go through all the elements of your expert background, the teaching of your staff, the assistance to your staff and to the individual teacher, and the evaluation process.
- You review the disclosure documents, exhibits, witness list, and reasons in detail.
- You work with legal counsel to prepare a basic outline of your testimony with questions on direct examination by your lawyer, and potential cross-examination questions by the teacher's attorney. Note: While you may have questions outlined, you must be prepared for the questioning to go off the text a bit. Thus, you must be disciplined in your listening and answering of questions to avoid getting off the issue at hand, the teacher's performance.
- You and legal counsel interview all witnesses, other administrators, and staff (teachers and classified) to prepare them for the hearing.

---

[153] *A Long Day's Journey into Night* is a drama play in four acts written by American playwright Eugene O'Neill in 1941–'42, first published in 1956. The "long day" refers to the setting of the play, which takes place during one day.

- You and legal counsel work together to prepare a summary of evidence and suggested findings to the board of education.
- You will be prepared and confident in your recommendation of nonrenewal/termination or cancellation based upon your work. As discussed in Chapter 15, it is your chance to shine, showing your board and community that you are the expert in education and assuring student learning is occurring.

The Hearing

Now that you are prepared for the hearing, it is time for the process to begin.

- *Procedural due process*: As discussed in Chapter 15, a formal due process hearing (remember, our practice is to provide same to both probationary and permanent teachers) is to provide that the teacher has the right to be represented and be given an opportunity to cross-examine all witnesses to examine all documents and to present evidence material to the issues.[154]

  Procedural due process requires that the school district follows proper procedure as to notice of a hearing and the right to be heard by a neutral fact finder. As the court has stated, a fundamental requirement of due process is "the opportunity to be heard" (*Grannis v. Ordean*, 234 US 385, 394).

  In other words, the same type of hearing that a trial in a court of law would require. As such, a formal due process personnel hearing generally walks, talks, looks like a trial in a court, and therefore passes the duck test: *if it looks like a duck, swims like a duck, and quacks like a duck, then it probably is a duck.*[155] ☺

  The trial format of a personnel hearing satisfies the requirements in the law to provide the teacher, who has a property interest in his/her continuing contract, procedural due process.[156]

---

[154] "79-832. Formal due process hearing; employee's rights; how conducted; school board decision.

"(1) A formal due process hearing for the purposes of sections 79-827 and 79-829 means a hearing procedure adopted by the school board which contains at least the following: (a) Notification to the certificated employee in writing at least five days prior to the hearing of the grounds alleged for action, cancellation, termination, or nonrenewal of the teacher's contract; (b) upon request of the certificated employee a notification, at least five days prior to the hearing, of the names of any witnesses who will be called to testify against the certificated employee and an opportunity to examine any documents that will be presented at the hearing; (c) the right to be represented; and (d) an opportunity to cross-examine all witnesses and to examine all documents and to present evidence material to the issues."

[155] See "If it looks like a duck, swims like a duck, and quacks like a duck, then it probably is a duck."

The duck test is a form of abductive reasoning. This is its usual expression: The test implies that a person can identify an unknown subject by observing that subject's habitual characteristics. It is sometimes used to counter abstruse arguments that something is not what it appears to be.

[156] The Due Process Clause of the Fourteenth Amendment provides that "[n]o State shall…deprive any person of life, liberty, or property, without due process of law…" Procedural due process claims require a two-step analysis: (1) whether the plaintiff has asserted a life, liberty, or property interest that is protected by the Due Process Clause and (2) whether the plaintiff was deprived of that interest without sufficient process. An employment contract with a public employer can give rise to an objectively reasonable expectation of continued employment (*White v. Busboom*, 297 Neb. 717, 728, 901 N.W.2d 294, 303-04 [2017]).

James B. Gessford: Substantive and procedural due process. "Teachers have a substantive due process right to be free from arbitrary, capricious, and irrational action on the part of their government employers in relation to their teaching positions." As a general rule, educators have a "latitude of discretion" in selecting the substantive and procedural requirements of a school district's evaluation model.

In addition to substantive due process challenges, teacher evaluation models have been attacked on procedural due process grounds as well. Some courts have held that procedural due process is satisfied, irrespective of any irregularities in the evaluation procedures, if the state statutes regarding teacher termination are adhered to. Nevertheless, in some states a teacher is entitled to a "hearing on both the substance and procedure of the evaluation. [The teacher] is entitled to receive proper notice of such hearing with sufficient time to gather. Evidence to support his position, and he has the right to present expert testimony and engage counsel to assist him in the presentation of his case"[157] (citations omitted).

- *Substantive due process*: The subtitle to this chapter is "A Long Day's Journey into Night" and finds its relevance to the fact that often personnel hearings last a long time, sometimes ten to twelve hours (we have had them go as long as twenty-five hours). Since board members work, hearings often do not begin until the late afternoon and early evening, say, 5:30 or 6:00 p.m. We often say that a formal due process hearing is like a three-day trial to the court compressed into one night. As noted above under the procedural due process section, the administration always goes first in the presentation of the matter to the board of education. Such a presentation will take anywhere from four to six hours, meaning the teacher does not get to present his/her case until well into the evening, 11:00 p.m. or later, even midnight or later. These circumstances bring into question the teacher's right to substantive due process, that is, a fair opportunity to present his/her case.[158] Both the attorney for the administration and the attorney for the board of education has a duty to protect the

---

[157] Gessford, National School Boards Associations, The School Law Review, 1995, 6-9.

[158] The meaning of substantive due process was discussed by the Eighth Circuit Court of Appeals in *Weiler v. Purkett*, 137 F.3d 1047, 1051 (8th Cir. 1998) (en banc) (quotations and citations omitted). "An alternative way to bring a substantive due process claim is to assert that the government's actions either 'shock the conscience' or 'offend judicial notions of fairness…or…human dignity.'" *Riley v. St. Louis County*, 153 F.3d 627, 631 (8th Cir. 1998) (citations omitted), cert. denied, 143 L. Ed. 2d 109, 119 S. Ct. 1113 (1999). In such a case, the plaintiff's "burden is to establish that the government action complained of is 'truly irrational,' that is, 'something more than…arbitrary, capricious, or in violation of state law'" *Singleton v. Cecil*, 176 F.3d 419, 425 n.7 (8th Cir. 1999).

record and progression of the hearing so that there is no violation of due process, procedural or substantive. This duty has given rise to The Pumpkin Rule.[159]

The Pumpkin Rule

The gym was oppressively hot! There was no air-conditioning. There was a fan at the open door, but it did not move much air. The hearing had started at 6:00 p.m. It was now 11:30 p.m., and the administration had finally finished putting on its evidence with regard to the teacher's conduct that gave rise to a recommendation to the board of education that his contract be cancelled. He was a popular coach, but had gotten his third DUI, was presently in jail, and was on work release, having to be picked up from the jail every school day by a friend, taken to school, and returned to the jail each evening. The administration was charged with establishing that the coach's off campus conduct had a nexus (connection) to his employment as a high school teacher and therefore an exemplar to students. It seemed a cut-and-dried case, but there was the juice factor at play in the community if not with the board. The attorney for the teacher began calling character witnesses (a common defense tactic in these types of cases) and announced that he had over thirty people who wished to testify. After two witnesses, it was midnight. The attorney for the board paused the proceeds and asked both attorneys to approach the board table. He said, "I turn into a pumpkin at midnight, and we are done here tonight unless you [the teacher's attorney] and your client agree to waive any claim of a violation of the teacher's substantive due process, as we are all tired, sweaty, and hot, *and it is fundamentally unfair to the teacher to continue.* The board is willing to continue, but you both need to agree to continue on the record."

The attorney for the teacher turned around and saw that all of his witnesses were still sitting in the bleachers waiting to testify. He knew he would not likely get all of them in one place again, and that this may be his only chance to get them all to testify to save his client. He consulted with the teacher and came back and said he would agree to continue past midnight and that he and his client would so state to the court reporter transcribing the hearing.

The principal, seeing many students in the audience, announced that any student who wished to stay at the hearing until conclusion would get a pass to come to school at noon that day (after all, it was after midnight, so the next day already). The students

---

[159] The pumpkin rule: from "turn into a pumpkin."

Etymology: From the story of Cinderella, in which the transformed coach reverts to its original state (that of a pumpkin) at midnight.

"Turn into a pumpkin" (idiomatic, colloquial): To go to bed; to go to sleep (especially at or around midnight). Used to indicate a curfew, or the time by which one must depart.

cheered and stayed. The principal later stated that he felt the hearing was a civics lesson and a teachable moment!

The hearing continued until 3:00 a.m. when the teacher rested his case. The board deliberated in closed session and came out with a decision at 4:30 a.m. cancelling the teacher's contract.

The lesson of this story is that substantive due process is not a static concept but measured by an "I know it when I see" premise. In the words of a court, does the "government's actions either shock the conscience or offend judicial notions of fairness…or…human dignity."[160] In short, substantive due process requires that the opportunity to be heard be fundamentally fair and meaningful.

"It is an opportunity which must be granted at a meaningful time and in a meaningful manner" Armstrong v. Manzo, 380 U.S. 545, 552, 85 S. Ct. 1187, 1191 (1965).

Always keep this in mind as you and your attorney proceed with the hearing process and prepare accordingly.

- "Order in the court [or gym]!": Section 79-832(2), requires that

> Due and proper notice of the hearing shall be given in accordance with the Open Meetings Act. Upon an affirmative vote of a majority of the school board's members present and voting and upon specific request of the certificated employee or the certificated employee's representative, the hearing shall be conducted in a closed session, but the formal action of the school board shall be taken in open session.

So, you must be sure that the board of education complies with the notice, agenda, and minutes requirements of the Open Meetings Law. As for an open or closed hearing, the hearings are almost always open to the public. As noted, it becomes a community event. As discussed below, the board can deliberate in closed session in performing a quasi-judicial function, but everything else is done in open session. Per the Open Meetings Law, the hearing must be in a location that can accommodate the public.[161]

[160] Id. at *Singleton v. Cecil*, 176 F.3d 419, 425 n.7
[161] Neb. Rev. Stat. §84-1412(3)(d).

The Deciders: The Board of Education

In the formal due process setting for a permanent teacher in a termination hearing, and a probationary teacher or permanent teacher in a cancellation hearing, the board decision must be based solely on the evidence presented at the hearing. As such, the administration *must* follow the protocol not to discuss confidential employee matters with the board (no matter how much the board wants you to). Courts have held that formal due process requires that the employee (teacher) be provided a neutral fact finder.[162]

At times, a teacher, through his/her attorney, may challenge the neutrality of the board of education. In those cases, the attorney for the board of education may have the board members sign what is called a voir dire affidavit.[163] A voir dire in legal parlance means a preliminary examination to determine the competency or impartiality of a witness or juror. Here, the board is acting as the jury, ergo, subject to questioning to confirm the board's neutrality and ability to judge the matter based solely upon the evidence presented at the hearing. Generally, the "voir dire affidavit asks the board members to confirm that they will base their decision solely on the evidence received as part of the hearing and exclude anything he/ or she may have heard or read about this matter prior to the hearing."

Board of Education Legal Counsel

In most formal and informal due process hearings, the board of education hires legal counsel to preside over the hearing on behalf of the board, rule on evidentiary matters (receipt of documents and objections), assure the teacher's due process rights are observed and protected, advise the board on any legal questions it may have, and assure that a record is made

---

[162] *Morrissey v. Brewer*, 408 U.S. 471, 488-89, 92 S. Ct. 2593, 2604 (1972). Our task is limited to deciding the minimum requirements of due process. They include (a) written notice of the claimed violations of parole; (b) disclosure to the parolee of evidence against him; (c) opportunity to be heard in person and to present witnesses and documentary evidence; (d) the right to confront and cross-examine adverse witnesses (unless the hearing officer specifically finds good cause for not allowing confrontation); (e) *a "neutral and detached" hearing body.*

[163] I, [Board Member], being first duly sworn on oath, states upon personal knowledge as follows:
1. I am a duly qualified and now-acting member of the Board of Education of the above school district.
2. In determining any and all questions presented at this hearing, I can be and will be fair and impartial. I will not indulge in speculation, conjecture, or inferences not supported by the evidence presented. I can and will approach this hearing with an open mind.
3. If I am personally acquainted with any material or fact not supported by the evidence introduced before me, I can and will put it aside and will not consider any such personal knowledge as a part of my decision. I can and will base my decision solely upon the evidence and will consider this evidence fairly and impartially.
4. I have no bias or prejudice or personal animosity towards or against [Teacher Name].
5. I have no personal or financial stake in the outcome of this matter.

FURTHER, AFFIANT SAYETH NOT.

in case of appeal. The retention of legal counsel is authorized by statute.[164] The attorney shall not function as a fact finder, simply a legal advisor.

The process to retaining and defining the role of board of education legal counsel should include the following:

- Retention: The attorney must be asked to serve as attorney for the board of education for the personnel matter.
  - o The attorney must do a conflicts check to assure that he/she does not represent any of the parties involved in the proceeding.
  - o The board of education should pass a motion to retain the services of the attorney and have a written agreement with regard to fees to be charge for such services.[165]

- Authority: The scope of the attorney's service and authority to act on behalf of the board of education should be clear to all parties—the administration (and attorney) and the teacher (and the teacher's representative or attorney).
  - o The attorney is provided the names, addresses, phone numbers, and e-mail addresses of the board members.
  - o The attorney advises the board of education on the hearing process and their respective responsibilities relative to the hearing process.
  - o The attorney initiates contact with attorneys for the administration and teacher.
  - o The attorney requests permission of the counsel for the administration and the teacher to review the evidence prior to the hearing. If granted, the attorney reviews the material to identify legal issues to enable him or her to advise the board, and such action necessary to protect the district and the board.
  - o The attorney coordinates issues with administration lawyer and teacher lawyer to assure a fair and time efficient hearing.
  - o The attorney serves as a quasi "hearing officer," as opposed to a statutorily provided "hearing officer" as the representative of the board of education in the hearing, ruling on receipt of evidence, objections, and otherwise providing for an efficient and fair process.

---

[164] 79-513. Legal services; payment authorized. "The school board or board of education of any school district in this state may pay from its school funds for the legal services of an attorney employed by the board when it deems legal counsel necessary or advisable." *Robinson v. Morrill County School District #63*, 299 Neb. 740, 910 N.W. 2d 752 (Neb. 2018) affirms practice of the board of education hiring a lawyer to preside over a personnel hearing, rule on objections, and receive evidence to be considered by the board. Key: The attorney did not function as a fact finder, and this was not the type of hearing officer statutorily authorized for Class IV (Lincoln) and Class V (Omaha) school districts.

[165] ACTION ITEM: MOTION TO RETAIN ADVISOR TO BOARD OF EDUCATION
Motion by _____, seconded by _____ to retain attorney [Insert Attorney Name] of [Insert Firm Name] Law Firm, for purposes of assisting and advising the Board of Education with regard to the personnel hearing requested by [Insert Teacher Name] scheduled for _____, _____ ___, 202_ at __:__ _.m.; and further authorize [Insert Attorney Name], or other attorney from his law firm, to serve as hearing officer for purposes of addressing all pre-hearing matters and conducting the hearing on behalf of the Board of Education at the hours rates set forth in the attached Letter of Retention.

o The attorney *does not* participate in making the decision for the board but may be in attendance in a closed session if invited by the board of education to address legal issues. (See discussion with regard to statement of the board's attorney above.)

Board Action

As noted above, generally a majority of the members of the school board shall render the decision to amend, cancel, terminate, or not renew a certificated employee's contract, *based solely upon the evidence produced at the hearing, shall reduce its findings and determinations to writing, and shall deliver a written copy thereof to the certificated employee.*[166]

It is essential that the board knows and follows the statute requiring them to make their decision based solely on the evidence that is provided at the hearing. The findings and determinations must reflect the evidence produced at the hearing (see voir dire affidavit terms above).

The foregoing raises the question of who prepares the board findings and determinations? The answer is the board with assistance from the board's legal counsel. Often, counsel for the administration will submit proposed findings and determinations based upon the evidence adduced at the hearing. The teacher's attorney may also submit findings and determinations for the board's consideration, usually very short, simply renewing the teacher contract.

Note that in a termination or cancellation matter a majority of the board must render the decision regardless of the number of board members participating. If there is a six-member board, there must be four votes for termination or cancellation regardless if a member is absent or has recused themselves.

The Right of Appeal

Finally, the teacher has a right to appeal the board's decision through the process mandated by state statute; compliance with these statutory processes by the teacher or his/her representative is essential.[167] The appeal process in Nebraska (and most other states) is an error

---

[166] Example, Neb. Rev. Stat. §79-832.

[167] Example, Neb. Rev. Stat. §79-833. Error proceedings; jurisdiction of court.

"In error proceedings to reverse, vacate, or modify a final order by a school board made pursuant to sections 79-824 to 79-842, the school district, school board, or both may be named as defendants in error in the proceedings."

§ 25-1905. Proceedings in error; transcript; abstracts of record not required in Supreme Court.

The plaintiff in error shall file with his or her petition a transcript of the proceedings or a praecipe directing the tribunal, board, or officer to prepare the transcript of the proceedings. The transcript shall contain the final judgment or order sought to be reversed, vacated, or modified. No written or printed abstract or any copy of an abstract of the records shall be required in any case in the Supreme Court of this state (Neb. Rev. Stat. Ann § 25-1905 [LexisNexis, Lexis Advance through the 2019 regular session of the 106th Legislature First Session (end)], [emphasis added]).

"Neb. Rev. Stat. § 25-1905 (Reissue 1985) requires that a transcript of the proceedings containing the final judgment sought to be reversed must be filed with the petition in error. A transcript of the proceedings in the lower tribunal must be filed

proceeding. What does that mean? From a practical point of view, it means that the only time you get to put evidence in the record is at the hearing, and the only evidence that the court can review is that record. As such, it is critical that you be prepared and make your case at the hearing as that is your only chance. Also, this is why you always have a court reporter to transcribe every word!

So now you know how a formal due process hearing works.

Your assignment: No more assignments!

---

with the petition in error in order to confer jurisdiction upon the reviewing court" (*Herzog v. Bd. of Educ. of Hitchcock Cty. Sch. Dist. No. 011 in Neb.*, No. A-90-637, 1992 Neb. App. LEXIS 187, at *1 [Ct. App. Sep. 1, 1992]).

CONCLUSION

"The expert [by knowledge, skill, experience, training, or education]!"

It is my hope that you have benefited from our sequential travels that provide the foundation for the effective evaluation of your assets so important to student learning. You now know the steps needed to

1. prepare yourself to be a principal;
2. lay the groundwork for your duties as the leader of your teaching staff;
3. inform your staff of their responsibilities and the means of measuring their performance to meet the standard of performance expected of each;
4. engage, teach, and lead your staff through the formative evaluation process, including enhancement of teaching skills, techniques, lesson planning, lesson presentation, classroom environment;
5. provide counseling, observation, and assistance;
6. document your work with your staff, individually and collectively;
7. effectively communicate with your staff through well-written narratives, both informally and formally;
8. complete and write accurate, candid, truthful, informative, and helpful summative evaluations based upon the science of teaching reflected in the educational model set forth in your evaluation instrument;
9. prepare meaningful and effective improvement plans;
10. commit the time to effectively provide follow-up support to your teachers, both those deficient and successful;
11. be confident in yourself and have pride in your efforts to make teachers better educators so our children learn and learn how to learn; and
12. if all else fails, be prepared to present your work to your superintendent and/or board of education in a due process hearing.

You may not yet have all the above capabilities, but you have taken an important step toward getting there.

The driving force for the writing of this book was to give principals the tools to effectively write improvement plans and evaluations. To know what to do, in what order, to a specified and hopefully positive end. To help you work toward improving every day, just as you ask of your teachers. If we have collectively accomplished these goals, success will follow.

You are and should not be in this alone. Effective teacher evaluation begins with the policy makers, the board of education. Those policies are then to be implemented by the superintendent of schools through his/her administrative team, which, of course, includes the principal(s). And the teachers are responsible to follow those policies in their professional performance to allow students to learn efficiently and effectively. So, each of the players have tasks, duties, and responsibilities. See Appendix F, "Who's on First—Tasks and Responsibilities."

Let me leave you with this. A sign sat on the desk of President Harry S. Truman displaying this motto borrowed from Mark Twain: "Always do right. This will gratify some people and astonish the rest."[168]

Rex

---

[168] AJ Baime, *The Accidental President: Harry S. Truman and the Four Months that Changed the World* (2017), 197–198.

ACKNOWLEDGMENTS

As with any effort of this type, there are so many people to thank for their assistance in the conception and eventual writing of this book. As most authors say in this portion of a book, I will probably miss some folks who helped or inspired this effort. That said, I must thank:

My partners here at the Perry Law Firm—Jim Gessford, of course, and Greg Perry, Josh Schauer, Derek Aldridge, Justin Knight, and Haleigh Carlson. All great lawyers and persons who truly care about the schools in all of Nebraska and the children those schools educate. Our firm practices preventative law, which seeks to assist schools in avoiding legal entanglements and helps provide a safe nurturing school environment for every child.

Mike Dulaney and Megan Hildebrand of the Nebraska Council of School Administrators for their initial support for the teaching of a class to administrators on teacher evaluations. Their support morphed into this book.

Maddie Fennel, executive director of the Nebraska State Education Association, for challenging me on the skill of school administrators and then willingly assisting in providing the teachers' perspective and desires for the evaluation process. Her ideas are directly quoted herein.

The educational experts that have graciously provided their expertise to advise me and provide substance to this book: Dr. Kim Saum-Mills of Millard Public Schools, Dr. Nick Pace, my brother, Mark Schultze, and Dr. Dennis Headrick, Vice President of Instruction for Southeast Community College here in Lincoln. Thank you, all.

Kelley Baker, a fellow school lawyer and friend who has mentored me throughout this project, and graciously edited the final product. Many thanks, Kelley.

Finally, my wife, Sharla, for her patience when I disappeared into the basement for hours, and our puppy, Truman (yes, named after my favorite president), for getting me to stop and play.

ABOUT REX R. SCHULTZE, J.D.

Rex Schultze is an attorney from Lincoln, Nebraska. Rex graduated from Kearney State College with a history degree in 1974 and went on to teach high school history at Omaha Bryan High School from 1974 to 1978. He decided to go to law school and graduated from the University of Nebraska—School of Law in 1981. Rex was hired by the Perry Law Firm in 1981. Over the next forty years, Rex worked with his fellow attorneys at the Perry firm in the school law area, helping school districts with the myriad of issues that come up every day. One area of focus has been assisting schools with personnel matters, including addressing the assistance to, evaluation of, and in some cases, the dismissal of teachers based upon competency. Over the years he has made numerous presentations and workshops on teacher evaluation and has written extensively on the subject. He serves as general counsel to the Nebraska School Activities Association and Southeast Community College and counsels and advises numerous public school districts throughout Nebraska.

If you want to know more about Rex's journey, go to https://issuu.com/ncsa-home/docs/ncsa_today_winter_2019_-_web_use, or the Perry Law Firm at https://perrylawfirm.com.

You can contact Rex by e-mail at rschultze@perrylawfirm.com, or by calling him at (402) 476-9200.

ABOUT JAMES B. GESSFORD

When discussing school law and school attorneys in terms of impact on our profession, Jim Gessford stands out as an authority who has positively contributed to the effectiveness of many Nebraska administrators.
—Dr. Stephen Joel, Superintendent of Schools, Lincoln Public Schools.

Jim's current legal practice is focused in school, education, and public institutions law.

Jim was born in 1951 in Holdrege, Nebraska. He graduated from Hastings Public Schools in 1969 and Hastings College in 1973. Upon graduating from college, Jim married Judi Prostok and moved to Lincoln where they have resided ever since. Jim and Judi have two children, Ben Gessford and Nikki (Perry), and three grandchildren.

Jim graduated from the University of Nebraska Law School in 1976. Between 1973 and 1976, while attending law school, Jim also spent a short time with the Kansas City Chiefs in the National Football League, and was a member of the Chicago Fire and the Chicago Winds in the World Football League.

Jim's forty-plus years of education and constitutional law experience is wide and varied in both litigation and practice. From school district reorganizations, a wide range of school finance and constitutional law litigation, countless school construction projects, interlocal cooperative and public-private partnership agreements as well as teacher and administrator disciplinary hearings, to placing schools into receivership and even creating a paper school-house. Gessford says there is never a dull moment.

"At least once or twice a week in conference with school personnel, I find myself saying 'Are you kidding me' or 'You just can't make this stuff up,'" he said. "At the current time, the COVID-19 Pandemic school closings have everyone in a tizzy as to potential liabilities, student and staff safety and protocols for reopening. And the new surges in distance learning, STEM, STEAM, the maker movement, blended learning, project-based learning, and software-driven adaptive learning environments are constantly presenting new challenges for evaluators and the teaching science."

Jim is a member and past president of the Nebraska School Board Council of School Attorneys, a past member of the board of directors of the National School Board Council of School Attorneys (COSA). He is an adjunct instructor, Doane College of Educational Administration Program, and frequent speaker and author in the school, education, and public institutions law areas at both the state and national levels.

ABOUT DR. KEVIN RILEY

The Walter Cronkite of Gretna. The most trusted man in town.
—Dr. Rich Beran, Superintendent of Schools,
Gretna Public Schools, Gretna, Nebraska

After more than three decades serving the families of Gretna, Gretna Public Schools Superintendent Kevin Riley will retire at the end of the school year.[169]

Riley came to Gretna in August of 1982 where he served as assistant principal at the junior-senior high school for three years.

He served as Gretna High School principal for the following 14 years before being named superintendent of Gretna Public Schools, a role he has served in for the past 20 years.

Riley knew he would go into education from the start.

"I never really thought about anything else," he said.

After attending Bellevue University to play basketball for four years, he finished up his education at the University of Nebraska at Omaha, moving on to student teach in Millard

---

[169] Dr. Kevin Riley's career as an educator:
1978–1982: Teacher/coach, Millard Public Schools
1982–1985: Assistant principal, Gretna Junior-Senior High School
1985–1999: Principal, Gretna High School
1999–2019: Superintendent, Gretna Public Schools
2019–current: Assistant professor, Department of Educational Leadership—University of Nebraska at Omaha

Public Schools and Omaha Public Schools. Before coming to Gretna, he taught and coached in Millard for four and a half years.

"I never thought I'd be a principal or superintendent, those things just happened," he said. "I've liked every job I've ever had in education."

He witnessed explosive growth in the district, watching the student body grow from about 900 students to more than 5,000.

"I think we're proud that people want their children to go to school here and that they move here for that reason," Riley said.

"I'm most proud that we're as much, or ever more so, dedicated to individual children as we were when there were 900 of them. Whether they're gifted or they struggle in school, whether they're academically inclined or more interested in the industrial arts, whether an athlete or performer, we've been able to maintain or even improve our commitment to individual children."

Another source of pride that Riley retires with is the success he has seen Gretna's graduates attain.

"Our graduates are all over the world doing amazing things," he said. "So much of it can be attributed to their parents and the homes they were raised in, but I know we made a contribution to that. I hold a special place in my heart for all the things they've accomplished.

"When they move back here because this is where they want their own kids to go to school, that means a lot to me."

Riley said he began to consider retiring about two and a half years ago. He remembers the quiet Christmas morning when the idea entered his mind as he sipped coffee in a quiet house where no one else was awake yet.

"It was the first time I seriously thought about it," Riley said. "I didn't know why. But people always said, 'You'll know when it's time.' When your heart and head are in the same spot, you know it's time.

"I was sure I would retire last summer. It's the right time for the district and for me to step away."

Though he is sure in his decision, Riley has no doubt retirement will take some getting used to.

"I've come to this plot of ground pretty much every day for 37 years," he said. "It's going to be very difficult for me because of the passion I feel for the children of this district, the staff, this Board of Education and the community."

Riley said he plans to teach part-time to pass on his administrative knowledge to aspiring school administrators.

"I still want to be involved," he said. "I still have some contributions to make to the profession."[170]

---

[170] Rachel George, editor, *Gretna Breeze*, May 23, 2019.

APPENDIX A

State Teacher Tenure Statutes

State	Statute	Additional Aid
Alabama	Students First Act of 2011	
Alaska	Alaska Stat. 14.20.095–14.20.215	Teacher Tenure in Alaska
Arizona	A.R.S. 15-501–516 and 15-531-553	Employee Rights—A Summary of Arizona Law for Teachers
Arkansas	A.C.A. 6-17-1501-1510	
California	CAL. EDUC. CODE §§ 44929.20 to 44988	
Colorado	COLO. REV. STAT. §§ 22-63-101 to 22-63-403	
Connecticut	CONN. GEN. STAT. § 10-144o–10-156ee	
Delaware	DEL. CODE ANN. tit.14, §§ Chapter 7, Chapter 13, Chapter 14, Chapter 39	
Florida	FLA. STAT. ch.120.68; 1012.22 to 1012.992	Education Commission of the States
Georgia	GA. CODE ANN. §§ 20-2-211; 20-2 211.1; and Article 17	
Hawaii	HAW. REV. STAT. §§ 89-6 to 89-11; 302A-501 to 302A-855	
Idaho	IDAHO CODE §§ 33-1201 to 1280	
Illinois	105 ILL. COMP. STAT. 5/10-24-1 to 5/24-26	
Indiana	IND. CODE §§ 20-28-1-1 to 20-28-12-5	
Iowa	IOWA CODE §§ Chapter 284 and Chapter 294, 294A	
Kansas	KAN. STAT. ANN. §§ 72-Article 21, Article 22, and Article 23	
Kentucky	KY. REV. STAT. Ann. §§ 161.720 to 161.810	
Louisiana	LA. REV. STAT. ANN. §§ 17:441 to 17:445 and 17:471	

Maine	ME. REV. STAT. ANN. tit. 20A §§ Chs. 501-511	
Maryland	MD. CODE ANN., EDUC. §§ 6-101 through 6-906	
Massachusetts	MASS. GEN. LAWS ch. 71 §§ 41 to 42	
Michigan	MICH. COMP. LAWS §§ 38.71 to 38.191	
Minnesota	MINN. STAT. § 122A.001–122A.175	
Mississippi	MISS. CODE ANN. §§ 37-9-1–37-9-81	
Missouri	MO. REV. STAT. §§ 168.011 to 770	
Montana	MONT. CODE ANN. §§ 20-4-201 to 20-4-214	
Nebraska	NEB. REV. STAT. §§ 79-824 to 79-848	
Nevada	NEV. REV. STAT. Title 34 Ch 391	Education Commission of the States
New Hampshire	N.H. REV. STAT. ANN. §§ 189.39 to 42 and 191:1 to 5	
New Jersey	N.J. STAT. ANN. §§ 18A:6-5 to 18A:6-136;	
New Mexico	N.M. STAT. ANN. §§ 22-10A-21 to 22-10A-40.1	
New York	N.Y. EDUC. LAW §§ 3001 to 3038	
North Carolina	N.C. GEN. STAT. § 115C-295 to 314	
North Dakota	N.D. CENT. CODE §§ 15.1-13-01 to 18.1-02	
Ohio	OHIO REV. CODE ANN. §§ 3319.07 to 3319.317	
Oklahoma	OKLA. STAT. tit 70, §§ 6-101–303	Education Commission of the States
Oregon	OR. REV. STAT. §§ 342.805 to 342.934 and 342.121–342.450 and 342.513–342.605	
Pennsylvania	PA. STAT. ANN. tit. 24, §§ 11-1121 to 11-1134	
Rhode Island	R.I. GEN. LAWS §§ 16-13-1 to 16-13-8	
South Carolina	S.C. CODE ANN. §§ 59-25-10 to 59-25-860; 59-26-40	
South Dakota	S.D. CODIFIED LAWS §§ 13-43-1 to 13-43-65	

Tennessee	TENN. CODE ANN. §§ 49-5-501 to 515	
Texas	TEX. EDUC. CODE Title 2, Subtitle D Chapter 21	
Utah	UTAH CODE ANN. 53G-11-101 to 518 and 53E-6-101 to 1011	Education Commission of the States
Vermont	VT. STAT. ANN. tit. 16, part 3	
Virginia	VA. CODE ANN. §§ 22.1-289.1 to 22.1-318.2	
Washington	WASH. REV. CODE §§ 28A.400, 28A.405, and 28A.410	
West Virginia	W. VA. CODE §§ 18A Arts 1-7	
Wisconsin	WIS. STAT. § 118.18 to 118.235	
Wyoming	WYO. STAT. ANN. §§ 21-7-101 to 21-7-701	

APPENDIX B

Model Lesson Plan Template[171]

Teacher:	School:
Class:	Date:
Unit:	Lesson Title:

Component 1: Lesson Planning, Alignment with State Standards and RC Curriculum, and Instructional Materials Prepared.
Component 1A: Lesson planning, alignment with state standards—Planning of daily instructional goals, strategies, and methods of assessment, and instructional content that is aligned with the local or state standards.
Component 1B: Unit or curriculum identification and lesson place in unit/curriculum structure—Provision of clear rationale for the design and sequence of units and placement of lesson within same.
Component 1C: List of prior concepts that support the concept that is the subject of the lesson—Plans establish that the instructional goal/objective are in sequence with the unit/curriculum.
Component 1D: Instructional materials to be prepared/provided—The lesson plan provides opportunities to accommodate individual student needs. The teacher is prepared for class with all necessary materials and equipment readily accessible.
Component 2: Analysis of Student Assessment Results and Meaningful Assignments (Homework)
Component 2A: Potential student challenges with material—Strategies to vary instruction for variety of learners. Lesson based upon analysis student assessment results and adjustment instruction or a plan intervention.

---

[171] While I have utilized the ideas of Danielson and the ITIP models, the template is an original work. This lesson plan template mirrors the summative evaluation form, Appendix C, with elements of the Madeline Hunter ITIP instructional framework and the Charlotte Danielson model template.

Component 2B: Assessment methods and tools—The various assessments and assignments to reflect desired goals/objectives.	

Instructional Framework (ITIP Model)	
Anticipatory set (action to pique interest, review information, focus student attention, and initiate the learning process).	
Objective to presented (concept to be learned, be able to do at the end of the lesson, why it is important, how it will help them	
Input and instructional strategies (information provided to students needed to achieve the objective).	
Modeling (demonstration on how to achieve the objective).	
Check for understanding (implementation of procedure to achieve the objective, include here higher level of thinking activities and questions [Bloom's Taxonomy]).	
Guided practice (support system to assure success with varied assistance for specific students or groups of students).	
Independent study (students capable to practice the concept learned, without support to gain skill, fluency, and flexibility in use of the achieved objective).	
Assessment (formative and summative—including sample questions, entire tests, portfolio guidelines, or rubrics if available submitted along with the lesson plan as attachments).	

APPENDIX C

Anywhere Public Schools Summative Evaluation Form[172]

[See Appendix B.][173]

Summative Report for [Insert Teacher Name]—[Semester], [Year]

The following Anywhere Performance Model Summative Report is based upon classroom observations, formal and informal evaluations, and review of instructional artifacts, including lesson plans, student assessments instruments, and other areas of the duties assigned to certificated teacher of the Anywhere Public schools, as set forth in Board of Education policy, administrative regulations, contract and job descriptions. The Summative report is cumulative and incorporates performance by the certificated teacher on a continuous basis during the employee's tenure with the School District.

Performance Rating Key:

Level of Performance	Numerical Rating
Unsatisfactory	1
Basic	2
Proficient (= Standard of Performance)	*3*
Distinguished	4

---

[172] The summative evaluation form is a slightly modified version of the form used by the Raymond Central Public Schools, Raymond, Nebraska. The original evaluation policy of the Raymond Central Public Schools references to the Danielson model and ITIP framework as the basis for the summative form but is original to that school district.

[173] [District standard of performance, expected level of performance by certificated staff: proficient level, rubric 3.]

PLANNING:

Component 1: Lesson Planning, Alignment with State Standards & Curriculum, and Instructional Materials Prepared.

Component—Proficient Level:

There is evidence of consistent planning of daily instructional goals, strategies, and methods of assessment. There is evidence of consistent planning of daily instructional goals, strategies, and methods of assessment. The teacher can provide a clear rationale for the design and sequence of units. Evidence indicated that instructional content is consistently aligned with the local or state standards. Plans indicate that the instructional goal of the curriculum are met. There is evidence of that the lesson plan provides opportunities to accommodate individual student needs. The teacher is prepared for class with all necessary materials and equipment readily accessible.

Level of Performance	Numerical Rating

Standard of Performance and Comment:
- There is evidence of consistent planning of daily instructional goals, strategies, and methods of assessment.
  - o   Comment:
- The teacher can provide a clear rationale for the design and sequence of units.
  - o   Comment:
- ITIP design consistently followed.
  - o   Comment:
- Evidence indicated that instructional content is consistently aligned with the local or state standards.
  - o   Comment:
- Plans indicate that the instructional goal of the curriculum are met.
  - o   Comment:
- There is evidence of that the lesson plan provides opportunities to accommodate individual student needs.
  - o   Comment:
- The teacher is prepared for class with all necessary materials and equipment readily accessible.
  - o   Comment:

Overall Comment:
Component 2: Analysis of Student Assessment Results and Meaningful Assignments (Homework)

Level of Performance	Numerical Rating

Standard of Performance and Comment:
- The teacher demonstrates proficiency in analyzing student assessment results in order to adjust instruction or plan intervention strategies.
  - Comment:
- There is evidence of consistent and meaningful engagement of student in activities and/or assignments.
  - Comment:
- The teacher varies assessments and assignments to reflect desired goals/objectives.
  - Comment:

Overall Comment:

Component 3: Quality of Feedback to Students

Level of Performance	Numerical Rating

Standard of Performance and Comment:
- Written and verbal feedback is timely, consistent, and positive while addressing individual student strengths and weaknesses.
  - Comment:
- The teacher circulates during instructional activities to support engagement, provide feedback, and monitor student work.
  - Comment:
- Feedback is targeted and tailored to how students can improve.
  - Comment:

Overall Comment:

Component 4: Context of the Lesson

Level of Performance	Numerical Rating

Standard of Performance and Comment:
- Context of the lesson is set with reference to prior knowledge/activities.
  - Comment:
- Learning objectives are written from content standards, are displayed, and verbally referenced.
  - Comment:
- Expectations for student learning are clearly stated. Instruction is purposeful.
  - Comment:

Overall Comment:
Component 5: Content Knowledge/Presentation

Level of Performance	Numerical Rating

Standard of Performance and Comment:
- The teacher displays strong content knowledge and can clearly explain the relevance of materials to students.
  - o Comment:
- Explanations are clearly stated.
  - o Comment:
- Student questions are followed-up by attempts to present material more effectively.
  - o Comment:

Overall Comment:
Component 6: Appropriateness of the Lesson/Pacing

Level of Performance	Numerical Rating

Standard of Performance and Comment:
- The pacing consistently offers opportunities for active student engagement with appropriate use of instructional time with intentional use of transition.
  - o Comment:
- Activities always reflect developmentally appropriate practices.
  - o Comment:

Overall Comment:
Component 7: Use of Technology

Level of Performance	Numerical Rating

Standard of Performance and Comment:
- The evidence indicated consistent and effective use of available technology and other resources when appropriate to meet the learning goals.
  - o Comment:

- The teacher utilizes new technology to involve students in their learning.
  - o Comment:

Overall Comment:
Component 8: Effectiveness of Instructional Strategies and Questioning Techniques for Student Achievement

Level of Performance	Numerical Rating

Standard of Performance and Comment:
- The evidence indicates knowledge and consistent use of a variety of instructional strategies with use of small groups, individualized instruction, and accommodations for special needs students.
  - o Comment:
- The teacher adapts teaching strategies to appropriately challenge students at their individual ability levels (differentiation).
  - o Comment:
- Teacher questioning techniques consistently provide the opportunity to assess most students' understanding, encourage higher level thinking skills, and promote active engagement.
  - o Comment:
- Students are guided through questions to construct their personal understanding.
  - o Comment:

Overall Comment:
Component 9: Expectations/Procedures for Student Success

Level of Performance	Numerical Rating

Standard of Performance and Comment:
- The teacher has high expectations for student achievement and consistently uses motivational techniques or strategies for all students.
  - o Comment:
- The teacher encourages students to learn from mistakes.
  - o Comment:
- The teacher initiates efforts to celebrate and recognize student success within the classroom.
  - o Comment:
- Explicit procedures for classroom and school safety are clearly communicated and understood.
  - o Comment:
- As the teacher manages the classroom, learning is the focus not the behavior.
  - o Comment:

Overall Comment:

Component 10: Student Interest, Engagement, and Classroom Climate

Level of Performance	Numerical Rating

Standard of Performance and Comment:
- Teacher and student interactions are positive and demonstrate mutual respect.
  - o Comment:
- The teacher is receptive to the interests and opinions of students.
  - o Comment:
- Student interest and engagement are high.
  - o Comment:
- There is consistent engagement of students in meaningful learning experiences relevant to student interests.
  - o Comment:
- The classroom environment is supportive of the learning of all students.
  - o Comment:
- The teacher demonstrates sensitivity to all students.
  - o Comment:
- Students are encouraged and comfortable to openly share ideas and examine mistakes.
  - o Comment:

Overall Comment:

Component 11: Alignment of Professional Development

Level of Performance	Numerical Rating

Standard of Performance and Comment:
- The teacher seeks out opportunities for professional development aligned with School Improvement goals and teaching assignment.
  - o Comment:
- The teacher can reflect on recently acquired areas of new knowledge or skills.
  - o Comment:

Overall Comment:
Component 12: Communication with Parents

Level of Performance	Numerical Rating

Standard of Performance and Comment:
- Interaction with families is consistently of high professional quality.
  - Comment:
- Areas of concern are addressed in a timely and positive manner.
  - Comment:
- There is consistent follow-up of parent contract.
  - Comment:
- The teacher regularly invites parental involvement in student learning.
  - Comment:

Overall Comment:
Component 13: Teacher's Records

Level of Performance	Numerical Rating
Unsatisfactory	

Standard of Performance and Comment:
- Teacher's records are consistently accurate and timely.
  - Overall Comment:

Component 14: Teacher Reflection
Standard of Performance and Comment:

Level of Performance	Numerical Rating

Standard of Performance and Comment:
- Teacher makes an accurate assessment of a lesson's effectiveness and the extent to which it achieved its goals and can cite general references to support the judgment.
  - Comment:
- The teacher makes a few specific suggestions about what may be done differently to meet the needs of students.
  - Comment:

Overall Comment:

Teacher Signature of Evaluator	Date

I hereby acknowledge that I have been advised and informed of the contents of this appraisal of my teaching performance and of my right to attach any personal comments that I feel are necessary.

Teacher Signature	Date

Teacher Comments Attached?	Yes ___	No ___

Teacher-Classroom Observation Form[174]

General Information

Teacher Name:	Evaluator Name:	Date:
School:	Grade and Subject:	Time of Observation: _____ to _____
Entire Instructional Period: _____ [Check to affirm].	Pre-Observation Conference: [ ] Yes – [ ] No*	Lesson Plan Provided Prior to Observation: [ ] Yes – [ ] No*

*Check appropriate box or provide other explanation in narrative portion of the form.

Lesson Planning Components 1 and 2: Review Prior to Lesson Observed

Plan Contains Required Components

Component 1: Lesson planning, alignment with state standards and RC curriculum, and instructional materials prepared.	Component 1A: Lesson planning, alignment with state standards.	Component 1B: Unit or curriculum identification and lesson place in unit/ curriculum structure.	Component 1C: List of prior concepts that support the concept that is the subject of the lesson.	Component 1D: Instructional materials to be prepared/ provided.	Component 2: Analysis of student assessment results and meaningful assignments (homework).	Component 2A: Potential student challenges with material.	Component 2B: Assessment methods and tools.
	[ ] Yes [ ] No	[ ] Yes [ ] No	[ ] Yes [ ] No	[ ] Yes [ ] No		[ ] Yes [ ] No	[ ] Yes [ ] No

[174] The teacher classroom observation form is based upon the summative evaluation form used by the Raymond Central Public Schools, Raymond, Nebraska. The original evaluation policy of the Raymond Central Public Schools references the Danielson model and ITIP framework as the basis for the summative form but is original to that school district. The teacher classroom observation form was created by me.

Plan Contains Lesson Framework

Anticipatory Set	Objective	Input and Strategies	Modeling	Check for Understanding	Guided Practice	Independent Study	Assessment
[ ] Yes [ ] No	[ ] Yes [ ] No*	[ ] Yes [ ] No	[ ] Yes [ ] No	[ ] Yes [ ] No	[ ] Yes [ ] No	[ ] Yes [ ] No	[ ] Yes [ ] No

Plan Contains the Required Rigor

	Yes	No	
There is evidence of consistent planning of daily instructional goals, strategies, and methods of assessment.	Yes [ ]	No [ ]	Comment
The teacher can provide a clear rationale for the design and sequence of units.	Yes [ ]	No [ ]	Comment
ITIP design was consistently followed.	Yes [ ]	No [ ]	Comment
Evidence indicated that instructional content is consistently aligned with the local or state standards.	Yes [ ]	No [ ]	Comment
Plans indicate that the instructional goal of the curriculum are met.	Yes [ ]	No [ ]	Comment
There is evidence of that the lesson plan provides opportunities to accommodate individual student needs.	Yes [ ]	No [ ]	Comment
The teacher is prepared for class with all necessary materials and equipment readily accessible.	Yes [ ]	No [ ]	Comment
The teacher demonstrates proficiency in analyzing student assessment results in order to adjust instruction or plan intervention strategies.	Yes [ ]	No [ ]	Comment
There is evidence of consistent and meaningful engagement of student in activities and/or assignments.	Yes [ ]	No [ ]	Comment
The teacher varies assessments and assignments to reflect desired goals/objectives.	Yes [ ]	No [ ]	Comment

Evaluator Listening and Scripting

See attached evaluator notes and scripting of teacher and student response to instruction during the observation.

Post-Observation Review of Instructional Components of Professional Model

The following review of components 3 to 10 reflect the evaluator's observation of the teacher's performance in each of the elements of such components.

Instruction: Component 3

Quality of Feedback to Students

Written and verbal feedback is timely, consistent, and positive while addressing individual student strengths and weaknesses.	Yes [ ]	No [ ]	Comment
The teacher circulates during instructional activities to support engagement, provide feedback, and monitor student work.	Yes [ ]	No [ ]	Comment
Feedback is targeted and tailored to how students can improve.	Yes [ ]	No [ ]	Comment

Instruction: Component 4

Context of the Lesson

Context of the lesson is set with reference to prior knowledge/activities.	Yes [ ]	No [ ]	Comment
Learning objectives are written from content standards, are displayed, and verbally referenced.	Yes [ ]	No [ ]	Comment
Expectations for student learning are clearly stated. Instruction is purposeful.	Yes [ ]	No [ ]	Comment

Instruction: Component 5

Content Knowledge / Presentation

	Yes [ ]	No [ ]	Comment
The teacher displays strong content knowledge and can clearly explain the relevance of materials to students.	Yes [ ]	No [ ]	Comment
Explanations are clearly stated.	Yes [ ]	No [ ]	Comment
Student questions are followed-up by attempts to present material more effectively.	Yes [ ]	No [ ]	Comment

Instruction: Component 6

Appropriateness of the Lesson/Pacing

	Yes [ ]	No [ ]	Comment
The pacing consistently offers opportunities for active student engagement with appropriate use of instructional time with intentional use of transition.	Yes [ ]	No [ ]	Comment
Activities always reflect developmentally appropriate practices.	Yes [ ]	No [ ]	Comment

Instruction: Component 7

Use of Technology

	Yes [ ]	No [ ]	Comment
The observation showed consistent and effective use of available technology and other resources when appropriate to meet the learning goals.	Yes [ ]	No [ ]	Comment
The teacher utilizes new technology to involve student in their learning.	Yes [ ]	No [ ]	Comment

Instruction: Component 8

Effectiveness of Instructional Strategies and Questioning Techniques for Student Achievement

The evidence indicates knowledge and consistent use of a variety of instructional strategies with use of small groups, individualized instruction, and accommodations for special needs students.	Yes []	No []	Comment
The teacher adapts teaching strategies to appropriately challenge students at their individual ability levels (differentiation).	Yes []	No []	Comment
Teacher questioning techniques consistently provide the opportunity to assess most students' understanding, encourage higher level thinking skills, and promote active engagement.	Yes []	No []	Comment

Instruction: Component 9

Expectations/Procedures for Student Success

The teacher has high expectation for student achievement and consistently uses motivational techniques or strategies for all students.	Yes []	No []	Comment
The teacher encourages students to learn from mistakes.	Yes []	No []	Comment
The teacher initiates efforts to celebrate and recognize student success within the classroom.	Yes []	No []	Comment
Explicit procedures for classroom and school safety are clearly communicated and understood.	Yes []	No []	Comment
As the teacher manages the classroom, learning is the focus not the behavior.	Yes []	No []	Comment

Instruction: Component 10

Student Interest, Engagement, and Classroom Climate

Teacher and student interactions are positive and demonstrate mutual respect.	Yes []	No []	Comment
The teacher is receptive to the interests and opinions of students.	Yes []	No []	Comment
Student interest and engagement are high.	Yes []	No []	Comment

There is consistent engagement of students in meaningful learning experiences relevant to student interests.	Yes [ ]	No [ ]	Comment
The classroom environment is supportive of the learning of all students.	Yes [ ]	No [ ]	Comment
The teacher demonstrates sensitivity to all students.	Yes [ ]	No [ ]	Comment
Students are encouraged and comfortable to openly share ideas and examine mistakes.	Yes [ ]	No [ ]	Comment

Summary and Notation of Exemplary Performance and/or Suggestions for Improvement

Signature of Evaluator

Name of Evaluator:	Administrative Position:
Signature of Evaluator:	Date of Signature:

Acknowledgment of Receipt by Teacher

Name of Teacher:	School Department
Signature of Teacher:	Date of Signature:

**Teacher has the right to submit a written response to this observation within ____ days of receipt thereof.

Expert Testimony

See "Expert Witness Defined by Marisa Tomei from *My Cousin Vinny* Is Credible" by Samuel Partida Jr., February 1, 2014 (https://illinoiscaselaw.com/expert-witness-defined-by-marisa-tomei-from-my-cousin-vinny/).

Who's on First—Tasks and Responsibilities

Actor	Task or Duty
Board of Education	
	Adopt evaluation instrument and procedure and underlying educational model *and file with the Department of Education.*
	Adopt job descriptions for all employees, particularly for superintendent, principal, teachers, guidance counselors, and other certificated staff.
	Adopt NDE Rule 27 Code of Ethics for certificated staff.
	Approve teacher handbook.
	Approve student handbook.
	Hire trained and effective school administrators.
	Support training of school administrators and teachers.
Superintendent	
	Prepare teacher handbook in consultation with legal counsel for approval of the board of education.
	Prepare student handbook in consultation with legal counsel for approval of the board of education.
	Review and understand evaluation instrument and procedure and underlying educational model.
	Develop, adopt, and train principals (and staff) a lesson plan template.
	Train principals and other building or program administrators on evaluation instrument and procedure.
	Lead entire administrative team and teachers in a commitment to student learning through in-services and professional development programs.

Actor	Task or Duty
	Support building principals in their efforts to teach and assist instructional staff.
	Evaluate building principals and administrators on the effectiveness of their leadership and knowledge and application of the evaluation instrument and procedure.
	Make improvement of staff teaching skills a priority of the school district as a whole—administrators, teachers, support staff, and students and parents.
Principal	
Summer before School Year	
	Review the evaluation instrument and process personally, a refresh knowledge of the educational model upon which it is based.
Preschool Year: August	
	Before each school year begins, review with and teach your staff your school's • teacher job description, • teacher contract, • teacher handbook, • evaluation instrument and process, • student handbooks, and • lesson plan template.
	Before each school year begins, review with and teach your staff Rule 10, the regulatory requirements which provides the areas teachers are to be evaluated on and in which they are to be competent: • Instruction (planning and delivery, assessment, and reteaching) • Classroom management • Professional conduct • Personal conduct
	Before each school year begins, review with and teach your staff the ethical standards for teachers.

Actor	Task or Duty
	In-service your staff: • Training your teachers on their duties and responsibilities. • Training your teachers on the instructional framework and educational model adopted by your board of education. • Giving your teachers notice of the standard of performance expected of them in your school district through in-services and review of the evaluation instrument and process.
During School Year:	
	Plan and use staff development to • Draw on in-house expertise, providing mentoring and demonstration opportunities with emphasis on differing degrees of teacher experience; • Provide enough time for follow-up support with marginal or less-experienced teachers to help them master new ideas, content, and strategies and integrate them into the classroom; • Focus initially on formative evaluation to support teacher growth and development; • Allow good and marginal teachers to interact and provide opportunities to explore, question, and debate new ideas about classroom practice; • Offer intellectual, social, and emotional engagement with ideas, materials, and colleagues.
	Identify each teacher's evaluator, and initiate system of providing ongoing instructional support to all staff, e.g., staff development calendar.
	Conduct brief observations in *all* classrooms to communicate, "I am around, I care, and I am here to help."
	Set up a computer filing system to accumulate various forms of documentation that reflect the performance of each teacher.

Actor	Task or Duty
First Semester	
	Do more than one observation of each teacher, and multiple observations of probationary staff, formal and informal and MBWA. *Do not forget.*
	Do summative evaluation of all probationary teachers and any teacher on a plan of assistance for the first semester *not later than end of November.*
Second Semester before Your Statutory Deadline for Giving Notice of Nonrenewal or Termination	
	Continue your staff development and planning. Remind staff of the basic" you provided them in August again.
	Again, do more than one observation of each teacher, and multiple observations of probationary staff, formal and informal and MBWA. *And again, do not forget.*
	Do summative evaluation of all probationary teacher and any teacher on a plan of assistance for the second semester *not later than end of March.*
Second Semester after Your Statutory Deadline for Giving Notice of Nonrenewal or Termination	
	Continue to assist and evaluate staff.
	Remind staff that while April 15 (or whatever date is set by the statutes in your state for notice of nonrenewal or termination at the end of the contract year) has passed and they are employed for the next school year, they must continue to work diligently to meet district standards, and that their evaluation for the next year starts now!
	Revisit the summative evaluation of every probationary teacher and permanent teacher on a plan of assistance before school ends and schedule a meeting at the beginning of the next school year to again review these documents and set expectations and goals for the ensuing school year.
End of School Year—Summer Break	
	Prepare to start again to continue the ongoing improvement of the instructional skills of yourself and your staff.

Actor	Task or Duty
Teachers (Yes, they have tasks and responsibilities in the process too!)	
	Each teacher must read and know the • teacher job description, • teacher contract, • teacher handbook, • evaluation instrument and process, • student handbooks, and • lesson plan template.
	Each teacher should know that they are to be evaluated and meet the district standard of performance in: • instruction (planning and delivery, assessment, and reteaching); • classroom management; • professional conduct; and • personal conduct.
	Each teacher should read and know the ethical standards for teachers in NDE Rule 27, "Professional Practices Criteria."
	Each teacher must know and be able demonstrate the ability to plan lessons and instruct students based upon the instructional framework and educational model adopted by the board of education.

CPSIA information can be obtained
at www.ICGtesting.com
Printed in the USA
BVHW090849110921
616362BV00006B/95

9 781649 521668